Studies
Modern Arabic Literature

دراسات فى
الأدب العربى الحديث

Edited by R.C. Ostle

ARIS & PHILLIPS LTD., Teddington House, Warminster,
Wilts, England.

ISBN 0 85668 030 3

Sole Distributor in the U.S. and Canada

International Scholarly Book Services Inc.,
10300 S.W. Allen Boulevard
Beaverton
Oregon 97005.

Printed in Great Britain by
Fysons & Co. Ltd., Bath

Contents

Foreword

It is rare that Western scholars of modern Arabic literature have the opportunity to come together with a group of Arab writers and critics for the discussion of themes of mutual interest. Indeed nothing quite comparable with the Colloquium on Modern Arabic Literature has taken place before; the two or three similar conferences that have been held to date were concerned only with the Arab view of modern literature and have resulted in publications only in Arabic.

The Colloquium was organised by the Centre of Near and Middle Eastern Studies at S.O.A.S. with myself as its academic director and the editor of this volume as its secretary, and with financial support from the School of Oriental and African Studies.

Although various organizational difficulties postponed the start of the Colloquium for a year, the summer of 1974 proved to be an ideal time for such a literary exchange since it corresponded with a changed attitude towards writers in certain parts of the Arab world.

These papers give some impression of the aims and methods of Arab writers as conceived by a number of their better known representatives, and of how those Western orientalists who concern themselves with modern writing are approaching the appreciation and analysis of recent literary achievement. It seems to me also that these papers taken as a whole make an original contribution to the history of modern Arabic literature, a detailed account of which still remains to be written, though sorely needed.

T. M. Johnstone
Professor of Arabic in
the University of London
and Chairman of the Centre of Near and Middle Eastern Studies,
School of Oriental and African Studies

Editorial Note

This volume contains the majority of the papers delivered to a colloquium on Modern Arabic Literature held in July 1974 at the School of Oriental and African Studies, University of London. Their range and variety pay tribute to the achievements of a literature which, in its modern forms, has matured with impressive rapidity since the latter years of the nineteenth century. All the major literary categories are represented here, and although no particular uniformity of approach underlies the separate contributions, a pleasing balance was struck between those papers which offer synthesizing, historical surveys, and those which devote themselves to close, applied criticism or concentration on specific themes.

The number of papers which concern poetry reflects accurately the strength of its tradition in Arabic Literature, and the merit of its achievements in the modern period: an appropriate point of departure is provided by the description of the literary polemics surrounding Ḥāfeẓ and Shawqī in Egypt during the early years of this century, and this is followed by a detailed, sensitive analysis of the work of ʻAbd al-Raḥmān Shukrī, a figure of great psychological complexity wracked by the dilemmas of his generation. After the discussion of general trends in Arabic poetry in the 'twenties and 'thirties, the papers on the post-war period present the same combination of a close critique of an individual poet, and the study of themes ranging over the whole spectrum of poetry since 1945. As for the single paper on folk poetry, the interest which it holds for students within and without the discipline of literature surely indicates the impact which this subject will have when it receives more attention than is at present the case.

The sections on the short story provide a mine of detailed information, both historical and evaluative, while the novel is represented by an analysis of one of the latest, and perhaps least typical, of Maḥfūẓ's works, and a contribution which treats the novel essentially as a means of social criticism, written by one who is both a creative writer and a professional sociologist. The problems which have beset the development of the drama as a literary form in Modern Arabic are accorded comprehensive treatment in three valuable papers: the question of the language of dialogue, for example, is one which is posed also for the novel and the short story, but it arises in its most acute form in the drama. One of the contributors to this section describes how some of the younger playwrights in recent years have been turning more to traditional dramatic forms in the Arabic heritage, while the paper on the Egyptian Theatre is highly thought-provoking and presents interesting reflections on the theatre during the Nasser era.

Although the transliteration of Arabic words has been standardised to a large extent, certain variations in the form and pronunciation of proper names have been left according to the preferences of individual authors. The editor wishes to thank Cambridge University Press for their permission to print the chapter on Shukrī, taken from Muṣṭafā Badawī's forthcoming book, *A Critical Introduction to Modern Arabic Poetry*.

R. C. OSTLE

Poetry and Poetic Criticism at the Turn of the Century

Introduction

Many writers who have discussed modern Arabic literature and the various influences which have affected its development have stressed the fact that its progress has been, in a sense, accelerated. Jabrā Ibrāhīm Jabrā has spoken in terms of a huge backlog which had to be made up in a short space of time, while Najīb Maḥfūẓ has described a process of catching up in a quarter of a century a span of five or six centuries.[1] The forward impetus and vigour of Arabic poetry today represents the culmination thus far of such a process, and it is to be expected that much critical and analytical attention should be focussed on the contemporary scene. Yet Muṣṭafā Badawī has underlined in a recent paper the need to take another look at the earlier periods in the development of modern Arabic literature - and particularly poetry - if only to provide a perspective for the current scene. It was his references to the criticism levelled by Muḥammad al-Muwailiḥī at Aḥmad Shauqī which first suggested to me that a closer investigation of the circumstances and nature of this criticism might be of interest.[2] My aim is to present the arguments used by both Shauqī and Ḥāfiẓ Ibrāhīm in the Introductions to the first editions of their *Dīwāns*, and to juxtapose comments and criticisms of critics at the turn of the century to both their ideas on poetry and their poetry itself.[3]

In his small and useful work, *Rijāl ʻAraftuhum (Men I Knew)*, ʻAbbās Maḥmūd al-ʻAqqād shows us convincingly that almost all the figures whose views we will be discussing here were involved in the politics of the day and indeed often in personal intrigues against each other.[4] Furthermore, in his choice of poems of Shauqī for criticism in *al-Dīwān* published in 1921, al-ʻAqqād demonstrates the occasional and/or political nature of much of Shauqī's poetry, something which has recently been further demonstrated by Mounah Khouri's study, *Poetry and the Making of Modern Egypt*. While the discussion which follows will attempt to restrict itself to the purely literary arguments, the nature of some of the personalities involved makes it almost inevitable and indeed necessary that some information of a historical and even anecdotal nature be provided.

The Criticism

Shauqī published the first edition of his *Shauqiyyāt* in 1898 and prefaced it with an Introduction in which he recorded his own views on poetry, as well as a rather pompous autobiography.[5] He begins with a survey of the merits of some of the great poets of the classical period: Abū Firās, Abū'l-ʻAlā al-Maʻarrī, Abū'l-ʻAtāhiya, to name just a few. Such poets, he says, were philosophers who also concerned themselves with loftier social values. Other poets perverted their talents by producing deliberately abstruse poetry; still others lost themselves in metaphors and similes, in the belief that the further they got from reality, the closer they were to poetry (*aḥsan al-shiʻr mā kān fī wād, wa'l-ḥaqīqa fī wād*). After discussing some patronised poets, Shauqī responds to the anticipated charge that he too wrote such poetry. This leads him to make one of his most controversial remarks. "I knocked at poetry's door," he says, "without knowing as much about it then as I do now. All I found were the *Dīwāns* of the dead, with no semblance of poetry to them and *qaṣīdas* by the living which merely imitated the ancients."[6] He tells us that he saw the light as soon as he went to Europe. He wrote a piece of *madīḥ* (his so-called *hamziyya*) in which he used new themes and style (*jadīd al-maʻānī wa ḥadīth al-asālīb*) and translated Lamartine's *Le Lac*. From that he turned to fables in the style of La Fontaine and he has since been trying new kinds of poetic composition. At this point, he pauses to express his appreciation of his friend, Khalīl Muṭrān, "a gifted writer who combines a European style with the method of the Arabs." Shauqī closes this section on poetry by saying that a poet should fulfil three conditions: firstly he must have the conviction that poetry is part of his own nature; secondly, he must have both learning and experience; and lastly, poetry should not be a frill (*ḥilya*) in his life, but an enduring occupation.

Muḥammad al-Muwailiḥī begins his criticism with some general remarks in a very gingerly fashion.[7] The purpose of criticism, he says, is to distinguish good from bad. Poets such as Abū Tammām went through the experience, and it is a routine matter in the West today for newspapers to publish critical reviews of literature. However, the Egyptian press, he maintains, ignores this idea, and is simply content to exaggerate the qualities of a work and to fawn on its author. He is sure that Shauqī, being the great writer that he is, will realise that he and Egyptian literature in general will benefit from the criticisms which are to follow.

With such niceties disposed of, al-Muwailiḥī proceeds with his task. He begins by criticising the prose usages of the Introduction. Shauqī is certainly no prose writer; either that, or else he has not bothered to check what he has written. How else could he claim that Imru'l-Qais is a *ghāzil* and confuse the meanings of *malakatun* and *salīqatun*? These and two other errors all occur on the very first page, we are told![8]

Turning to the discussion on poetry itself, al-Muwailiḥī says that he finds the whole thing very confused. How, for example, can Shauqī praise poets like al-Ma'arrī and al-Mutanabbī and then claim that he has knocked at poetry's door and only found a collection of unpoetic *Dīwāns*? Furthermore, how can he omit the names of Abū Tammām, al-Buḥturī and Ibn al-Rūmī from the discussion, while mentioning Ibn al-Aḥnaf and Bahā' al-Dīn Zuhair? Such odd priorities in the choice of exemplary poets, in al-Muwailiḥī's opinion, calls Shauqī's judgement into question.

al-Muwailiḥī now broaches what is for him the crux of the issue. What Shauqī is telling us, he says, is that he discovered the way to Arabic poetry in Europe and that he began composing poems in this 'European' Arabic style. Amazing, says al-Muwailiḥī! Poetry is made up of words and themes (*alfāẓ wa ma'ānī*), and so reference to the Arabic language is inevitable. In any case, al-Muwailiḥī claims to have read as much European poetry as he can and says that he finds its ideas and themes no better; in fact, they are forever borrowing from the Greeks, Romans and Persians. If Shauqī really believes that Arabic poetry does not treat all the subjects which it might, then he should go away and read some more *Dīwāns*!![9]

In the third article in the series, al-Muwailiḥī broaches the second part of the Introduction; Aḥmad Shauqī's autobiography. The article is prefaced by the quotation *A'ūdhu bi 'l-lāhi min qaulat ana* , and this marks the general tone of al-Muwailiḥī's comments. This section, he says, contains vanity, errors and sheer padding (*zaḥw, sahw wa ḥashw*). Shaikh 'Alī al-Laithī told Shauqī's father about his son's future talents before his birth; Shauqī's eye disorder as a child was cured when the Khedive Ismā'īl ordered gold coins to be scattered on the floor (small wonder that he recovered, quips al-Muwailiḥī, when the Egyptian treasury was his oculist!). Other details of Shauqī's life, his education in France, visits to England, Belgium and Algeria, are all passed over, as is the information that Shakīb Arslān suggested the title *Shauqiyyāt* for the first time.[10]

With the fourth article, we leave this personal bickering and look at examples of the poetry itself. This is prefaced by a significant comment about some criticisms which have already been levelled at the critical articles themselves. al-Muwailiḥī declares that he intends to carry on regardless. The remainder of the article is devoted to some comments about individual words in the poem mentioned by Shauqī in his Introduction:[11]

Khada'ūhā bi qawlihim ḥasnā'u wa'l-Ghawānī yaghurruhunna 'l-thanā'u.

The first line strikes al-Muwailiḥī as contradictory; if there has been deception, then the girl cannot be a beauty. Other lines however earn al-Muwailiḥī's unqualified admiration, a fact which needs perhaps to be emphasized, bearing in mind the reactions of some literary scholars to his criticism.

In the fifth and last article, the subject is the famous description of a ball, *Athar al-Bāl fī 'l-Bāl.*[12] Here again, many of the lines are cited by al-Muwailiḥī as being excellent, both from the point of view of language and treatment of theme (he mentions, for example, the buffet and wine descriptions). His criticisms again focus on individual words or lines. In lines 22 and 23, he finds the use of darkness of a flag as a simile when talking about the morning sun to be inappropriate, unless, that is, he has Abū Muslim and the 'Abbāsid flag in mind! Another line which al-Muwailiḥī criticises contains the use of the word 'Umar:

Fahwa baynahum 'Umaru wa'l-wufūdu tantadibu.

Unless 'Umar ibn Abī Rabī'a is intended, he says, this reference is highly inappropriate. Significantly, the line is no longer found in the text, perhaps suggesting that some of these criticisms were heeded. As further evidence of that suggestion, we may point out that line 46 used the word *ānatan* twice. al-Muwailiḥī pointed out that one may say *āwinatan*, but not *ānatan*. The text now reads *marratan.*[13]

With this short article, the series ends. The final article contained a statement that the series would be continuing, but, bearing in mind that criticisms had already been voiced, it seems probable that powerful forces were brought to bear on al-Muwailiḥī to stop. al-'Aqqād suggests that it was Ibrāhīm al-Muwailiḥī (Muhammad's father) who prompted his son to write this series because of his thwarted desire to become a court writer and Shauqī's own appointment as *Ra'īs al-Dīwān al-'Arabī* (there being no budget for a court poet under Cromer's administration!); in which case, the palace itself would, of course, have been anxious to see the series concluded.[14]

But, in spite of the presumed suppression of these articles, al-Muwailiḥī did not stop his defence of the canons of classical

Arabic poetry or his attacks on 'Westernised' styles. After a discreet pause, he began to restate his points in a new and less personal way. In December 1900 (the last article in his criticism of Shauqī appeared in May), he published an article in *Miṣbāḥ al-Sharq* entitled 'A Word About Poetry' *(Kalima fī 'l-Shi'r)*. The best poetry, he says, should be eloquent and have good themes, should be neither obscure nor complicated, so that its effect will be immediate and penetrating. In every language poetry has its own garments *(libās)*; it is the task of the poet to compose his themes in those garments. Some contemporaries suggest that Arab poets of old did not follow the same course as Europeans, but stuck to specific and restricted topics *(abwāb mu'ayyana wa ṭuruq maḥdūda)*. They claim that the old poetry cannot convey the ideas of the modern period, and so have started producing what they term *shi'r 'aṣrī*. As a result, their work does not combine the two major elements of poetry.[15]

Four weeks later, another article was published under the title 'A Sentence to Follow a Word About Poetry' *(Jumla Ba'da Kalima fī 'l-Shi'r)*.[16] In it these two above mentioned elements are specified: firstly, poetry is *kalām mauzūn*, 'speech in metre', and secondly it is 'one of the conditions of the spirit' *(ḥāla min aḥwāl al-nafs)*. After defining metre by comparing it as an aural phenomenon with symmetry to the eye, he proceeds to the second element. He mentions the attribution by numerous Greek and Roman poets of their talents to the 'Muses', the Arabic equivalent of which is the *shaiṭān*; lines by Ḥassān ibn Thābit, al-A'shā and al-Farazdaq are cited as examples. If a poet has something to say about a whole variety of subjects, if he deals with experiences, if he uses eloquent expressions to convey his themes as well as accurate phraseology *(alfāẓ muḥkama)*, all this being combined in such a way that themes and words which express them fuse into a whole, then that is a line of poetry. One presumes that Shauqī was supposed to take particular note of the words *alfāẓ muḥkama*, while we may also draw attention to the fact that the basis of this definition remains the *bait* or single line. Poetry, al-Muwailiḥī continues, is intended to reveal to the listener hidden aspects of themes and to clarify them in a variety of ways. However, people who put words together in metre are not necessarily poets; indeed prose can be poetic. Many writings in metre are not poetry at all; as examples, he cites some textbooks written in rhyme so that they can be easily memorised. Finally, to keep up his campaign against the importation of Westernised ideas into poetry, he quotes a poem by an unnamed Spanish poet - describing a Moorish palace - to show that classical Arab poets were as capable of beautiful descriptions as Western poets. How, he asks, can any of today's poets prefer Western views of poetry to Arab ones?

As a final article in this continuing campaign, al-Muwailiḥī published *al Shi'r al-'Aṣrī* , in which he describes the way in which some poets are writing in a Western guise, using strange, foreign words and expressions, and then terming the result 'contemporary poetry' (one wonders whom he has in mind!).[17]

With the outlines of the discussion between the 'modern' poets and the more conservative elements thus delineated in the writings of Shauqī and Muḥammad al-Muwailiḥī, the third protagonist now comes on scene: Ḥāfiẓ Ibrāhīm, 'the poet of the Nile' and, like Muḥammad al-Muwailiḥī, a great admirer of the classical Arab poets and in particular al-Ma'arrī and al-Mutanabbī. Ḥāfiẓ was a close friend of al-Muwailiḥī and with him attended numerous meetings of literary circles such as that of Princess Nazlī Fāḍil and less serious circles such as that of Shaikh Ḥasan al-Ālātī.[18]

In August 1901, the Introduction to the *Dīwān* of Ḥāfiẓ Ibrāhīm was published in *Miṣbāḥ al-Sharq*, and it sparked a prolonged debate in the columns of the paper which came to be entitled *Munāqashāt al-Udabā'* ('Arguments Among Littérateurs'). The opening of the Introduction is, to say the least, arresting. Poetry, says Ḥāfiẓ Ibrāhīm, is a science to be found along with the sun. It remains hidden in the souls of men, like electricity, it is to speech what the soul is to the body. After this identification - one can hardly term it a definition - the poet proceeds on his way through the classical Arab poets, as Shauqī had done earlier. Ḥāfiẓ Ibrāhīm chooses to survey them by genre, *ghazal, fakhr, ḥikma* and *madīḥ*. After that, he repeats the views of al-Muwailiḥī in slightly different form. Prosodists who claim that poetry is speech in rhyme and metre *(kalām muqaffan mauzūn)* are wrong. Poetry is in essence anything which creates an effect on the soul, and the best examples are in metre. However, some writers can write poetically in prose; he cites Bashshār, al-Mutanabbī and al-Ma'arrī. The best poetry is that which contains no artificiality; the best poets are those who know when to be concise and when to be prolix - he cites Ibn al-Rūmī, Bashshār, Abū Nuwās, Abū Tammām, al-Buḥturī, and al-Mutanabbī.

Following this short Introduction, the compiler of the *Dīwān* Muhammad Ibrāhīm Hilāl, adds a few pages of introduction of his own.[19] After the first four centuries of Islam, he says, the *badī'* spoiled the spirit of Arabic poetry, and this process continued until recently, when a number of poets have tried to write poetry while placing severe limits on it. He cites al-Sa'ātī, al-Bārūdī, Nāṣīf al-Yāzijī and al-Najafī (among others). He then claims that Ḥāfiẓ shows the greatest mastery of them all; only he combines skill in versification with an ability to use unusual themes *(gharīb al-ma'ānī)*.

Readers of *Miṣbāḥ al-Sharq* had only one week to wait before reading a criticism of his Introduction. The first article was prefaced by a word from the editor (either Ibrāhīm or Muḥammad al-Muwailiḥī) to the effect that, following the tradition in Europe (as detailed in the fifth of the articles criticizing Shauqī), they intended to publish a series of articles on the subject of poetry. Their only caution is that any personal references *(shawā'ib al-Munāẓarāt al-shakhṣiyya)* should be avoided; al-Muwailiḥī's earlier comments about Shauqī seem to have been conveniently overlooked!

Bearing in mind the potentially interesting avenues of criticism which al-Muwailiḥī was exploring when his series of articles on Shauqī was abruptly curtailed, it is perhaps all the more unfortunate that the cudgel of criticism against Ḥāfiẓ Ibrāhīm is taken up by a pedantic scholar named Maḥmūd Wāṣif, who is yet more conservative in his views on poetry than the man whom he is criticising. As a result of Wāṣif's concern with individual words, the series of articles seems mostly concerned with Ḥāfiẓ' competence at writing proper Arabic rather than with his poetry.[20] In particular, Wāṣif finds Ḥāfiẓ' striking opening statement about 'poetry being found along with the sun' inaccurate! Does that mean, he asks, that it comes from the *jinn* or angels or something? However, Wāṣif's major point concerns the very nature of poetry itself. He claims that it is indeed exclusively *kalām muqaffan mauzūn*, and that the whole purpose of prosody is to differentiate poetry from prose. Such things as *balāgha* and *khayāl* (imagination) belong to other disciplines. Both al-Khalīl and al-Zamakhsharī would support *his* definition, he claims.

The main response to Wāṣif comes from the compiler of the *Dīwan*, Muḥammad Ibrāhīm Hilāl, although he is assisted by a number of other correspondents, including Muṣṭafā Luṭfī al-Manfalūṭī. As Hilāl, al-Manfalūṭī and others point out, the statement concerning 'poetry being found along with the sun' is simply a poetic exaggeration about which there is no point in arguing. The major point (on which all correspondents agree, save Wāṣif) is that metre and rhyme are not the basis of poetry. As Hilāl says, such a definition is merely that of prosodists; poetry is NOT versification, but an expression of that imaginative spirit which pervades literature in both poetry and prose. Rhyme and metre are the inventions of later Arab writers in a more recent period of Islam. Other correspondents point out that poetry can be found in anything which has a pleasurable effect on us: birds singing, trees rustling or waves pounding. The effect of poetry is the result of themes *(ma'ānī)*; metre and rhyme are merely verbal fetters and are not sufficient by themselves to make anything into poetry. Poetry was there before all the rules in any case.

In his final article in the series, al-Muwailiḥī expresses his regret that the criticism has been so pedantic and vituperative, since it was his hope that the series might perform a service for literature. Rather than express his own views any further, he simply republishes the major points from his earlier article.[21]

The final stage in this short succession of poetic discussions involves Ḥāfiẓ' views on the *Shauqiyyāt*.[22] In 1906, he published his *Layālī Saṭīḥ* which owes an obvious debt to al-Muwailiḥī's work *Ḥadīth ʻIsā ibn Hishām* (which had not yet been published in book form), a debt expressed through the inclusion of part of al-Muwailiḥī's own text in *Layālī Saṭīḥ* itself.[23] The latter work is made up of a number of nights during which a narrator meets a character called Saṭīḥ, and together they discuss a current problem of Egyptian society. The sixth night contains a discussion of the *Shauqiyyāt*, although Ḥāfiẓ avoids direct and obvious criticism by making Shauqī's ideas about poetry the subject of a three-sided discussion.[24] The narrator (Ḥāfiẓ himself, if we can draw any comparison with al-Muwailiḥī's ʻIsā ibn Hishām) meets a poet who is reciting his own verse which would do justice to Abū Tammām himself (presumably also implying that his poetry conforms with the canons of classical poetic analysis). When the poet is asked why he has not collected his *Dīwān*, his reply is that he would do it, were it not for the fact that people in Egypt read things because of their author's fame, and not for their intrinsic value. This leads the poet to rue the praise which was heaped on the *Shauqiyyāt* when they were published, something which even surpassed the Istanbul press talking about ʻAbd al-Ḥamīd in person. All the marvellous themes which Shauqī has written about, the poet declares, are simply Western.

The narrator cautions the poet about being too hard on *shāʻir al-sharq*, as Shauqī is termed. The narrator says that Shauqī writes well and that writing poetry is easy for him. The problem is that he is garrulous *(mikthār)*, and such people can rarely avoid mistakes. Shauqī's poetry fits exactly the words of al-Aṣmaʻī describing Abū 'l-ʻAtāhiya's lines: 'It's like a sovereign's courtyard; pottery falls to the ground, but so does gold.' To this rather weak defence, the poet replies that he is not convinced. How can Shauqī be said to be garrulous, when he has so much spare time and yet writes so little and uses so few rhymes!?

At this point, the third character, the supernatural figure of Saṭīḥ himself, appears and claims that neither of them is right. One is praising him too much, the other criticizing. Shauqī, he says, is the most skillful craftsman of them all, but his range is narrow, *(ḍayyiq al-majāl)* even though his imagination is broad. If only he had *daqqat al-mabānī* to go with *raqqat al-maʻānī* (the work is partially in *saj'*!), then his poetic style would be fine.

The poet immediately returns to the argument. Shauqī, he says, is forever pirating and distorting both Arabic and Western themes. Even if his style is as good as Saṭīḥ claims, then his themes belong to someone else. As 'Abd al-Qāhir al-Jurjānī says in *Dalā'il al-I'jāz*, eloquence is not simply a question of words and themes, but of style. Anyone who reads Shauqī needs a geomancer or astrologer to tell him what is meant by the poetry! He had decided to limit himself to certain phrases which act as his trade-mark. Poor al-Mutanabbī will be groaning in his grave to hear what Shauqī has been writing. All this is not to mention the lines by al-Mutanabbī which Shauqī has pirated, simply by changing a single word.[25]

Saṭīḥ now accuses the poet of only mentioning Shauqī's bad points, to which the latter replies that, if Saṭīḥ wants to hear a list of his good points, it will only take up a quarter of the night, while the faults will take up the rest! Saṭīḥ concludes by saying that Shauqī remains the best poet in the East and deserves to be considered as such.[26]

In spite of the somewhat tepid defence of Shauqī by Saṭīḥ, Ḥāfiẓ Ibrāhīm has here carried his friend, al-Muwailiḥī's earlier criticism of Shauqī a stage further. In addition to the previous objections about the use of Western ideas, we now have the additional complaint of a lack of variety and even plagiarism from classical poets. However, the choice of al-Mutanabbī as the figure who would be groaning is hardly convincing for those who had read the Introduction of Ḥāfiẓ's own *Dīwān*. For, in spite of his admiration for al-Mutanabbī, even he is charged there with writing poetry, the style of which was inconsistent with that of Arabic poetry - if it were not for that, Ḥāfiẓ says, he would have been the most poetic of poets in Islam.[27]

Discussion

While the logic of some of Shauqī's statements may have raised al-Muwailiḥī's hackles, we can hardly dispute the former's views when he talks of '*qaṣīdas* by the living which merely imitated the ancients'. This seems to fit exactly into the first of four phases identified by al-'Aqqād whereby he sees the written Arabic poetic tradition passing from its prolonged stagnation to a lively and vigorous modern development.[28] This first phase he terms 'weak imitation' *(taqlīd ḍa'īf)*, and within it we would place such early nineteenth century poets as al-Khashshāb (d. 1815) and ʻAlī al-Darwīsh (d. 1853), and also Shaikh ʻAlī al-Laithī (d. 1896) from a later period - the last of them being mentioned by Shauqī in an anecdote in his Introduction to the *Shauqiyyāt*.[29] Along with this went a tradition of poetic criticism which seems to be represented in these discussions by the verbal pedantries and rigid formalism of Maḥmūd Wāṣif. The motto of this tradition was presumably *kalām muqaffan mauzūn* as a means of differentiating the poetic and non-poetic and great emphasis was put on the elements of the *badīʻ* and the elaborate word play which was a natural product of such emphasis. As a result, the formal aspect of the line of poetry as a group of words strung together all but obliterated the content, and even the theories on imagery formulated by such earlier scholars as ʻAbd al-Qāhir al-Jurjānī were lost in a flood of sheer rhymed verbiage.

All but the most conservative criticisms voiced in the debates discussed above would seem to fall within the spectrum, the poles of which are Al-ʻAqqād's second and third phases: the second is called 'firm imitation' *(taqlīd muḥkam)* - whereby poets would produce traditional poetry which paid as much attention to content as to form - and the third 'creativity through feelings of national freedom'.

The person who is generally recognised as the precursor of a modern poetic revival and who combined a concern for the revival of the old tradition with a desire for a new creativity was the poet and statesman Maḥmūd Sāmī al-Bārūdī (d. 1904), while many of the critical principles involved in the revival were formulated by Shaikh Ḥusain al-Marṣafī (d. 1889). Among contributors to the present discussions, both Muḥammad al-Muwailiḥī and Ḥāfiẓ Ibrāhīm can be seen as adherents to the principles practised and analysed by these men.[30] It was al-Marṣafī who cited numerous examples from al-Bārūdī's poetry as well as that of the classical poets in his work *al-Wasīla al-Adabiyya lil-ʻUlūm al-ʻArabiyya* to support his statements about the nature of the poetic art. About al-Bārūdī himself, he says in a much quoted comment:

> (al-Bārūdī) read no books on the arts of Arabic. However, when he reached intellectual maturity, he found that he had a penchant for reading and creating poetry.[31]

al-Marṣafī states quite clearly that poetry is not *kalām muqaffan mauzūn;* the definition of the prosodists will not suffice. Poetry is *kalām balīgh*, being based on metaphor and description. In other words, the individual poet's ability to combine the elements of *balāgha* with those of versification is what is involved in the poetic art.

Within the present discussions, Maḥmūd Wāṣif places himself outside the bounds of al-Marṣafī's criteria, while al-Bārūdī himself, with his talk of 'an imaginative spark radiating in the mind and dispatching rays to the heart',[32] and al-Muwailiḥī, with his reference to 'a condition of the soul', along with many other writers, seem through varying, and often poetic, phraseology to fall within the terms of al-Marṣafī's definition.[33]

In addition to precise definitions of all the traditional elements of poetry and prose, al-Marṣafī explains the best way of gaining mastery of the poetic art. The would-be poet should steep himself in the poetry of the classical period and gain experience in that way, rather than learning the various devices of the *badī'* in a mechanical fashion.[34] In this connection, it is interesting to note that al-Muwailiḥī delivered a lecture in 1893 on precisely this topic, pointing out that the memorisation of poetry is a stimulus to general creativity because it brings the reader into contact with varieties of themes and imagery.[35]

al-Marṣafī's codification of this revival of the classical poetic tradition was thus based on well-established principles: memorisation and the line as the basic unit are both examples of this. It was this neo-classical tradition, with its renewed vitality, which al-Muwailiḥī and Ḥāfiẓ Ibrāhīm are defending in our current context against what they regarded as alien interpolations. To which considerations should probably be added the fact that al-Bārūdī, Ḥāfiẓ Ibrāhīm and al-Muwailiḥī were all deeply committed to the nationalist causes of their day, so that any attempts to incorporate alien elements into this poetic tradition may well have been regarded as more than a mere literary threat.

All of which brings us to the object of al-Muwailiḥī's and Ḥāfiẓ' criticism, the poetry and views on poetry of Aḥmad Shauqī.[36] The preceding arguments seem to have identified as the major points: firstly, the purpose of the Introduction itself; secondly, the validity of Shauqī's comments about Western poetry vis à vis that of the Arabs; thirdly, the question of Shauqī's 'borrowings' from the classical poets; and lastly, the validity of the criticism itself.

As far as the purpose of the Introduction is concerned, Shauqī is quite explicit in stating that it is in answer to public demand; he tells his readers that he has refused out of modesty to respond to a request for the inclusion of his photograph as well.[37] However, if Shauqī's purpose is also to acquaint his readers with his views about poetry, then al-Muwailiḥī is surely correct in declaring the result a confused jumble. Ṭāhā Ḥusain declares that he is unable to detect in it any frank credo about poetry, and considers Haikal's comment on Shauqī, that he is a modernist at times and a traditionalist at others, simply an evasion of the issue.[38] Even a more recent and detached critic can write:

> Shauqī is convinced there is something new which Arab poets need to be affected by, but does not study it very closely. (In his Introduction), he seems more perplexed than an innovator with a clear goal. He says that there is a world of literature beyond our horizons from which we should benefit, but what are the lines and limits of this world? And what does he want to transfer from it? That seems obscure ...[39]

In fact, it seems that Shauqī, with a certain youthful impetuosity, made certain rather unguarded remarks about classical Arabic and European poetry (in the latter case, on the basis of a superficial knowledge in the view of Ṭāhā Ḥusain),[40] and, as a result, brought down the critical wrath of al-Muwailiḥī on him. We have already shown that al-Muwailiḥī was no hater of European culture *per se*, nor indeed was he out to criticise Shauqī merely for the sake of it; in fact, he praises many of Shauqī's lines very warmly. What al-Muwailiḥī demanded was that every importation of Western ideas should be the product of a reasoned discussion of its merits. It is unfortunate that Shauqī's rash comparison of the two literatures provided no such rationale and provoked an equally unreasoned retort from al-Muwailiḥī.

In raising the question of Shauqī's 'borrowings' or imitations of al-Mutanabbī, Ḥāfiẓ Ibrāhīm is raising an issue which was to be raised again by later critics such as Ṭāhā Ḥusain and al-ʻAqqād, one which, ironically enough, seems to indicate ā more conservative side within the duality of Shauqī's poetic nature as portrayed above in the quotation from Haikal. For the concept of *muʻāraḍa* was well-known in the classical tradition; the aim was to use a line by a previous poet in order to *outdo* him, and, according to the classical theorists, only in certain very specific cases was this to be construed as plagiarism.[41]. To the kind of comment which is made by one of the speakers in *Layālī Saṭīḥ* Shauqī would presumably have replied that his imitations of al-Mutanabbī (not to mention Ibn Zaidūn and al-Būṣīrī) were firmly within the classical tradition.

al-Muwailiḥī's criticism of the poetry itself thus emerges as being firmly within the canons of classical criticism as revived by al-Marṣafī. Whether dealing with prose or poetry, he is primarily concerned with words in their context, as syntactic and semantic units within the framework of the line. He is dealing with the grammatical correctness of the word, and, equally as important, its suitability to the context in question, but larger issues such as the unity of the entire poem do not concern him.

In quite striking contrast to the Introduction of Shauqī and Ḥāfiẓ, both from the point of view of format and tone, is the 'Brief Statement' *(Bayān Mūjaz)* with which Khalīl Muṭrān prefaced the first volume of his *Dīwān* in 1908.[42] Muṭrān says that he finds classical Arabic poetry sterile. But then, instead of extolling European literature, he gives vigorous expression to his own ideas on poetic composition: he will use the words of his own era, not be a slave to rhyme or metre, and look to the unity of the poem - its form, themes and imagery - rather than to the individual line.

Here is not the place to assess Muṭrān's role in the development of modern Arabic poetry. This résumé of the Preface to his *Dīwān* is quoted merely to demonstrate that he took ideas from European literature and stated them in unequivocal terms within the context of his own view of Arabic poetry, something which Shauqī seemed unprepared to do. Perhaps it was fortunate for Muṭrān that by 1908 Muḥammad al-Muwailiḥī had retired to the seclusion of his home, only to raise his pen on two other occasions, both of them political. However, al-Muwailiḥī must have been gratified when his most famous pupil, al-ʻAqqād, mentioned his name as being one of the few genuine critics of the early part of this century when the latter embarked on his famous criticism of Shauqī in *al-Dīwān*.[43] As a final footnote, when I asked Ṭāhā Ḥusain in 1967 if he had ever met al-Muwailiḥī, he replied with a wry smile that he had indeed - at Shauqī's house in 1927. The animosities and intrigues of earlier days had apparently been forgotten, and, in any case, the accelerated process in the development of modern Arabic literature had gathered momentum and essentially left these two personifications of neo-classicism behind.

Roger Allen

1. Jabrā Ibrāhīm Jabrā, 'Modern Arabic Literature and the West', *Journal of Arabic Literature* 2 (1971), p. 81; Najīb Maḥfūẓ, *al-Marāyā* (Cairo: Maktaba Miṣr. 1972), p. 66.

2. Muṣṭafā Badawī, 'Convention and Revolt in Modern Arabic Poetry', in *Arabic Poetry: Theory and Development*. ed. Gustave E. von Grunebaum. (Wiesbaden: Otto Harrassowitz Verlag, 1974), pp. 181 ff. See also 'al-Bārūdī Precursor of the Modern Arabic Poetic Revival', *Die Welt des Islams* N.S. XII (1969), p. 228.

3. I would like to take this opportunity to thank the Director of Dār al-Kutub in Cairo, Dr. Maḥmūd al-Shinītī, for his kindness in allowing me to microfilm the necessary materials for this paper from books and newspapers which are rarely, if ever, available elsewhere.

4. ʻAbbās Maḥmūd al-ʻAqqād, *Rijāl ʻAraftuhum*. Kitāb al-Hilāl no. 151. (Cairo: Dār al-Hilāl, 1963).

5. For a suggestion concerning this kind of Introduction to the Dīwāns of this period, see ʻUmar al-Dasūqī, *Fī'l-Adab al-Ḥadīth* (Cairo: Dār al-Fikr, 1966), II: p. 215.

6. Aḥmad Shauqī, *Shauqiyyāt* (Cairo: Maṭbaʻa al-Iṣlāḥ, 1898), p. 7.

7. The articles *Naqd Dīwān Shauqī* were published in the al-Muwailiḥī newspaper, *Miṣbāḥ al-Sharq*, nos. 99, 100, 101, 102 and 104, 6th April till 18th May, 1900. The series is reprinted in Muṣṭafā Luṭfī al-Manfalūṭī, *Mukhtārāt al-Manfalūṭī* (Cairo: Maktaba al Tijāriyya al-Kubrā, n.d.), pp. 139 ff. al-Muwailiḥī is of course mainly remembered as a journalist and author of one of the early monuments of modern Arabic literature, *Ḥadīth ʻIsā ibn Hishām*. However, the careful reader of this latter work will notice the author's great interest in poetry: the text is filled with lines from the great poets of the classical period, and the wedding episode concludes with an ode, presumably written by the author himself.

8. al-Manfalūṭī, *Mukhtārāt*, p. 146.

9. al-Manfalūṭī, *Mukhtārāt*, p. 148.

10. Shauqī, *Shauqiyyāt* (1898), p. 22.

11. Shauqī, *Shauqiyyāt* (Cairo: Maṭbaʻa al-Istiqāma, 1961), II p. 111. See also Ṭāhā Ḥusain, *Ḥāfiẓ wa Shauqī* (Cairo: Maktaba al-Khānjī, 1966), p. 212.

12. Shauqī, *Shauqiyyāt* (1961), II p. 10.

13. Shauqī, *Shauqiyyāt* (1961), II p. 12.

14. al-ʻAqqād, *Rijāl ʻAraftuhum*, p. 99. Ṭāhā Ḥusain says (Ḥāfiẓ wa Shauqī, p. 193) that Shauqī 'did not dare to chide his critics, but would treat them like snakes *(arāqim)*, not meeting them face to face but dealing with them from behind with the edge of the hand'.

15. *Miṣbāḥ al-Sharq*, no. 132, 7th December 1900.

16. *Ibid.*, no. 136, 4th January 1901.

17. *Miṣbāḥ al-Sharq*, no. 138, 18th January 1901.

18. For the former circle, see ʻAbd al-Laṭīf Hamza, *Adab al-Maqāla al-Suḥufiyya fī Miṣr* (Cairo: Dār al Fikr, 1966), 3: p. 26; and my article, 'Writings of Members of the Nazli Circle', *Journal of the American Research Center in Egypt* Vol. VIII (1969-70), pp. 79 ff.

19. Muḥammad Ibrāhīm Hilāl is described by Khalīl Muṭrān as a writer of prose and poetry, and a follower of al-Bārūdī. See *al-Shuʻarā'al-Muʻāṣirīn* in al-Manfalūṭī, *Mukhtārāt*, p. 69.

20. For examples, the articles contain a long discussion about the use of the word *ʻilm* to describe poetry. Wāṣif insists that its current use as 'science' is inappropriate; others point out that its basic meaning is 'to know', which is also the basic meaning of the verbal root from which *shiʻr* (poetry) is derived. This argument, fluctuating between meaning and usage, continues fruitlessly throughout the series of articles.

21. *Kalima fī Khitām al-Munāqasha*, *Miṣbāḥ al-Sharq* no. 177, 25th October 1901. See also the article in note 16. It is now published as *Jauhar al-Shiʻr* ('The Essence of Poetry') in al-Manfalūṭī *Mukhtārāt*, p. 196 ff., where it is wrongly attributed to Ibrāhīm al-Muwailiḥī.

22. An episode which occurred in November 1922 is worth recounting in that it was in all probability a contributing factor in al-Muwailiḥī's decision to retire from the public arena. He was involved in a café incident after allegedly insulting a young nobleman, Muḥammad Nash'at, who slapped him in the face. ʻAlī Yūsuf, the editor of the newspaper *al-Mu'ayyad*, now began a column in his paper called *ʻĀm al-Kaff* ('The Year of the Slap'), and numerous poets contributed scurrilous verses to it. Readers of the *Dīwān* of Ismāʻīl Ṣabrī

(in the *Fukāhāt* section) will discover that the anonymous poets 'Subḥī' and 'Isḥāq' were none other than Ṣabrī himself, who shared Shauqī's admiration for French literature.

23. Ḥāfiẓ Ibrāhīm, *Layālī Saṭīḥ* (Cairo: Dār al-Qaumiyya, 1964), pp. 29-30.

24. *Ibid.*, pp. 33 ff.

25. *Layālī Saṭīḥ* (1964), p. 36.

26. *Ibid.*, p. 38.

27. Ḥāfiẓ Ibrāhīm, *Dīwān* (Cairo: Maṭba'a al-Iṣlāḥ 1901), Introduction, p. 12.

28. al-'Aqqād, *Shu'arā' Miṣr wa Bī'ātuhum fī 'l-Jīl al-Māḍī* (Cairo: Maktaba al-Nahḍa al-Miṣriyya, 1965); p. 120.

29. See Shauqī Ḍaif, *Shauqī, Shā'ir al-'Aṣr al-Ḥadīth* (Cairo: Dār al-Ma'ārif, 1953), p. 43; Ṭāhā Ḥusain, *Ḥāfiẓ wa Shauqī*, p. 1; 'Umar ad-Dasūqī, *Fī'l-Adab al-Ḥadīth*, I: pp. 51 and 129; Muṣṭafā Badawī: 'Al-Bārūdī ...' *Die Welt des Islams* N.S. XII (1969), 229-30.

30. Furthermore, al-Muwailiḥī dedicates *Ḥadīth 'Isā ibn Hishām* to al-Bārūdī among others; see the *Ihdā'* to all editions. Abū Shādī is at some pains to point out that Ḥāfiẓ is a member of al-Bārūdī's school; see *Qaḍāyā-'l-Shi'r al-Mu'āṣir*, (Cairo: al-Sharika al-'Arabiyya li'l-Ṭibā'a wa 'l-Nashr, n.d.), p. 46, also Ṭāhā Ḥusain, *Ḥāfiẓ wa Shauqī*, pp. 196 and 198.

31. al-'Aqqād, *Shu'arā' Miṣr*, p. 13; Muḥammad Mandūr, *al-Naqd wa 'l-Nuqqād al-Mu'āṣirūn* (Cairo: Maktaba Nahḍa Miṣr, n.d.) p. 18; Shauqī Ḍaif, *al-Adab al-'Arabī al-Mu'āṣir fī Miṣr* (Cairo: Dār al-Ma'ārif, 1961), p. 87.

32. al-'Aqqād, *Shu'arā' Miṣr*, p. 142; Muṣṭafā Badawī, 'Al-Bārūdī' 'Die Welt des Islams' N.S. XII (1969), 233.

33. For example, Muṣṭafā Ṣādiq al-Rāfi'ī: 'poetry is nothing but the heart's own tongue addressing the heart,' al-Manfalūṭī, *Mukhtārāt*, p. 98; Shakīb Arslān: 'poetry is mankind's natural vision in the mirror of his own nature,' *Ibid.*, p. 117; al-Manfalūṭī: 'poetry is a talking image, and since the constant factor is *effect*, that is the balancing factor in judging its worth,' al-Dasūqī, *Fī 'l-Adab al-Ḥadīth*, II: p. 218.

34. He cites ʿUmar ibn Abī Rabīʿa, Jarīr, Abū Nuwās, Abū Tammām, al-Buḥturī and the *Kitāb al-Aghānī*, among others, as good sources.

35. *Iktisāb Malaka al-Inshā' bi Ḥifẓ al-Ashʿār* given to *al-Mujtamaʿ al-ʿIlmī*, *al-Muqaṭṭam*, 18th August 1893. This theory was of course nothing new; see, for example, Ibn Khaldūn, *Muqaddima*, chapter VI, section 34.

36. It should be observed at this point, in view of the extent of Shauqī's career, that discussion here is confined to the *Shauqiyyāt* of 1898.

37. Aḥmad Shauqī, *Shauqiyyāt* (1898), p. 13.

38. Taken from Haikal's Introduction to the *Shauqiyyāt* which was added to later editions in place of the poet's own. Neither the Introduction of Shauqī nor of Ḥāfiẓ Ibrāhīm are included with their poetry now; nor is the article of al-Muwailiḥī (see notes 16 and 21) which was printed in the second edition of the *Dīwān Ḥāfiẓ*. The *later* Introductions are the subject of Ṭāhā Ḥusain's chapter 'Muqaddimāt', *Ḥāfiẓ wa Shauqī*, pp. 10 ff.

39. Shauqī Ḍaif, *Shauqī, Shāʿir al-ʿAṣr al-Ḥadīth*, p. 87.

40. Ṭāhā Ḥusain, *Ḥāfiẓ wa Shauqī*, p. 201.

41. See Gustave E. von Grunebaum, 'The Concept of Plagiarism in Arabic Theory, '*Journal of Near Eastern Studies*' III (1944), pp. 234 ff.

42. Khalīl Muṭrān, *Dīwān al-Khalīl* (Cairo: Maṭbaʿa al-Maʿārif, n.d.). Robin Ostle points out that Muṭrān made no changes to the text of his preface even in 1949 when a second edition of his *Dīwān* was published; 'Khalīl Muṭrān: The Precursor of Lyrical Poetry in Modern Arabic', *Journal of Arabic Literature II* (1971), p. 118. In view of the sentiments expressed in the Preface, it is amusing to note that Muṭrān decided to write this piece in rhyming prose, for which he is chided by Ṭāhā Ḥusain, *Ḥāfiẓ wa Shauqī*, p. 12.

43. Al-ʿAqqad, *al-Dīwān* (Cairo: n.d., 1921), p. 2.

Shukrī the Poet - a Reconsideration

Of the three poets generally referred to as the *Dīwān* group of poets Shukrī is undoubtedly the greatest: in spite of their many interesting poems, the genius of al-Māzinī and al-'Aqqād reveals itself more clearly and convincingly in the sphere of prose. Shukrī, much of whose poetry reminds one of Edward Young's *Night Thoughts*, is perhaps one of the most fascinating and complex personalities in the history of modern Arabic poetry. The clue to his personality probably lies in his hypersensitivity, a quality which al-'Aqqād justly noted in his obituary of the poet.[1] This is the impression one amply receives from a perusal of his clearly autobiographical book of *Confessions* (1916)[2]. It is because of Shukrī's hypersensitivity, which borders on the abnormal and pathological, that al-Māzinī accused him of madness in the unkind attack he launched on him in the critical work *al-Dīwān*, which was provoked by Shukrī's strictures on his many obvious borrowings (or plagiarisms) from western writings. In an interesting attempt to universalize his problem, Shukrī claims in the introduction to the *Confessions* that the author of the book is typical of Egyptian youth at that juncture in the history of Egypt, alternating between excessive hope and utter despair (as a result of the state of Egyptian society which inspired both extremes) and being exceedingly suspicious (and this is the product of ages of despotic rule), weak of resolve, given to day-dreaming, and to entertaining wild hopes and ambitions which they can never realize because of their inactivity. They are capable only of spasmodic acts of courage and are generally timid. They are excitable but without profundity, vain and exceedingly sensitive, impatient and fond of complaining. Despite their vanity they are confused, perplexed and full of doubts, not certain which of their outworn beliefs and traditions are harmful superstition and which of their newly acquired modern ideas and attitudes are true and useful, with the result that they are harmed both by the old and the new. In his further description of the author, he says that despite the sardonic expression on his face he was a very kind and compassionate man. He was in turn proud and humble, but generally melancholic because he was misunderstood and mistrusted by his society whom he in his turn misunderstood and mistrusted.

This sketch of the author and his cultural (or sociological) background shows that Shukrī had a good deal of honesty and insight into his own character. There is no doubt that Shukrī's malaise is in part a reflection of the malaise of contemporary Egypt, caught as it was in the clash between traditional Islamic and western values in a period of cultural transition. But equally Shukrī's own psychological make-up has contributed to it. The book fills in various details which either provide or explain themes treated in his poetry. He begins with the assumption that happiness and great sensitivity are mutually exclusive, that a man of feeling is inevitably a man of suffering (C.p.13), that the taste of the masses in poetry and the fine arts is corrupt, and that the conventional poetry of eulogy, elegy, satire and description of daily political and social occurrences, in short the poetry of the Establishment at the time, is poetry of the false heart and that the true poet 'describes the passion of the soul' (C.pp.19-20), that the soul is full of contradictions (C.p.74) and is 'a temple inhabited by God who illustrates it with His light, but is also Satan's cave lit up by his fire'. (C.p.85). On the different stages of the development of the poet's mind we read the following:

> In my childhood I was very superstitious seeking the company of old women to hear stories about the supernatural to the extent that their stories filled every corner of my mind which became a huge world teeming with magic and demons ... Later I went through a phase of religiosity during which I became immersed in books of devotion which described the characteristics of wickedness as well as God's horrible punishment. The full horrors of this unbearable punishment are so vividly depicted in these books that whenever I dreamed about them I used to wake up with a start ... Yet my obsessive preoccupation with prayer and devotion did not put an end to my pursuit of sensual pleasures which, if anything, was intensified the more I prayed and worshipped. It only served to double my terror of the consequences in the next world; in my fear I used to think that every word or deed I was the author of was a cardinal sin with the result that I used to cry and lament in fear of God's punishment ... I even used to imagine as I lay on my bed that above me there were scorpions and serpents sent by God to punish me, and at times it seemed that the bed was full of glowing coals, so I used to wake up screaming and terrified.
>
> I subsequently turned to reading books of poetry and literature, so I became aware of the beauty of the world and my terrors which had been inspired by religion grew less. I then passed through the stage of doubt and quest ... I denied the existence of God with the same fascination as that with which others asserted their faith in Him. Yet my denial alarmed me without satisfying my mind, for it never explained to me what I am, why I exist, and whither I shall be

> going. My soul is such that it is never satisfied with atheism: it has religious needs which it cannot dispense with, and that is why my atheism only yields me despair and sorrow. I used to roam the streets of the city at night (for night seemed to accord with my feelings of despair and sorrow) looking at the stars, asking them about life and death, God and man, this world and the next. But the stars merely looked back at me as if in pity and in sadness ... and life then felt heavier than a nightmare or a horrifying dream ...
>
> Eventually I regained my faith, having learnt that the universe has a huge spirit with its own life and personality and that this spirit inspires its will to the various individual spirits and that the Fates are its subalterns. Yet despite my strong rejection of popular beliefs I experience moments in which I can accept anything, even magic and what violates or suspends the operation of the laws of nature ... I loathe the laws of nature because they stand in the way of my ambitions and hopes. That is why I find no harm in breaking them. This happens mostly in times of calamity or sickness when fear humbles the heart and weakens the resolve. Sometimes I am so scared lest Satan should appear before me and deceive me just as he had deceived Faust, so I turn around to make sure that he has not yet appeared. Likewise I sometimes believe in the existence of other devils and jinn as I used to do in my childhood. (C.pp.21-25)

I have used the above quotations, despite their length because of their great importance to our subject. They underline the fact that the change in the conventional idiom of Arabic poetry is, like all genuine changes in artistic expression, not simply a matter that affects the external and artificial features of style. It presupposes a change in the whole of the poet's *Weltanschauung*, his general attitude to life, man and God. What we find in these quotations is the psychological dislocation and the spiritual turmoil and confusion which attend the change from the relatively comfortable and comforting world of neoclassicism with its traditional values, in which a certain measure of agreement obtained on the major issues of life. In *Confessions* Shukrī records the impact of such a change on a man of sensibility. Shukrī's hypersensitivity, coupled with his vivid imagination and a tendency towards self-dramatisation remain salient features of his poetry. On the subject of imagination we find this interesting comment in *Confessions*, revealing a significantly ambivalent attitude, the relevance of which we shall see later on:

> Imagination has a great effect upon our life, whether we are awake or asleep. Man is governed by his

imagination in his thoughts and opinions, his endeavours and hopes, in what he alleges to be established facts and in his transactions with others. Consequently I used to question my opinions with disastrous results, for it meant that I hesitated and refrained from going on with whatever I was trying to do. Imagination enables man to share other people's feelings and conditions, which leads to sympathy and mutual understanding, but it can also magnify the minute and minimize the important. Imagination is both the paradise and the hell of our dreams. Do we not spend our life alike in our dreams and our daydreams, alternating between roses and thorns, between angels and demons? At times I feel as if I had been transported to a world other than this world, where the air is perfumed and water fragrant and people are perfect in beauty and virtue ... I see in my reveries visions so beautiful that I cannot adequately describe them. But at other times I see black dreams of despair and sorrow, then I fear all the disasters of life which can be pictured by the imagination in its countless different forms. I anticipate them and feel their painful impact ... The pain which I endure is the result of the folly of fear engendered by imagination. That is why it is a manifestation of God's mercy that in the mass of mankind imagination is like a caged eagle, not allowed to rise to the sun and prey on other birds. (C.pp.68-70)

Already in vol.I of his *Dīwān* which appeared in 1909, when the poet was only twenty-three years of age, and before his departure for England we notice sometimes in embryo many of the main themes which were to characterize Shukrī's subsequent poetry. It is true that we find a number of poems dealing with topics of public interest. He wrote elegies on the nationalist leaders Muṣṭafā Kāmil, Qāsim Amīn and Muḥammad ʻAbdu (*Dīwān*, pp.47, 53, 54, 58). He made an appeal for fund raising in order to help establish a secular Egyptian university, a plea for national unity and for the sinking of differences between Copts and Muslims in the national interest, for the unity of political factions in an attempt to restore past glory, an exhortation to the people of Egypt to shake off their stagnation and humiliation and to learn to be steadfast and resolute (pp. 39, 40, 48, 69, 71). Likewise he poses as a stern moralist. The very first poem in the collection 'Chosroes and the Princess' opens with an address to young women asking them to heed the story he is about to tell showing how a young beautiful woman can protect her honour and overcome the importunities and threats of even a tyrant. He calls his story 'a tale with a moral'. The next narrative poem entitled 'The Lover of Money' and given the sub-title 'How women are deceived' tells the story of a man, who has been professing his love for a wealthy woman he is courting, but who ruthlessly spurns her once he learns of the loss of her fortune (pp. 19, 22). He warns against the danger of despair and preaches the need for resolution *(ḥazm)* a recurrent word in his poetry which is imbued with a spirit of stoicism (p. 40). Yet in the entire volume there are no more than the handful of poems listed above on public themes, and of a poem like 'The Lover of Money' more than one third is taken up by a long detailed description of the background of nature against which the story takes place. Nature and the poet's subjective emotions, his thoughts and his attitudes provide the main themes of the vast majority of the poems. Already Byron struck a responsive chord in the poet to the extent that he elicited from him a poem in praise of his moving poetry (p. 74).

In 'A Stranger's Nostalgia at Sunset' the sight of sunset arouses feelings of sorrow and nostalgia both in the stranger and in the poet. Nature acts as a catalyst for the poet's identification with the stranger, thereby emphasising his feeling of alienation from his society. This is how Shukrī describes the poet or creative writer:

> At home and amidst his own people he lives like a sad stranger
> Nought in his heart but love, sorrow and anger against these untrusted times. (p. 25)

Shukrī can be more cheerful as in his description of the sea or his hymn to the sun at sunrise (pp. 27, 33), but the mood is generally a sombre one; even when nature has a liberating effect upon the poet as in 'The Meadow at Night': in 'The Garden' we are told that 'unlike man's joy, the joy of the birds is unmixed with sorrow' (pp.37-38). In 'Complaint against the Times', one of many plaintive poems, the poet is in a state of near despair in which he is 'spurned by God's mercy while being so young' (p. 40), for such is the lot of poets as he says in 'The Poet and His Beloved' God has ordained that 'sweet hope flees from a poet's thoughts just as a healthy man flees from a leper' (p. 49). The theme of the lover as a worshipper of beauty already appears here in 'The Worship of Beauty' (p. 63). There is a large number of short poems in this volume, expressing meditations and aphorisms mainly about love and the sufferings of the lover mostly couched in conventional idiom and the volume ends with a long poem in what he describes as *shi'r mursal* (blank or rhymeless verse), entitled 'Words of Passion' and containing his observations on various causes of the poet's sufferings and his reflections and aspirations towards a higher and happier state of affairs in the world, in a rather prosaic language which is not characterized by many verbal felicities (p. 85).

Shukrī's second volume which appeared in 1913, after his return from his studies in England, prefaced with an enthusiastic introduction by al-'Aqqād, contains much of his mature work and is more typical of his productions until 1919, the date of the appearance of the last volume he published in his own lifetime. Contrary to prevalent opinion, in his mature work Shukrī never loses interest in public or social issues altogether. He urges his people to accept change and progress and not to stagnate (p. 107), pointing out to them that it is only false religion that preaches resignation, while true religion means heroic struggle and endurance (p. 109). He preaches the value of work and the danger of despair in his didactic poem 'Life and Work' (p. 113), draws a painful contrast between dynamic Europe and his own stagnant society (p. 305) and stresses mankind's need for visionaries and dreamers to achieve great things (p. 298). He writes on the suffering of an orphan child (p. 111), the fear of death and the unknown expressed in a sick child's conversation with his mother (p. 122), pleads for educating criminals in prison instead of sentencing them to death, and for showing mercy to those who commit crimes driven by poverty and need (p. 134). He attacks the veiling of women (p. 152) and the attitude which regards them as mere chattels and their husbands' private property (p. 141). He describes his country's ancient monuments like The Sphinx and the Great Pyramid, although here he is simply moralizing on man and time and the transitoriness of human life and achievements (pp. 440; 444). In 'The Voice of Warning' we have a passionately committed poem in which, in ruthlessly frank terms, he laments the weakness of the Egyptian character and tries to rouse his fellow countrymen to improve their lot through scientific, technological and economic enterprise (p. 277). An equally angry criticism of his backward nation for their neglect of science and knowledge, the only means to glory, appears in 'Science and Dignity' (p. 415). 'The Awaited Hero' is a Messianic poem which is an invocation to the long awaited hero, the saviour of his nation, to come and revive the spirits of his people who will then shed their lethargy and identify themselves with him, and be infected by his determination and resolve (p. 387). In his last published volume of his Poems we still find a movingly committed poem like 'The Youthful Hag' in which the poet, ever loyal to his country and hopeful of her resurrection, persists in his attempts to rouse her from her deep slumber despite the unpopularity that this will bring him. 'I have not been negligent in my preaching, but have been let down by deaf ears'. (p. 557)

Likewise, Shukrī never manages to drop the stance of a moralist. In 'Black Flowers' he attacks the pleasures of life which ultimately bring pain, regret and sorrow in their wake (p. 227). In the epigraph to vol.IV he points out that the function of poetry is to ennoble and raise the soul above all that is base (p. 284). Furthermore, in the poetry written after 1919, Shukrī became excessively moralistic and often his poems were no more than a string of moral observations and meditations and his satires grew more savage and direct, as in 'Dead People' (p. 643) published in 1938, although as late as 1935 he was capable of writing such a remarkably lyrical and evocative poem as 'A Lovely Night' (p. 612). No doubt his attitude as a moral teacher was later enforced by his career as schoolmaster and educationist.

But from the second to the seventh volume of his *Dīwān* there is undeniably a growing concentration on the poet's inner world, his subjective and spiritual experiences. His complaints against his times increasingly sounded less like those of a social reformer and more like those of an 'outsider', who is at odds with a society that was incapable of either understanding him or appreciating his efforts. In 'The Poet and the Ruined Times' (p. 157) lack of appreciation and the difficulties put in the poet's path end by destroying his hopes, and render his heart 'like a ruined mansion'. The same feeling is expressed in countless poems such as 'A Poet's Complaint', 'A Poet's Prophecy', 'Agitation of the Soul', 'Fear and Terror', 'Poetry and Nature' and 'A Poet Dying' (where the chief source of the young poet's sorrow is his failure to attain fame before death) (pp. 164, 167, 169, 221, 226 and 235). Shukrī's agonizing awareness that he was living in a period of great cultural upheaval, where the clash between traditional and modern values had a devastating effect upon society, and especially the sensitive individual (which is fully expressed in the *Confessions*), often made him like Hamlet feel that 'the time's out of joint', and touched the metaphysical roots of his existence.

Shukrī's early feeling of alienation, which as we have seen, is discernible in 'A Stranger's Nostalgia at Sunset', was enforced by his experience in Sheffield where he spent three years (1909-1912). His poems 'A Poet in a Strange Land' and 'Nostalgia of a Stranger' show that he felt very much like an exile there, cut off from his home, friends and familiar surroundings, missing the sunshine and clear sky in a gloomy city where 'Above us the sky is in mourning like the vault of a tomb' (pp. 154, 155). In 'The Humiliation of Old Age' the poet's feeling of being a stranger among his kith and kin drives him to desire death before he becomes a despised old man (p. 418).

The main themes of Shukrī's poetry are philosophical and moral meditations, interesting or unusual states of mind, beauty in general and nature in particular, love, death, and the creative imagination. He wrote about man's belief in the golden age (p. 574); in 'Man and Time' (p. 136) he wonders if man's desire for a better world is the result of his soul remembering a less imperfect prenatal existence; in 'Mixed Needs' (p. 139) the body is described as 'the gateway to the soul' while 'The Eternal Seeker' (p. 292) represents allegorically the value of the eternal quest for truth. 'The Voice of God' is a religious and mystical comment:

> Listen, in listening the soul communes, for God's eloquent voice is so near.
> Each of us is a Moses. In the eyes of the Lord all pure souls are great. (p. 349).

In the introduction to vol.VII Shukrī denies the charge of lack of religious faith levelled at him, claiming that 'Doubt or questioning does not betray insufficient faith; on the contrary, it is the highest degree of faith', and that belief in God and in good is 'a basic need necessitated by the enormity of evil and misery' in this world (p. 505). This enormity prompted a compassionate angel, in the poem entitled 'The Rebellious Angel' (p. 537), to rebel against God and decide to turn his back on his blissful life in heaven and seek the earth in order to alleviate human suffering and combat evil. On earth he met with the same fate as Christ, but because he had rebelled his soul was condemned to an eternally restless existence, neither in Heaven nor in Hell. According to the poet, God's wisdom, which the angel had failed to see, lies in making evil an occasion for good to reveal itself.

But it cannot be said that Shukrī is as sensitive to the good as he is to the evil in man and in human society. 'The Mirror of Conscience' shows his unusually keen awareness of evil in the world of man (p. 235). Poems like 'The Nature of Man' (p. 228) and 'The Friendship between the Dead and the Living' (p. 232) show the extent of his misanthropic feeling: in the latter he says that we forget the enmity of those who die and passionately lament their death thinking that they are loyal to us, but if they were to return to the world of the living they would prove to be faithless in their affections. Another poem is entitled 'The Mirage of Friendship' (p. 250). This sentiment is expressed in countless other poems. In 'The Futility of Life' (p. 251) he writes 'If man were to know the full extent of his misery in life he would not have wished to be born'. In 'Boredom with Life' boredom sets in as a result of the poet being suddenly assailed by the disease of doubt when he was in the midst of his enjoyment of a comfortable easy life (p. 161). Shukrī composed poems on the duality of passion, the love/hate relationships, repentence and crime which reveal his fascination with unusual states of mind (pp. 146, 282). Despite the low opinion of human nature which he held, Shukrī was not a cynic; on the contrary, his poetry is imbued with a strong feeling of pity, as is clear in, for instance, his poem 'The Murderer' (p. 383), a dramatic monologue in which the poet evinces a deep-rooted sense of sin, together with great compassion for human suffering, in some ways reminiscent of Shakespeare's portrayal of Macbeth, by which it may very well have been inspired.

Among Shukrī's other themes nature occupies a large space. In 'The Magic of Spring' he claims that 'To be fully human man must love the beauty of nature, otherwise he is no better than a stone' (p. 217). 'The worship of beauty', he once wrote in an essay in 1916, 'frees man from the bondage of prejudice, obtuseness and narrow-mindedness, and bestows upon his soul a light which illuminates for him the secrets of life and opens the gates of his heart to every aspect of the beauty of nature.'[3] And as late as 1936 he wrote a poem entitled 'Truth and Beauty' (p. 623) in which the poet's sense of human misery makes him turn away from Beauty to Truth, but he soon realizes that beauty is designed to be a consolation enabling man to withstand sorrow and that it is the ideal which inspires man to improve his lot, and gives him hope, fortitude and love. 'The Voice of Night' opens with the words

> You have filled the world with your deep breathing
> Which all who have a wakeful heart could hear. (p. 118)

The term'wakeful heart' is significant and it recurs in his verse ('a happy wakeful heart', p. 121). In 'A Description of the Sea' the poet is struck by the teeming sea and by its changing moods which make him feel it has a life of its own (p. 118). 'Narcissus' which is about both the mythological figure and the flower at one and the same time, reveals the poet's 'romantic' ability to respond to nature and yet to transcend it (p. 342). A number of poems on birds, like 'Elegy on a Sparrow', in which there is a genuine feeling of bereavement at the death of a sparrow, and 'The Caged Songbird' show Shukrī's powers of empathy, of feeling for non-human forms of life (pp. 162, 301). His poem 'To the Wind' (p. 401) is Shelleyan in its dynamic Dionysian quality and in the author's desire to identify himself with the wind. As in nature Shukrī, like Wordsworth and other romantics, found in childhood a source of joy which has a healing power for the soul: 'The Child' treats the innocent and divine joy of childhood while in 'Children's Laughter' he writes: 'The laughter of children, like the words of the Lord, wipes off sin and guilt'. (pp. 571, 114).

But it is love and beauty that provide the themes of the vast majority of Shukrī's poems. To explain the preponderance of love poetry in his work he wrote in the introduction to vol.IV of his *Dīwān* (p. 290):

> I have noticed that some readers do not understand the high place accorded to love poetry. The value of love poetry is due to the fact that to love beauty is to love life. The greater a man's love of beauty is, the greater is his love of life. Love of life and beauty is one of the powerful social factors that lead nations to progress and advancement. By love poetry I do not mean the poetry of lust or sexual passion, but that of spiritual love which rises above all descriptions of the body except those which reveal the working of the soul. Love is the passion most intimately related to the soul, from it derive many passions or emotions such as hope, despair, envy, regret, bravery, cowardice, love of glory, munificence or meanness. Because of this, love has a great place in poetry ... it is not a condition that love

> poetry should involve loving any one individual alone, although this may be the cause most likely to produce it. The love poetry I have in mind is caused by the passion which enables man to feel keenly Beauty in all its manifestations alike in a beautiful face, or a body, a flower or a river, in the beauty of lightning, in the clouds, the beauty of night and stars, morning and its breeze, or the beauty of the soul or character, an attribute or an event, or the beauty of the images created by the human mind. The love of one human being for another is only one aspect of this extensive passion which embraces all visible beauty in life. This poetic passion bestows its light upon everything, even upon those loathsome dark aspects of life, giving them an artistic beauty ... Like the painter, the love poet draws upon the images of beauty in his mind ... Who knows, perhaps Qais ibn al-Mulawwaḥ was singing not about the real Lailā al-ʿĀmiriyya, but about the one who inhabited the inner world of his soul.

As is to be expected Shukrī's love poetry is marked by its excessive idealization of the beloved. In 'Smiles' (p. 148) we read that her smile brightens up his soul and nearly unveils the unknown secrets of the invisible world, enables him to hear myriad songs in his soul, and her glance breathes life in him as the sun causes the hidden seeds to germinate. The terms in which she is described suggest that she is more than a mere human being. In 'To the Beloved' (p. 177) the lover's attitude is one of utter humility. He addresses her in 'I have no other concern but You' (p. 240) saying:

> My life is now dark, so grant me a ray of light,
> A word, a greeting that I may reap when we meet.
> My soul is a sapling which you have planted,
> It can only hope for your munificence.
> My soul is the lowly earth beneath your heights
> You are the target of all creatures, no one lives but you
> So have mercy upon me, my beloved. Do not disappoint one
> Who has been offering you his prayers.

Clearly the object of love is almost divine here and just as in 'The Sought Beauty' (p. 321) where he says:

> I saw in a dream your face which I adore
> Crowned with the stars of night.

or in 'Love and Eternity' (p. 269) the poet's love is love of Beauty and not of an individual human being. But although he claims 'I am not one who loves fair maidens, nor do my eyes shed tears when they desert me' ('Love and Affection', p. 271) there are moments when the passion seems to be for a human being. For instance, in the deeply moving 'A Lover turns away his glance' (p. 172) the poet is agonizingly aware that the object of his desire is, for some mysterious reason which he dares not disclose, unattainable and that he therefore ought not to indulge in daydreams about him or her. Could it be that the poet was suffering from a homosexual passion? This is not at all a fantastic theory, although Shukrī's general tendency to use the traditional Arabic masculine pronoun in his love poetry cannot help us to decide either way. However, we do know that Shukrī never married, and what is more interesting, there is a morbid fascination with death and the gruesome aspects of physical decay and dissolution in practically all his love poems, especially where beautiful women are mentioned.

In the powerful poem 'Beauty and Death' (p. 115) the poet, trouble and unable to sleep, sees in the dark of night a vision of his recent dead beloved, but as he embraces her she once more dies in his arms, her beauty vanishes and her flesh disintegrates, leaving behind a skeleton smelling strongly of decay. The image of the poet kissing a dead corpse occurs again in his poetry ('Memories' p. 162). In 'Women in Life and in Death' (p. 132) he sees the ugly and the dead behind the beautiful and living, expressing a somewhat diseased sensibility:

> They rose, swaying in their clothes in the dark nights
> After they had become food for worms ...
> They came in the dark, and struck the eyes of beholders
> with disease
> Echoing the shrieks of owls till the air grew sick,
> Wearing their shrouds for modesty, lest their ugliness
> be seen.
> Alike in death and in life they hide defects that make
> their modesty a mockery.

This hysterical, melodramatic, nightmarish vision brings out the strong connection in the poet's mind between beauty and decay and his ambivalent attitude towards women. In his prose work *Kitāb al-Thamarāt* (Book of Fruit), a book of meditations sometimes couched in poetic prose, on man, nature, society and art, some of which are close to the themes of his poetry, Shukrī defines love as 'an animal whose upper half is a beautiful woman and whose lower part is a serpent'.[4]

Nearly every poem on love and beauty ends with thoughts on death. Examples are so many that they can be chosen at random. One poem is given the title 'Love and Death' (p. 211), 'Beauty, the Mirror of Nature' (p. 216), 'Love's Paradise and Hell' (p. 218) and 'The End of Love' (p. 223) and 'After Beauty' (p. 268), all, particularly the last two show the poet unflinchingly facing the most unpleasant aspects of physical decay. 'Would we were' (p. 257) begins with:

Would I were a breeze and you a bloom
We would then love one another for ever
We would neither quarrel nor part.
Would I were a meadow and you the rain,
Would I were the water and you the wine,
We would then contain one another.
With neither jealousy nor deceit.

and it ends with:

Would I were a dead man and you were my tomb
There would then be neither longing nor despair
Neither prohibition nor reprimand.

Just as there is death imagery in his love poems, death conversely is often seen as a woman, sometimes with sexual overtones felt in his courtship of death. In 'Death' (p. 542) he prays to death to deliver him from a life which is a painful riddle and invokes death by the most appealing epithets and descriptions, calling it a mother that for long has been deaf to her son's entreaties and whose breasts he wishes to suck. He loves death as a man loves the face of his beloved and yearns to quench his passion by kissing its lips. And, of course, it is fairly often that the poet invokes death. In 'The Misery of Life' (p. 405), as the title suggests, the poet is writing about his sufferings. Though living amidst his people he feels as if he had come to them from another planet, new and strange. Tired of his life he calls upon death to relieve him, although death here is viewed in romantic pleasurable terms. 'Moonlight on the Tombs' (p. 145) depicts the moon weary and wan, inspiring the same sensations in the beholder, and likens it to a fair maiden worn out by disease and lying on her death bed. In 'The Voice of the Dead' (p. 151) the poet stands amidst the tombs and hears the voices of the dead sounding now like the rustling of winds in leaves, or the bubbling of water, now like the beating of drums, the wailing of bereaved women, the howling of desert wolves or the roaring of the enraged sea. 'Between Life and Death' (p. 213) gives us the lonely figure of the poet standing by the raging sea in the middle of a thunderstorm on a dark night, a perfect 'sublime' setting for the poet whose thoughts turn to the subject of death and suicide: he admits to love of death being 'an overwhelming secret disease' and addresses the sea saying:

O save me from an unjust and wicked world,
My misery is teeming like your waves.

In 'Buried Alive' (p. 215) he explains that the secret of his unhappiness is a great sorrow deeply seated in his heart; he feels that the wide world is too confined for him and that he is buried alive. It is as if in his sleep his relations, mistaking him for dead, buried him in a deep grave and piled earth and stone on top of him and the poet woke up not knowing whether he was awake or had just had a nightmare. Finally his well known 'Dream of Resurrection' (p. 241) is a macabre poem giving the gruesome details of dissolution and betraying his low opinion of men, for it shows the persistence of human greed and strife when the bodies, risen from their graves, quarrel over the missing limbs and parts on the Day of Resurrection.

In 'Ideas Beyond the Reach of Words' (p. 121), as the title suggests, Shukrī deals with the mysterious aspects of the psyche which cannot be logically discussed or formulated in words:

> Part of the soul they are and how can the soul be seen
> by the physical eye?
> You know them only when your wakeful heart is fortunate
> enough to feel them.
> They are often attained by the one who keeps silent, for
> silence yields much eloquence
> and is full of peace.
> The soul speaks only to those who listen in humility.

These unknown and 'virgin' regions of the soul had a deep fascination for Shukrī, as they did for his Romantic successors. He even wrote a poem entitled 'To the Unknown' (*ilā'l-majhūl*, a word which became very potent in Romantic vocabulary) (p. 396), which shows this fascination (the didactic and moralistic prose introduction to the poem in which he links this passion to the healthy and useful scientific curiosity was added more than twenty years later). In 'The Marriage of Souls' (p. 392) the soul of each individual is felt to be an island, a *terra incognita*, a painful mystery and a riddle, yearning for communion with its like through love without which it becomes an arid desert, without water or vegetation. 'In Paradise', a poem seen by one scholar to be intimately related to D. G. Rossetti's *The Blessed Damozel* on the one hand and to the Moslem tradition of the Heavenly Bride, *ḥourī*, on the other, the poet cannot be happy if he is divorced from his soul-mate.[5] Hence the poet's constant quest for the ideal object of his desire. 'The Poet and the Image of Perfection' depicts a poet who in the pursuit of the ideal (which is ultimately Perfect Beauty - the creation of his imagination) is lured to his destruction (p. 130). ʿAbd al-Ḥai thinks this poem is inspired by *Alastor:*

> As in the case of Shelley, the theme of Shukrī's poem is self-alienation and the pursuit of a perfect image of the self which, in spite of its evasive nature, is the only means of attaining self-authenticity. It is not so much a pursuit of Ideal Beauty as an attempt of the mind to counter self-alienation by an image which the mind itself has evolved.[6]

This may be so, but surely the poem is also a variation on the theme of *La Belle Dame sans Merci*. Imagination is regarded as a tool of insight into a higher order of reality - a reality, however, which may render those who have glimpsed it incapable of coping with this mundane world:

A tale they told of a gifted poet
Whose verse was good and whose speech was noble,
Who loved not maidens, but was enthralled
By a virgin, a daughter of his Fancy,
An image of beauty his mind had formed
Perfect and peerless in loveliness,
Like a child he was who has glimpsed a light
That aroused his yearning for what cannot be,
He stretched out his hand to the distant star
Thinking it was within his reach.
Wherever he turned she was there before him
Shimmering like a deceitful mirage,
Her image so close to him, hovering around
As though it was not hard to grasp.
Perchance his fancy clothed her in flesh
For many a fancy has strange power.
Desolate, he shunned the company of men
And took to roaming on the mountain cliffs,
Pondering on the ways of love
Holding communion with spirits.
And as he was climbing a high cliff
Whose sublime view fills the soul with terror,
He glimpsed her whom he had painted in his mind
Like the fond worshipper of beauty he was.
She said to him, 'If your love be true
Then follow me, let fancy be your guide.'
So he followed and walked distraught,
(And lost is the man whose fancy is his guide).
He strove to hold her in his anxious arms,
Running towards her as fast as he could
Till at last he fell down the precipice.
May God have mercy on the soul of a poet
Who died a martyr to his impossible dreams. (p. 130).

The poem clearly shows Shukrī's ambivalent attitude to imagination which we have already encountered in his book of *Confessions:* he is both fascinated and frightened by it: 'lost is the man whose fancy is his guide'; it was left for a later, younger generation of more thorough-going Romantics to accept imagination without any reserve. In 'The Mouthpiece of the Invisible' (p. 128) true imagination is said to be the mouthpiece of the invisible; and because the poet feels and suffers, he sees what others cannot see and communes with the Divine. Likewise, 'Death and Imagination' (p. 153) shows the value of the imagination in conferring beauty on life, making both life and death easier to bear:

There is in poetry many a pleasurable dream which
enables us to endure life or death.

The poet's vision can be a source of bliss: 'The Angel's Visit' (p. 480), for example, describes the poet, uncertain whether he was awake or asleep, receiving a host of angels who cure him of his despair, purify his soul and give him a whiff of eternity. But visions can also be a source of terror. For instance, in 'A Step away from the World of the Senses' (p. 419) the poet while awake dreams that he has departed from the world of the senses, but the fearful vision he sees which indicates to him the full extent of the dominion of death, drives him to seek frantically to return to the real world and after several unsuccessful attempts he manages to do so. He wishes he would never again in his life have a similar experience and advises others never to stray from the concrete and secure world of the senses. Moreover, in 'The Shadow of Madness' (p. 402) the poet feels the constant presence of the image of the beloved to be painfully oppressive, like an obsession or a disease and wishes in vain he could break free from his enthralment.

There are perhaps too many poems about the theme of idealized love in Shukrī's work and their cumulative effect tends to be rather monotonous, especially as the tone is generally solemn and unrelieved by any humour. Furthermore, they are mostly in the first person: there is not enough variety in them which could have been achieved if the poet had made a greater use of the narrative and dramatic poems. Not that Shukrī's poetry is entirely lacking in formal variety. He uses the narrative and the dramatic monologue, deriving his material from well-known Pre-Islamic Arabic stories and legends, or from more modern sources (pp. 142, 156, 180, 201, 205). He experiments in the use of the multiple rhyme, the alternate rhyme or rhyming couplet. He even attempts to write blank (rhymeless) verse on a number of occasions (pp. 200, 201, 203, 205) though the result cannot be described as successful and in one case he finds himself slipping into monorhyme in eleven consecutive lines (p. 91). The poem which adheres to the monorhyme and monometre remains Shukrī's norm.

Stylistically, too, despite the profound influence of English Romantic poetry on him, Shukrī's style remains in many respects traditional: the vocabulary is still quite difficult and needs a glossary and the verse does not flow smoothly enough for the particular themes it tries to express. As has already been mentioned, Shukrī addressed the beloved in the traditional masculine form, and now and then uses conventional love and desert imagery. He has an unmistakable tendency to express himself in generalisations, sentiments, and moral precepts in the manner of traditional gnomic verse. Once or twice when as a young man he talked about his great ambition he struck the note of traditional boastfulness *(fakhr)* (pp. 46, 55). He sometimes complains of his times in the manner of Mutanabbī, and even in a poem expressing *ennui*, a specifically modern disease, we hear verbal echoes from Mutanabbī's verse (p. 161). It is true that Shukrī can attain a high degree of lyricism as in his most accomplished poem 'The Bird of Paradise' (p. 266), but this does not happen frequently enough. On the contrary, he can easily descend to the level of what is largely poetry of mere statement, even in a poem about a Romantic theme, such as 'The Ideal' (p. 460), which is an unabashed defence of the infinite inner world of dreams and the imagination, against drab and limited external reality.

M. M. Badawī

1. ʻAbd al-Raḥmān Shukrī, *Dīwān ʻAbd al-Raḥmān Shukrī*, ed. Niqūlā Yūsuf (Alexandria, 1960), p. 16. All references between brackets will be to this edition.

2. ʻAbd al-Raḥmān Shukrī, *Kitāb al-Iʻtirāf* (Alexandria, 1916). The references between brackets preceded by the letter C are to this edition.

3. ʻAbd al-Raḥmān Shukrī, *Kitāb al-Thamarāt* (Alexandria, 1916), p. 6.

4. *Ibid.*, p. 8.

5. Muḥammad ʻAbd al-Ḥai, *Tradition and English and American Influence in Arabic Romantic Poetry*, unpublished D.Phil. thesis (Oxford, 1973), p. 265.

6. *Loc. cit.*

Īlyā Abū Māḍī and Arabic Poetry in the Inter-War Period

This paper proposes to present a not too extensive account of the literary career of Īlyā Abū Māḍī (1890? - 1957), and then this will be used as a basis for the discussion of trends and movements in modern Arabic poetry in more general terms. He is an appropriate subject for such an approach because of the quality, range and variety of his work, and the fact that much of it echoes or anticipates themes and styles which have been important features in the story of Arabic poetry in the course of this century up to 1945.

Although Abū Māḍī belonged to that school known as the *mahjar* group of poets with the result that the greatest part of his work was produced in North America in New York, the real significance of this *mahjar* poetry - apart, of course, from its own intrinsic merit - lay within the development of Arabic poetry inside the Arab world. The fact that this verse was written in an environment separated both physically and culturally from its native context meant that experimentation both in form and content could take place in an atmosphere more devoid of literary traditions, social prejudices and political pressures, than would have been the case in Beirut or Cairo. Many of the salient features and ideas developed by the *mahjar* poets between 1910-25 reappear inside the Arab world, particularly in Egypt. For example the book on literary theory and criticism, Nuʿayma's *al-Ghirbāl*, was first published in Egypt in 1923. Appropriately its first edition begins with a preface by ʿAbbās Maḥmūd al-ʿAqqād, the self-styled leader of the *dīwān* group in Egypt, who took issue with Nuʿayma on certain points, in particular the delicate question of the Arabic language and its correct, disciplined usage in poetry.[1] Here then, is one of the earliest notable examples of a creative dialogue between the *mahjar* group and poets inside the Arab world.

The *Mahjar* poets, deeply aware of their situation as first-generation immigrants in New York, tended to develop to an extreme degree certain themes which derive from obvious feelings of alienation from their native social and cultural surroundings. At the same time their work often lacks many of the subjects current among their counterparts in Damascus, Beirut and Cairo, in particular those themes which suggested that poets were still very active and concerned members of society in practical terms. Īlyā Abū Māḍī's work, however, belongs to both of these categories: he was the most prolific and gifted of the *mahjar* group and his work provides some of the most satisfying examples of certain very typical features of this verse. At the same time, unlike his other colleagues, he demonstrates an enduring contact with the culture, people, and problems of the Arab World. He is a much less 'Europeanized' figure than either Mīkhā'īl Nu'ayma or Khalīl Jibrān, both in terms of his background and education, and in terms of the poetry which he produced.

The years of his adolescence were spent in Alexandria, in apparently humble circumstances, before he emigrated finally to the USA in 1911-12, and it was at the end of this early period in Egypt that his first *dīwān* was published, just before his departure when he was about twenty years old. This volume, entitled *Tadhkār al-Māḍī* is on the whole brief and unexciting save for the contrast which it forms with his later, more mature works, and also for the early signs which it shows of the talent and the originality to come. The first section of this book, 'Literature and Society', contains nine poems which are rather heavy, moralistic compositions, all strongly didactic in tone. They show a deep concern for the moral fibre of society and Man's shortcomings: the first poem, *al-Insān wa'l-Dīn*[2] dwells dolefully on how people fall short of the demands and injunctions made upon them by religion, and how dramatically they fail to conforms with its ideals. The poet continues in this vein throughout the section: inner beauty and purity of soul are praised, as opposed to handsome physical attributes; he commends true pride as that stemming from hard work and diligence, not from vain futile pastimes of pleasure and frivolity. On more than one occasion the solid virtues of learning and education are highly praised. This, of course, is a form of *zuhd* poetry which has a long tradition in Arabic: here solid social virtues are constantly emphasised as the moral condemnation of man and his shortcomings continues. Men are slaves of gold and riches, they prostrate themselves not in prayer but before the face of a *dīnār*,[3] and much is made of people's obsession with *al-Dunyā* to the detriment of *al-Ākhira*.

This volume, however, is not without other more interesting features: the second section is a collection of poetic narratives, some of which remind one strongly of the work of Khalīl Muṭrān, in particular the piece by Abū Māḍī entitled *Maṣra' Ḥabībayn*.[4] Naturally Muṭrān was living and working in Egypt at that time and his first *dīwān* published in Cairo (1908) contained several such narrative poems. Even in the more obviously traditional passages of *waṣf* contained in *Tadhkār al-Māḍī*, there are sections of natural description in which the author has frequent recourse to pathetic fallacy, with close identifications between the mood and emotions of the poem and the atmosphere of the surrounding scenery. Again these examples are reminiscent of some of the more striking work of Khalīl Muṭrān in well-known poems such as *al-Masā'* or *Badr wa Badr*.

The second *dīwān* by Abū Māḍī was published in New York in 1919, and provides the initial signs of his contacts with other of the *mahjar* writers such as Khalīl Jibrān, Mīkhā'īl Nu'ayma, and Nasīb 'Arīḍa. The preface to this book was written by Jibrān who speculates primarily on the nature of the poet and poetry, thoughts which introduce more than one example of poems by Abū Māḍī on the same subject. The poet is seen as a strange, peculiar being who has special gifts and insight; one who through the unique powers of his thought and vision is capable of rising above this world and the existence of ordinary men. Most writers on Jibrān have seen the origins of these ideas in European romanticism and in the career of William Blake particularly, with whom Jibrān identified closely. As far as Jibrān himself is concerned, this may well be correct, although it is worth mentioning that there is little in such ideas which would be greatly at variance with a medieval Arabic context. In the 11th century AD, Ibn Rashīq al-Qayrawānī described the nature of the poet and poetry in very similar terms.[5] What is more specifically European - as far as the writer can judge - is the anguished predicament of the poet as an individual who becomes progressively estranged from a society which is heedless of his message and the benefits of his special vision. This is most feelingly illustrated in a poem from this *dīwān* - *Lam Ajid Ahadan* - a dialogue between the poet and a mysterious female voice.[6] She asks him persistent, urging questions, exhorting him to action in a manner highly reminiscent of de Musset's Muse in *Les Nuits*. What is the point of one who has the power of visionary contemplation if he does not expose his thoughts for the benefit of his fellows? Roughly the poet replies:

> What is the point in raising a voice, if there is no
> echo to it?
> What is the point in shedding and spreading light, if there
> is no guidance for people in it?

He explains that the fault did not lie in the nature of his contemplation or the quality of his vision, but in that people took no notice of his verse. When young he had been filled with hope and optimism for his mission and in the relevance of his message. Now this has given way to disillusion and pointless solitude:

> But when I stretched out my hand, and looked around, I found
> not a soul.

This image of the despised and rejected prophet is also portrayed in the poem *al-Shā'ir*[7] in the same *dīwān*, but the attitude of estrangement and isolation is not maintained consistently by Abū Māḍī. In *al-Shā'ir wa'l-Umma*[8] he is not so depressed about the role of the poet, who is presented here as the living conscience of the people, not so unlike the idealistic adolescent who had written *Tadhkār al-Māḍī* back in Egypt. He encourages the people when they are in despair, sees more clearly than they do and points out the error of their ways.

Many of the love-poems in the second *dīwān* can certainly be described as 'traditional', but there should be nothing of the pejorative implications which have usually attended the phrase *shi'r taqlīdī* as far as many of these poems are concerned. In *Ammā Ana* the poet strives to express the nature and strength of his desires for his beloved. The descriptions and images are frankly sensual and explicit in the best and richest tradition of Arabic amatory poetry, while the lack of abstruse, conceited allusionsremoves all barriers to the immediate impact of his feelings and desires on the reader.[9] Unlike his *mahjar* colleagues such as Khalīl Jibrān, Mīkhā'il Nu'ayma or Nasīb 'Arīḍa, Abū Māḍī had no extensive knowledge of literature outside his own Arabic heritage, and in cases like this poem, or *Ana wa Ukht al-Mahā wa'l Qamar*,[10] he writes easily and skilfully within his own tradition.

In addition to this amatory poetry, one finds in his second *dīwān* numerous poems about Syria and Lebanon, many of them falling within the category of occasional poetry. They often display the usual nostalgia of the emigrant for his homeland, but they are also deeply concerned with the political and military crises which convulsed the area during the First World War. Numerous are the titles such as *al-Ḥarb al-'Uẓmā*, 'Events of 1914', 'Events of 1916' and so forth.[11] He was particularly conscious of the sufferings of his countrymen at home while he and his colleagues were in the relative security of the *mahjar*. The sober tones of the historian who describes the harrowing facts of the famine which afflicted Syria and Lebanon during the war, cannot quite compare with the vivid lines by Abū Māḍī on the same subject, taken from the poem *Umma Tafnā wa Antum Tal'abūn*:[12]

> 'Many a tiny one like the chicks of the sand grouse, perish
> from severe famine.
> Their sinews are weak when it attacks; and hunger will destroy the strength of lions.
> Have you seen a necklace when it comes apart? thus are the
> tears on their cheeks.
> Their spirits have run away like water
> through grief; God what a cruel fate.'

It is *al-Jadāwil*, the third *dīwān*, (New York 1927) which is regarded by many as the peak of Abū Māḍī's achievement, but this is true only for that type of poetry which was most typical of the *mahjar* writing. In this book he continues and develops to an extreme degree the tendency which began to appear in the second *dīwān*, namely an obsession with his individual perplexities, combined with an ever increasing sense of loneliness and isolation. The first poem in the book - *al-'Anqā'*[13] is all mystery, constant searching, doubt, and urgent but undefined aspiration. The legendary bird is a symbol for something about which people have heard and know, which they constantly seek but which always eludes them. The object of the poet's frenzied search is referred to usually by the feminine pronoun and the whole atmosphere of evocative mystery is typical of the malaise of the individual which is such a feature of this *mahjar* verse. The search of the poet assumes cosmic proportions as he looks along numerous different courses: the life of ascetic religious piety provided no ultimate satisfaction, nor did his world of visions, dreams and imagination. Throughout the poem, the mystery remains vague and unsolved.

A poem which has enjoyed a great reputation is *al-Ṭalāsim*,[14] perhaps the most lengthy, detailed, exposition of the painful mysteries which surround the isolated figure of the poet. The sole aim and justification of this work is to express a state of confusion and perplexity, without offering any hopes of solution or indulging in deep and detailed speculation. Yet in spite of its great reputation and popularity, one feels bound to say that as a work of art this is not Abū Māḍī's most successful poem. It is too long and detailed to sustain the reader's interest at a consistently high level. The constant re-iteration of the answer *Lastu adrī* to the different situations, becomes eventually boring as it loses its initial quite impressive effect. The poem as a whole would have benefited from a contraction in length by means of more judicious choice of the numerous details and situations. It is really a type of manifesto in verse of the various themes used by the *mahjar* writers, and probably for this reason it became a significant poem for the many poets and writers within the Arab world who found in it echoes of their own perplexity and experience.

Even in *al-Jadāwil* where one finds Abū Māḍī at the height of his introspective brooding, he finds it impossible to cut himself off from society and the rest of mankind as some of his other colleagues do. The poem *Fī'l-Qafr*[15] describes an attempt at a typical Jibranian flight into nature, to escape from people and their society, full of corruption and unhappiness. The blissful state of solitude in nature is idealized in the true pastoral tradition, but in spite of this, Abū Māḍī recognizes with rare honesty that it is futile to escape from other human beings and all their shortcomings, since all those things exist within himself either actually or potentially. The rather unforgiving, if not to say puritanical, author of *Tadhkār al-Māḍī* has obviously travelled a long way in terms of human experience. In the volumes of verse subsequent to *al-Jadāwil* one finds further variations on the theme of the subjective introspection of the perplexed and isolated individual, as well as further evidence of how Abū Māḍī maintained a strong identity with Syria and Lebanon. Some *mahjar* poetry showed an unwillingness on the parts of these authors to project anything beyond the limits of their own tortured personalities - one could think of Nasīb ʻArīḍa in particular. Īlyā Abū Māḍī certainly did demonstrate this tendency, but only to a certain extent and as one aspect of his work as a whole.

When evaluating the effects of the *mahjar* writers on the development of poetry within the Arab world from the 1920s onwards, one can say with comparative safety that their influence on poetic diction and imagery was of paramount importance, leading Mandūr to express the admiration of a whole generation of Egyptian writers and critics for this new type of *adab mahmūs*.[16] Further they had a role to play in modifying the traditional structures of the *qaṣīda* and the *bayt*, although this was a more gradual rather than dramatic contribution on their part. Then perhaps most of all there was their predominant concern with the crisis of the individual alienated within his society, their idea of the poet as a rejected and misunderstood prophet, preaching to the deaf ears of his fellow men in a corrupt, inhuman society. This attitude certainly struck echoes within the Arab-Islamic context, but there remains something very European about this predicament belonging to the tradition of Rousseau, Blake and Baudelaire.

The increasing trend towards a similar kind of subjectivity in Arabic poetry since the late 19th century has been a major preoccupation of critics and writers both in the Arab world and the West. Reference was made above to Khalīl Muṭrān and the possibility of some contact (probably indirect) between him and Abū Māḍī in Egypt. Muṭrān has been singled out from the generation of Ḥāfeẓ and Shawqī as a poet of particular talent and originality, especially because of his concentration on the personality of the writer, the scenes where his own sentiments and emotions are uppermost. Evidence for this is usually quoted from poems such as *al-Masā'*, *Wafāt ʻAzīzayn*, *al-Shāʻir wa'l-Ṭā'ir* or *Badrī wa Badr al-Samā'*.[17] Yet Shawqī's own *dīwān*, for example, is by no means devoid of poems of brooding introspection or romantic reminiscence; this cannot be said of the author of *Maṣāyir al-Ayyām* or *Ghāb Būlūnyā*.[18] The two poets are certainly very different: Shawqī was for almost twenty years a trusted member of the court circle of the Khedive ʻAbbās II, perhaps the last great court poet in Arabic literature. He lived in a context where the poet still had an active and practical role socially and politically, at a time when he or his contemporary Ḥāfeẓ Ibrāhīm in two pages of verse could concentrate the feelings of a nation more effectively than any other medium. Muṭrān, on the other hand, was a Christian Lebanese immigrant to Egypt, coming from a background where the cultural ties with Europe had always been strong. The two are most dissimilar even in poems of a like type and theme; Shawqī usually reveals his emotions in a more calm and controlled manner, while Muṭrān's outbursts tend to be more violent and climactic. One can reasonably say that Muṭrān is at his best in the type of highly subjective poem referred to above where his individual voice is of prime importance, and he implies in the preface to his first *dīwān* that this is the poetry which he prefers.[19] This has probably made it more natural in Muṭrān's case to concentrate on such poems rather than on the eulogies, elegies and poems for all manner of social and political occasion which in fact make up the bulk, indeed the majority of his complete works. But differences of temperament, cultural formation, and background cannot alone be sufficient criteria of judgement in literature. Shawqī was a much more universal poet and his great gifts are distributed more evenly throughout the corpus of his work. Whether it was a *madīḥ* for the Khedive, a fiercely political piece such as that written on Lord Cromer's departure from Egypt, a poem revealing the past glories of Pharaonic or Islamic Egypt, or lines of his own personal feelings and reflections, Shawqī's talent and technique are nothing short of remarkable.

Shawqī was of course the alleged arch-exponent of *shi'r taqlīdī* attacked so bitterly by 'Abbās Maḥmūd al-'Aqqād and his colleaques. It is of great significance that the term *taqlīdī* has implications as much sociological as literary, if not more so. The most complete statement of their attack on Shawqī lay of course in *al-Dīwān, Kitāb fī'l-Naqd wa'l-Adab* (Cairo 1921), a book which is essentially destructive by nature as al-'Aqqād admits that they give precedence to the destruction of permanent idols, rather than the detailed exposition of new principles. The attack on Shawqī is much more personal than scientific. One thing which the book emphatically does not prove is that Shawqī was an inferior poet in terms of skill and technique: al-'Aqqad in particular tries to do this, but his arguments are neither disciplined nor convincing. In fact he and al-Māzinī were reacting more against a way of life and a certain type of society, than against good or bad poetry. Shawqī, both in his style and in his practical function as a poet, epitomized that society for them. The new generation of Wafdist supporters after World War I could never quite forgive Shawqī, who had been the court poet of 'Abbās II under the British. The fact that when Shawqī returned from exile after the war, he no longer fulfilled such a role, made no difference. That a poet should be chosen as the object of their attacks demonstrates how important a means of communication and propaganda it still remained, beyond the range of strictly personal predicaments or purely literary criteria. In the light of these remarks, one is justified in considering *al-Dīwān* ... by al-'Aqqād and al-Māzinī of much the same category as *Fī'l-Shi'r al-Jāhilī* by Ṭāhā Ḥusayn, or *al-Islām wa Uṣūl al-Ḥukm* by 'Alī 'Abd al-Rāziq - books which must be judged not so much for their intellectual discipline and scientific arguments (or lack of them), but rather as manifestations of the cultural and political crises of their time.

The 'Diwan' poets are described in Mounah Khouri's book *Poetry and the Making of Modern Egypt* (Leiden 1971) as those who created the poetry of *wijdān*, of emotion, where themes of social and political significance gradually give way to verse of a subjective, highly individual nature, presumably similar to that practised so much by Abū Māḍī and his colleagues in the *mahjar*. He concludes that the link between the social and literary aspects of most of their compositions is very tenuous. To apply such a statement even to the *mahjar* poets would be hardly appropriate, but to draw such a conclusion about the *dīwān* poets is somewhat misguided. First, it is hardly surprising that poetry should have been showing more subjective, egocentric tendencies throughout a period when the writings and activities of figures such as the feminist Qāsim Amīn and the political theorist Luṭfī al-Sayyid were concerned basically with the significance of the individual in social and political terms. Muṣṭafā Kāmil and Sa'ad Zaghlūl were establishing a tradition of political figures in Egypt who could be described as popular leaders, who gave broad sections of the Egyptian population the conviction that they too as individuals had a part to play in the struggles and the destiny of the newly emerging nation-state. It is against this background that one must view the poetry of the *dīwān* group.

'Abd al-Raḥmān Shukrī was the member of the group who both by temperament and his personal history seemed much more fitted to the life of a recluse in his ivory tower than either of his two associates al-'Aqqād or al-Māzinī. Yet the poetry composed by Shukrī between 1910 and 1920 is in many ways as socially relevant as that written by Aḥmad Shawqī, but Shukrī speaks on behalf of different people and a different generation. A poem such as *al-Shā'ir wa Ṣūrat al-Kamāl*[20] could be seen as a typical example of the poet's most introspective, egocentric aspirations, ending in despair and disillusion, a true poem of *wijdān* where the ideas and the concepts of the English Romantics appear most clearly. Yet this constant theme of aspiration and disillusion, the frustration born of an impotence to realize ideals, is so authentic for that period of Shukrī's life and time. This is particularly so if one considers this poetry together with his small pamphlet entitled *Kitāb al-I'tirāf*, which claims to be a record of the thoughts and feelings of a young Egyptian faced with all the dilemmas of his time.[21] He is pessimistic about the changing forms of tyranny which his country endures. He had grandiose hopes and dreams, but a frustrating incapacity to put them into effect. He is a prey to doubt and bewilderment, between the two stools of the old and the new, not knowing which ideas and customs are harmful fantasies, or which are the proper bases for further development.

Quite a different spirit lay behind the poetry and activities of the man whose career in Egypt was to culminate in the founding of the Apollo society: Aḥmad Zakī Abū Shādī. This is the other main group of poets within the Arab world usually associated with subjective, romantic poetry akin to that which Īlya Abū Māḍī and his colleagues brought to such a peak in the *mahjar*. The broad-mindedness of the man and the aims which he hoped his society would pursue are indicated by the fact that Aḥmad Shawqī became the first President in 1932, even though the style and way of life with which he had been identified were doubtless alien to the more progressive members of the group. The key word to associate with Abū Shādī and his colleagues is that of co-operation *(al-Ta'āwun)* between writers who did not necessarily have the same ideas or objectives in poetry. Because poetry was still very much one of the voices of society, perhaps Abū Shādī saw Apollo as an attempt to bridge the gap between those whose cultural and political orientations were increasingly at variance. This interpretation would seem to correspond with the character and intentions of the man himself, one who hoped that poetry would be a means of communication open to the different sections of society, and perhaps even a means of bringing them together. His early *dīwāns* of the mid-20s represent a broad range of themes and styles: there are many of the lyrical love poems of the type one would normally associate with the Apollo society, *(Zaynab* 1924*)*, but there are numerous pieces on political and social change, poems of patriotism, and nationalism, and 'occasional' poetry in the most traditional sense. He acknowledges his debt to Shawqī, to Ḥāfeẓ, to Muṭrān as well as to European poetry. (See the *dīwāns Miṣriyyāt*, 1924 and *Anīn wa Ranīn* 1925).

His huge tome *al-Shafaq al-Bākī* was published in 1926-27, containing more than thirteen hundred pages of poetry. In view of their drastic variations in quality, the only reasonable explanation which one can derive from the innumerable prefaces and poems contained in this book is that their author considered poetry as a possible means of linking together the increasing ramifications of modern life. He seems to have feared the break-down in communications between different sections of society as it became more complex and as the Islamic way of life in all its traditional forms came increasingly under attack, or did not respond positively and intelligently to the demands being made of it. For him, poetry had to be firmly rooted in its society, it must take account of and reflect its religion, its patriotism, and its modernising processes. It had to play its part in preserving the position of the Qur'ān, *ḥadīth* and the purity of the Arabic language. The poet must indeed be a prophet amongst his people, but emphatically not after the *mahjar* fashion. Jibrān and some of his colleagues (here one should make an exception of Abū Māḍī) were apt to glory in the idea of the prophet who was despised and rejected. For Abū Shādī, the poet is a prophet who must be constantly in accord with the needs and tastes of his times. He goes in fear of the situation in which the poet could become estranged from his people by speaking in a language and terms which they do not understand.

Throughout this huge book it is true there are many love poems which one can identify readily with the predominant fashion of the Apollo poets, and there are nature poems written rather after Romantic European models; but there are many others about innovation in literature, the cause of feminism, prison reform, the place of Islam in society and so forth. In fact the versification of Abū Shādī displayed the same omnivorous voracity as did the prose of al-ʻAqqād, and inevitably it suffers from lapses in quality. The contemporary reader has the instinctive reaction that many of these would have been more successful as prose articles, but at least as far as Abū Shādī was concerned, poetry was still a natural vehicle for the treatment of such subjects, quite as much as prose. Later in the 1930s he was to learn to his cost that his ideal of the all-embracing medium of poetry was not capable of surmounting the divisions and factionalism of social and political life in Egypt, and he could no longer maintain his original optimism about how poetry would be an instrument of bringing people together. In *Ashiʻʻa wa Ẓilāl* there are poems which suggest that the Islam which he had espoused enthusiastically in the mid 1920s was now losing its great creative capacity for re-interpretation and re-formulation, he accuses it of losing touch with life, people and relevance. (See the poems *al-Mu'adhdhin*, *ʻĪd al-Islām*).[22]

It is true that poets such as Ibrāhīm Nāgī and ʻAlī Maḥmūd Ṭāhā in the 1930s developed a much more escapist type of poetry, often though not always after the pattern of European romantic models which had great appeal and many imitators. This was the trend which in the eyes of many modern poets of the post-1947 era has been stigmatized by an 'ivory tower' irrelevance, the sort of verse which should have little or no place in the era of new departures characterised by revolutions in prosodic form and socio-political commitment. Yet that particular trend was not the whole story of the Apollo society, nor did it represent the totality of the spirit and ideas which led originally to its foundation. Poetry has always been that remarkable combination of an aesthetic, emotional creation which may have a universal appeal in human terms; then there is its peculiar relevance to its own context, offspring as it is of the frictions and harmonies of its creator. This has been as true of Arabic poetry in the inter-war period, as at any other time in this century.

R. C. Ostle

1. M. Nu'ayma: *al-Ghirbāl* (Cairo 1923), pp.11-12.

2. Īlyā Abū Māḍī: *Tadhkār al-Māḍī* (Alexandria 1911, p.3).

3. *Ibid.*, p.16.

4. *Ibid.*, pp.28-29.

5. Ibn Rashīq: *Kitāb al-'Umda fī Ṣinā'at al-Shi'r wa Naqdih* (Cairo 1907). pp. 19 ff.

6. *Īlyā Abū Māḍī, Shā'ir al-Mahjar al-Akbar* (Ed. Zuhayr Mīrzā, 1963) pp.307-10.

7. *Ibid.*, pp. 434-37.

8. *Ibid.*, pp. 447-51.

9. *Ibid.*, pp. 477-79.

10. *Ibid.*, pp. 353-59.

11. *Ibid.*, pp. 734-38, pp. 327-31, pp. 583-86.

12. *Ibid.*, pp. 694-700.

13. *al-Jādāwil*, (New York, 1927) pp. 5-8.

14. *Ibid.*, pp. 89-112.

15. *Ibid.*, pp. 29-31.

16. Muḥammad Mandūr: *Fī'l-Mīzān al-Jadīd* (Cairo n.d.) pp. 69-91.

17. Khalīl Muṭrān: *Dīwān al-Khalīl* (Cairo 1908), pp. 119-21, 45-8, 175-9, 14-15.

18. *al-Shawqiyyāt* Vol.II (Cairo n.d.) pp.146-9, 27-8.

19. See Preface to *Dīwān al-Khalīl* (1908).

20. *Dīwān ʻAbd al-Raḥmān Shukrī* (Ed. N. Yūsuf, Alexandria 1960) pp.130-31.

21. ʻAbd al-Raḥmān Shukrī: *Kitāb al-Iʻtirāf* (Cairo 1916).

22. A. Z. Abū Shādī: *Ashiʻaʻʻwa Ẓilāl* (Cairo 1931), pp. 36, 66-67.

Contemporary Arabic Poetry - Vision and Attitudes

Introductory Note

This paper deals with some aspects of vision and attitudes in *avant-garde* contemporary Arabic poetry. By 'contemporary' I mean the period from 1948 up to the present time. It falls neatly between two wars, and has been throughout its twenty-five years well punctuated with events which have had a profound influence on the development, outlook and vision of modern poetry. It begins with the Palestinian débacle of 1948, and ends with the October war in 1973. Such landmarks as the following are important: the Egyptian revolution of 1952, the Algerian revolution (1954-1962), the Suez aggression of 1956, the Iraqi revolution of 1958, the union between Syria and Egypt in 1958 and its dissolution in 1961, the rise of an official Palestinian representation in 1965, the June war of 1967, the strengthening and growing seriousness of the movement of armed resistance after this war, the civil war in Jordan in 1970, then the above-mentioned October war of 1973, and, in between, several *coups d'état* in Syria and other Arab states. All through this time, a definite and important shift in society was taking place, and intellectual and literary life was undergoing numerous developments.

It was poetry in particular that underwent the most drastic changes. One can say, in fact, that there is an Arabic poetry before the 'fifties, and there is an Arabic poetry after the 'fifties. *Avant-garde* poetry of the period is a sign of the inner vitality and dynamic need to change things completely and in all spheres. The poets, who want to be the prophets of the Arab world, have anticipated the profound changes that will eventually take place in all aspects of Arab life. The secret of *avant-garde* Arabic poetry lies in its dramatic intercourse with the universe around the poet. The poet is no more a figure in solitude; he is now the prototype, even sometimes the archetype, whose personal experience is rarely so private as to have no relationship with the world around him, with the moment in history, with a sense of the past and future.

However, this paper can only deal with one particular aspect. I have chosen to focus my discussion of vision and attitudes in contemporary Arabic poetry on the relationship of these elements to time. As far as I know, this relationship in modern Arabic poetry has not been discussed. Since the concept of time in this poetry, and the attitudes it reflects towards the various periods of time are very important, I hope to be able to throw some light on the subject.

The Present, the Immediate Past and the Future

The relationship of *avant-garde* Arabic poetry with time and change is usually dynamic. Time is no longer an element of disintegration and dissolution, of permanent change as it was, for example, in pre-Islamic times. Then, the poet, looking at the abandoned camp-sites, could only see the elements of tragedy, of irrevocable change, of the permanent dissolution of a once happy existence. The pre-Islamic man's whole life yielded to the element of change as inherent in the very nature of desert life: springs drying up, pastures becoming arid, loved ones departing, youth withering away. It was the poet's wonder and bewilderment at the realisation that everything was subject to change and ruin that coloured his long and insistent grief as he stood on the deserted ruins of the camp, where only the traces of life and love remain, where the wind has almost swept away all that was left of a once happy tribe. In this poetry there is little adherence to the soil, to a permanence beyond time and change, a permanence that can defy and defeat time and change.

In the Islamic periods, with the profound changes that Islam introduced - urbanisation, the diminishing importance of desert life, the constant immigration of poets to the towns - this nostalgia, while keeping its basic emotional *motifs* all through the history of Arabic poetry, relinquished or diverted some of its external features. However, if the camp-sites or at least their pre-Islamic concept, were gone, the nostalgia for the departed loved ones remained, and so did the anguish at the passing away of youth and its joys. It has remained an integral part of the general mood of Arabic love poetry (formal and folk) that the present is arid and meaningless, and that in the words of Proust 'the only paradise is a lost paradise'.

In contemporary Arabic poetry the interpretation of time has changed drastically. As has been said, it is no more an element of disintegration by which the very essence of life is consumed. An attitude like this towards the immediate past, for example, would be dangerous, for it would mean finalising its main issues -

accepting the loss of all the precious elements that constitute the Arab nations' struggle for a dignified existence after 1948, the loss of Palestine, of honour, of freedom. There could be no finality, therefore in the poet's attitude towards this past. Life cannot, any more, lose its substance; what has been lost must be replaced, what has disintegrated must be made whole again. Life is not a rigid machine that can be destroyed forever. It *must* contain the possibility of rebirth, otherwise the whole nation is doomed. Memory, therefore cannot be involved only in contemplating what has been tragically lost. It is a memory that refuses, rather, to forget both the loss *and* all the political implications of the loss. These implications prescribe the present and the future. Forgetting them means the death of a people and a cause. This memory, therefore, connects the immediate horrific past with the present (often horrific too) in order to prepare the ground for a brighter future to emerge.

The poetry for the 'fifties in particular concentrated on the idea of the change of the seasons which, more than anything, marks the passing of time. This gave hope to the winter of Arab discontent after the Palestine disaster of 1948. The idea was that winter *will* give birth to spring, and death will eventually produce life and resurrection. This was particularly inspired by the sudden acquisition and quick popularity of the mythology of Phoenicean fertility cults among some poets. The idea came to them from contemporary Western poetry, particularly from T.S. Eliot's theory and application of the myth of Adonis in *The Waste Land*.[1] However, the rapid adoption of this and other myths can only be explained by the need of the moment for an interpretation of present Arab history in positive and concrete terms. Al-Sayyāb's implicit use of the Tammūz myth in his famous poem 'Unshūdat al-Maṭar' (1954) was a supreme example which triggered forth various experiments using either the same myth (under different names such as Ba'al in Khalīl Ḥāwī, the Phoenix in Adonis), or Biblical stories such as the story of Christ's crucifixion and resurrection which al-Sayyāb also exploited, or that of La'āzar (Lazarus) employed by Ḥāwī. All these poems span time and are dynamically and basically concerned with change, with transcendence, with the eventual arrival at fertility and fruition. The past, whenever invoked, and I am still talking here of the immediate past, is usually a dark abyss, an intolerable memory of a terrible fall that has produced an intolerable present. The present is still a time of failure, of stupor, of terror, of tyranny, where innocence is devoured, and freedom curtailed, where man is crucified and tortured. It is therefore a time of death, a petrified existence. However, it is never total death, not in the 'fifties, since out of this lifeless winter the great festival of spring will emerge.

Despite the insistence of the poetry of the 'fifties on remaining conscious of the immediate past, there was a domination of the moment over permanence and continuity in all spheres. A feverish appetite for modernism took hold of the poets. They aspired to cut the umbilical cord which linked them with the poetic past and to direct poetry, dynamically, towards the present moment. Artistically, the poets felt that their epoch was superior to all previous epochs and they rejected and disqualified the Classical as well as the modern poetry previous to their work, attacking among other things, the aesthetic involvement and aloofness of the symbolists, the self-centred escapism of the later romantics, and neo-classical bombast and rhetoric. The new poets were not homogenous in their outlook on the world. Some were Marxists, some were Arab or Syrian nationalists, some were liberals, but they all agreed on one thing: that poetry had to abandon the self-contained aesthetic world of a previous generation and look for broader horizons.[2] Poets were expected to involve themselves with the immediate problems of their age, and the present became crucially important. They had to look for answers to the searching question: 'How can the Arab world emerge from the dilemma in which it suddenly discovered itself?' The Palestine disaster, it was soon found out, was not an accident, nor was it the core of the dilemma. It was, rather, a witness and a proof. Suddenly the ground of the old life began to shift, and with this nervous instability of life and faith, the poets, who were the first to discover and announce their rebellion and anger in the Arab world, became a group by themselves. Neither the established literary circles accepted them, nor the broad masses at first, nor for that matter did the official circles. There never has been, perhaps such a deep divergence between official circles and the *avant-garde* generation of poets as that which has existed since the 'fifties.

Studying the poetry of this decade, one finds such words as *ḍayāʿ, ruʿb, qalaq, ghurba, rafḍ,* repeated over and over again. A mood of alienation from contemporary Arab existence took hold of poets and artists. The present seemed to be empty and disgusting, and they felt uprooted and lost. Alienated in many spheres, they in turn rejected the old world around them, which belonged to the dead past. Rejection in the 'fifties, however, was not a totally blind rejection, for, as has been already pointed out, it had its positive side which believed in the inevitability of rebirth, but a rebirth apart from all connections with the past.

The outlook of *avant-garde* poetry in the 'fifties towards the future seems to us now naive and simplistic. The *Tammūzian* poets who wanted to be the *voyants* of their generation seemed to stumble too easily on the happy solution. They decided that time which had wrought so much havoc and ruin on our lives, and which would eventually bury our generation among its ruins, would reward our children.

Their theme of hope established a firm and confident relationship with the future. However, these poets did not back their vision with a coherent system of thought. Furthermore, their intuition was not able at that early time to give them a lucid vision of the highly complex political situation in the Arab world, of all the abortive streaks that had been woven for so long into the make-up of social and political life.

Confidence in the future abated the edge of the tragedy inherent in the situation, but did not do away with a general tragic tone. The poetry of the decade contained the poles of rejection and acceptance, denunciation and celebration, anxiety and confidence. Mixed with a basic optimism was a partially tragic outlook sustained by two tragic *motifs*: the inevitability of sacrifice and death, and the unavoidable doom of this generation. So that the happy children in Ḥāwī's poem, 'Al-Jisr', crossing the river of time from this horrific present to the future shore of safety, will only do so on a bridge built from the ribs of this generation.

This tragic tone pervaded the poetry even of the most optimistic and futuristic of these poets: al-Bayyātī. However, it was al-Sayyāb who was again the first to tear the curtain, and in some individual poems expose a more complete tragic vision. His poem, 'Jaikūr wa 'l-Madīna', for example, also written in the 'fifties, is a tragic realisation that the individual, battling with 'the world order', is nothing but a weak, mortal man made of flesh and blood. The poem has a universal vision of the powerlessness of man and his vulnerability. al-Sayyāb was a highly perceptive poet who, even in his more optimistic poems divining a happy future for the oppressed (e.g. the Marxist inspired 'Unshūdat al-Maṭar'), could discover all the universal laws of necessity that combine to break a man and eventually to destroy him. His genuine grief in this poem for the dead sailor drinking salt water from the gulf, for the fate of the fugitive immigrants battling in vain the stormy waves of the sea, for his dead mother drinking rainwater in her grave, for all the paradoxes of life and death, reveal a tragic vision more involved with the universal condition of man than Marxist strictures usually sustain, a vision consistent with his entirely tragic poem, 'Jaikūr wa 'l-Madīna'. In the latter, the village poet finds himself and numerous village boys trapped in the heartless City, within the iron walls that block the road to his village, Jaikūr, an archetypal symbol of lost innocence and happiness. The past in this poem is a happy memory of a life impossible to regain, the entire concentration is on the present with its hopelessness and anguish. The future is blank and impossible to perceive behind the stubborn walls of the City. Both al-Sayyāb's conversion to and subsequent defection from communism were perhaps prompted by the tragic sense of life he so keenly possessed, by the intuition of what life is at its most crucial moments. This had led him to the quest for a solution to man's dilemma in his country, but the Marxist answer, stubbornly favouring an optimistic conclusion and a rationalistic understanding of these dilemmas, conflicted too acutely with his basic tragic sensibility and his vigilant awareness of *all* forms of human suffering. His early poetry represents most authentically this conflict.

By the beginning of the 'sixties, however, most of the once optimistic poets had already begun to lose heart. They now realised what they had failed to realise earlier: that the complexity of the problem and the full appreciation of the conspiracy had eluded them. Much of the old confidence was abandoned, particularly when faced with the deceptions of certain situations in the Arab world which had given to millions a rapturous hope in the future, such as the union between Egypt and Syria (1958) which was dissolved in 1961. A feeling of utter political inadequacy dominated the early 'sixties, and the present became even more unbearable. A poet like Khalīl Ḥāwī, for example, who was one of the most optimistic of the Tammūz group, reversed his attitude and wrote poems of utter despair. In his poem, 'La'āzar 'Ām 1962,[3] the Biblical figure of Lazarus is depicted rising from the dead only as the gloomy, dead spirit of a man. The climate of contemporary poetry was no longer one of optimism. Faith in the future was clouded, and the psychological climate was ripe for more tragedy and violence.

As has already been said, there were elements of tragedy and counter-tragedy in this poetry. What enhanced the tragic aspect was the silent avoidance in *avant-garde* poetry of any religious interpretation of the various political problems and of the Palestinian debacle, a kind of interpretation which was popular in less sophisticated poetry and in folklore. 'In tragedy', says I.A. Richards, 'the least touch of any theology which has a compensating Heaven to offer... is fatal'.[4] To the *avant-garde* poets, it was not God's just hand that wrought the Palestine disaster, for example, and that would perhaps amend it in the future, but human hands: the betrayal of values, the murderous treachery, the shortsightedness of individuals who were in a position to influence the course of events, combined with the ignorance and stupor of millions. And it would be only the atonement of men in combat, not in worship, that would undo the wrong.

Inherent in the Palestine catastrophe and as a result of it, there were certain situations that are as a rule particularly conducive to a tragic vision: the premature but willed death of heroes, the constant failed endeavours, the personal suffering and death of simple innocent people, uprootedness, enforced partings, declines of fortune and former status, the voiced or silent rejection and degradation of the refugee in many countries of the Arab world, the physical and spiritual alienation. However the tragedy inherent in these situations was usually diluted because, when the poets spoke directly of the Palestine tragedy, they more often than not offered a kind of communal solution that anticipated a hopeful future. Rarely was a situation depicted in *avant-garde* poetry merely in the light of the human condition in which men are destined to suffer their individual experiences. Even the mass murders of the Qibyas and the Kufr Qasims did not seem complete tragedies except for the victims themselves, and *their* personal tragedies were usually overlooked by poets in favour of the renewed determination to repair the wrong which the brutal assaults produced in the nation. 'Tragedies', says George Steiner, 'are irreparable'.[5] They are final and conclusive. 'There isn't any hope', writes Anouilh, 'You're trapped. The whole sky has fallen on you, and all you can do about it is to shout'.[6] However, the fall of the Palestinian City (Jaffa, Jerusalem, Acre, Safad...) can only be temporary for the poets. It was impossible to admit the contrary. On a national basis, the Palestinians were facing their own dilemma with mounting tenacity, with a stubborn refusal to accept the situation as final. The themes of 'return' 'vindication', and the idealisation of 'heroism' and 'resistance' dominated much of the poetry written in this period. So long as the future carried the promise of encounter and restitution, the tragedy was incomplete, and there could be no admission of a final loss.

The National situation therefore, was denied a final tragic verdict. Some of the numerous individual tragedies which the general situation bred, however, were well portrayed in creative prose writings such as Ghassān Kanafānī's novelette, *Rijāl fī 'l-Shams*, (1962). The question which imposes itself here is: why was the theme of individual tragedy sacrificed in poetry, in favour of a communal message that expressed itself either through the abstract medium of ideas, or through communal symbolism and ritual? For there was, on the whole, no particularisation of experiences as they affected individual lives.[7] This is a point worth discussing at length in a separate study. Muṭrān, at the turn of the century, expressed his deepest social and political rebellion through the objective delineation of individual experiences, and in two long poems in the early 'fifties, al-Sayyāb portrayed the tragic situation of the blind prostitute in 'al-Mūmis al-ʻAmyā'', as well as the grave digger's tragi-comical situation in 'Ḥaffār al-Qubūr. He has exploited both experiences to give concrete backing to an ideological point of view. In the 'fifties too, Ṣalāḥ ʻAbd al-Ṣabūr wrote his famous poem, 'Shanq Zahrān', on the hanging of a young villager, Zahrān, choosing to describe the ordinary life and tragic death of one of several victims of British aggression on the village of Dinshawai in 1906, thus particularising the tragedy of the village in images warm with life. Why then, when it came to the question of the Palestine catastrophe was such a kind of treatment generally overlooked? The answer might lie partly in the fact that the depiction of complete tragedy with regard to the Palestinian question was avoided by poets who wanted to be the *voyants* and prophets of the future, but it may also have some important artistic motives.

Perhaps violence, the wish to destroy, is the other face of tragedy. The poetry of the 'sixties displayed a great propensity to violence. Khalīl Ḥāwī's collection, *Bayādir al-Jūʻ*, in 1962, to give a single example, is an experiment in extreme violence. There is no ambivalence in this. The tragedy was caused by an evil which destroyed things of great value and it is natural to respond with the wish to destroy this great evil, both that which came from the outside, and that which sprang from internal indigenous mistakes.

Violence, however, did not only emerge from feelings of resentment for being some of the world's victims in the twentieth century, but also from a feeling of guilt for allowing ourselves to be victimised. The feeling of guilt, in fact, has prevailed in modern Arabic poetry ever since the nineteenth century, expressed in the tone of chastisement and astonished anger at the stupor and weaknesses of the modern Arab world. However, this feeling of guilt rose to a high pitch after 1948, arriving at its volcanic outburst in the aftermath of 1967, and merging with the wish to destroy.

In the aftermath of the June war of 1967 there was an unvoiced desire in the nation to be flaggelated. Qabbānī's famous poem, 'Hawāmish ʻalā Daftar al-Naksa' was the first important work that accomplished this. He unleashed all the self-hate, shame, and inner feelings of guilt which the whole nation felt. In this poem and in several others that followed, the poet, using an abusive, highly emotional language, tore down the ramparts of present Arab culture and the lingering ills he believed helped to cause the defeat. Al-Bayyātī who in most of his poetry had sustained a universal outlook, also turned his whip now on the decadent values which he believed betrayed the cause of man, abandoning for a while the intricate symbolic approach he had already achieved, and addressed his readers in simple, angry and emotionally abusive language. In December 1968, Adonis published his long, devastating poem on the war, 'Hādhā huwa Ismī', in which the drama of defeat is portrayed in sophisticated, oblique terms, and the present and past mutilated beyond repair. This poem will be discussed again in the next section, but the recognition of guilt in all these poems carried with it a kind of redemption which helped people to rid themselves a little of an unbearable psychological situation.

Pain was expressed also through irony and sarcasm, rare emotions before 1967. These elements have begun to infiltrate Arabic literature after the defeat, but are stronger in creative prose works than in poetry. It is interesting to note that amongst the Syrians, with their typical blasé attitude (a result perhaps, of too many upheavals in political life), have emerged two outstanding ironists: Zakaria Tāmir in the short story, and Muḥammad al-Māghūṭ in poetry. al-Māghūṭ[8] depends greatly on the comical image, rather than on the element of tone and direct sarcastic approach. In his poem on the war, entitled 'Marwaḥat al-Suyūf' he mixed bitter sarcasm with a pained, even tragic attitude, expressing himself through a series of comical images strung together like beads in a necklace. He chose his images from city life, the city life of an emigrant whose eye is more on its sordid aspects. It is a symbolic poem which alludes to the Arab world waiting hopefully for the war in the guise of an aged eagle waiting for the storm, sitting silent and alone like a coachman, his beak worn-out like a shoemaker's thumb. When he moves, he does so hesitantly, like a prostitute at the door of an inn, and keeps tasting the remnants of clouds (old Arab glories) like an old cook, his white feathers getting dirty all the time like a servant's apron. However, when the storm comes, it defeats him, and leaves him behind, crumbling on the horizon like a drunkard in front of a washstand.

In a poem like this, it is the present which is of crucial importance, and if history and the past are ridiculed, the future is completely ignored. Perhaps it is a feature of irony and sarcasm not to span time in the future, for one can only ridicule with conviction that which has already happened.

It was in the second half of the 'sixties that Palestinian poets writing in Israel appeared on the scene. Before that, the only Palestinian poetry known in the Arab world was that of the Palestinian poets writing in exile. These wrote about their country and their dispersion. Their first objective was to keep alive the memory of their country: its vegetation, its customs, its cities, constantly alive in the minds of a new generation growing up in exile. The memories of cities in particular gave a touchstone to their sense of place, and to their constant vigilance over time, for those cities seemed in this poetry unchangeable and immortal. When the Palestinian poets writing in Israel came on the scene (they became a full force after the 1967 war), they added a further flavour to revolutionary poetry in Arabic, and gave to post-war dizziness and shock a new focus, a new stabilising force. Having grown up under Israeli occupation, they were more accustomed to physical confrontation with the aggressors, and to their ruthless manner in dealing with the Arabs. They now seemed to transcend the new, post-war situation with defiance. Their tone remained high, their confidence unperturbed. It was greatly refreshing to read post-war poems and see their vision of the present less clouded, of the future still optimistic: 'You (to the Israelis) build for the present', shouts Tawfīq Zayyād. 'We erect our edifice for the future. We are deeper than the sea, higher than the lamps of the sky'.[9] Another poet, Samīḥ al-Qāsim, says, 'On the fifth of June, we were born again'.[10] There is much rhetoric in most of this poetry, yet it belongs in varying degrees of authenticity to the modern tradition in Arabic poetry. However, poets like Maḥmūd Darwīsh, Samīḥ al-Qāsim, Tawfīq Zayyād, Sālim Jubrān and the emerging ʿIzzidīn al-Manāṣira, broadly speaking form a group by themselves. Their poetry is characterised by a fiery imagery, a positive and challenging tone, and often by a subtle simulation of the intonations and syntactical constructions of the Palestinian dialect, which aims to produce a warm, unifying effect among the Palestinians themselves.[11]

These poets have been in constant touch with their country and its life. They did not need, as did the Palestinian poets in exile, to 'remember'. In one of his loveliest poems after the 1967 war, Darwīsh says: 'We have no need to remember; Mount Carmel is in us... and we are in the flesh of our country...'[12] The country itself becomes a beloved, almost of flesh and blood. A Mystical fusion of love for woman and love for country characterises much of the poetry of this very talented poet. His lyrical fantasy transcends all the easy clichés of patriotic poetry in Arabic to give to his verse a new attraction. It is not a poetry of ideas and analysis, but of vision and passion, revealing an immense inner excitement and a heightening of sensibility. Because of his fluid rhythms, his lucid images, his familiar tone, his warmth and ardour, and above all his simpler language, he is perhaps the most popular poet writing now after Nizār Qabbānī.

The difference in tone between the poetry of the resistance written by this group of poets, and that of many other Palestinian poets in exile, might stem from the fact that these poets have established a tradition in different surroundings. The confrontation with the aggressor on one's own land produces a greater defiance and asserts daily the difference in identity and situation. It has been characteristic of modern Arabic poetry since its renaissance to show greater and more direct defiance, and to exhibit less obliquity of style when confronting a foreign power on Arab land. The conflict is sharper, more straightforward, more openly violent and above all more personal and concrete because there is no doubt as to the identity of the aggressor. It is only when the conflict becomes internal, with indigenous ruling bodies that proclaim slogans of liberty and progress, yet who can unleash their hatred in open and even more frequently in clandestine ways on those who oppose them, that poetry turns to allusion and symbolisation. The tone becomes oblique, the approach more subtle. The poet suffers from alienation and retorts by rejecting his world. In the poetry of the resistance, the rejection is directed mainly towards the aggressor and towards those who have openly betrayed the cause. A greater tendency to integrate with their world and to preserve it is displayed.

However, the general attitude in all Palestinian poetry towards time has been an attitude of resistance against time, against the disintegration of ties and roots, and the fading away of memory. One's present identity depends on what one was. The Palestinian poets, therefore try to assert their own Palestinian past in order to preserve their identity intact. Since, in fact, the only hope this nation can ever have lies in the liberation of their land one day, the future assumes crucial importance.

The Remote Past

The treatment of the remote past, the past of Classical times, in modern Arabic poetry is interesting. The vision of this 'past' has been present in modern Arabic poetry since its renaissance in the nineteenth century. In the poetry of the early pioneers, i.e. the neo-Classical school, the past was glorified and perpetuated with love. This was to be expected in artistic terms, for the modern poetic renaissance was accomplished only by modelling the poem on past examples from various poetic epochs in Classical times. To these poets the past meant mainly two things: the eras of perfection of the poetic technique, and the epochs of the glory of conquests and empire of Arab and Islamic civilisation. The attitude towards these two concepts was highly deferential and was, implicitly or explicitly, compared with the present, eyeing with concern and regret the obvious change, even degeneration, of the politics and poetics of the modern period. In the neo-Classical poetry, the adherence to past models of 'poetic perfection' was fanatically expressed in the adoption not only of the old two-hemistich form, but also of old attitudes and, in part, of the old language as well. The poetical vision embraced all the paragons of public glory, and the memory of the race was illuminated by the epic tales of conquests, of great deeds, of pomp and power and progress and justice, which characterised the golden periods of Arab civilisation.

However, generations vary in their choice of historical periods from which to draw inspiration and analogy. The present generation of poets have moved to a different kind of national archetype, selected with care and often after deliberate research into the annals of Arab history. The glorious, heroic models had come easily and naturally to the former generations of poets, and in their exercise of memory they high-lighted the more positive aspects of the past, with the intention of drawing encouragement, example, and probably consolation from them. Now the role was generally reversed, for it was the less positive aspects of Arab history that were explored with the intention of drawing a lesson from them, of showing how history has repeated itself. The former 'glorious' models were hardly symbolic by nature. They might have given the poems some epic colouring, since the use of history and of the archetype in poetry is more akin to 'epic' than to 'lyrical' constructions, but the mytho-symbolic aspect is hardly present. The heroic models were mentioned as paragons of their particular qualities, but not as symbols of what still takes place under different names and in various disguises. On the contrary, their very mention drew a breath of nostalgia and regret, as if to suggest that their equals could not be found today. Now, in the present period, the poets chose to remember particular events: tragedies, great feats of endurance, persistence, courage, sacrifice, and resistance against either the odds of history, or against characteristic oppression, tyranny, lust, treachery and personal ambition. The new archetypes were now the lone heroes fighting the world: Ṣaqr Quraish, ʻAlī b.Abī Ṭālib, al-Ḥusain, al-Ḥallāj (skilfully used by ʻAbd al-Ṣabūr in drama), Dīk al-Jinn, Abū'l-ʻAlā'l-Maʻarrī etc., or ambitious tyrants and their agents forcing their power on the world. It is true that tyranny in the early twentieth century was alluded to symbolically, but it was the foreign archetype of the tyrant that was usually employed, such as Muṭrān's Nero (1924). Old Arab history was hardly touched on, except to show its positive and glorious side. Now, both the crucified and the crucifier were chosen from Arab history. The fact that Ṣaqr Quraish in the famous poem 'Al-Ṣaqr' by Adonis succeeds eventually in fleeing his enemies and in building a new empire does not detract from the fact that, as a fugitive, his struggle was a lonely and frightful experience.

In this sense, *avant-garde* contemporary poetry which employs these historical archetypes is mythical by nature. The resurrection of such personages from the past and their projection into the present make an immediate link with historical periods and give the feeling of continuous progression from past to present to future, a progression that unifies experience and illustrates the similarity and the potential occurrence of the same experiences, whether they are achievements, failed endeavours, malignant attitudes or even passive submission. This kind of pre-occupation with the past, its employment in a mythical symbolisation that throws light on the present, had its beginnings early in the period under discussion, but it became a constant method of dealing with the present in the 'sixties after the dying away of the Phoenician fertility cults which dominated much of *avant-garde* poetry in the 'fifties. In the mid'fifties al-Sayyāb, a pioneer in the use of myth and archetype in contemporary Arabic poetry, wrote his famous poem, 'Fī'l-Maghrib al-ʿArabī' (1956) which used archetypes from Arabo-Islamic civilisation. It was written in celebration of the Algerian revolution. The theme of the dead god being revived as in the Phoenician myths, is present. The Prophet Muhammad is the archetypal hero whose past glory does not save him from dying now, in the twilight of a once great civilisation. With his death God himself retreats from the world, and the whole world dies.[13] This God is seen weeping in an evacuated house in Arab Jaffa, and is found wounded and hungry, begging for alms. However, the Algerian revolution revives His spirit. Strength and virility return to the nation with His revival. The once dead land, full of living graves, experiences a resurrection of millions of symbolically dead people, and God lives again in the Arab world.

Because of the general predominance of the present over the past during the 'fifties and the stigmatisation of the Classical past, this poem acquires a particular flavour and importance. Other poets began looking into this past and at the turn of the decade, Adonis published his third collection, *Aghānī Mihyār al-Dimashqī* (1961) in which a definite link with the historical past was made. Adonis, in this collection, broke through the resistance of the 'fifties to this past and recovered the balance. This attitude developed into a broad and deep sense of history in his poetry, a mythic sense in which the immanence of the past in the present, and the constant flowing together of the different periods is skilfully portrayed. Other poets began showing the same tendency. They had been looking into Arab legendary history for Arabic myths which they had hoped to find alive among the people, for they realised that such myths would be more effective than the 'imported' ones. However, modern Arabic culture, they soon found out, is not particularly rich in mythic tales. It is true that every nation has its own mythology with which it interprets some vital aspects of life, but the interpretation of life, death, human endeavour, human suffering, and all the great experiences of man, was almost wholly taken over by Islam, and the present *Weltanschauung* in the Arab world is basically Islamic. Since highly significant myths tend to yield greater poems, the limited number of such myths in Arabic had driven *avant-garde* poets in the 'fifties to use myths from ancient Phoenician and other sources. However, despite the interesting treatment of these myths by some poets, they remained an intellectual acquisition. On the other hand, the Arabic myths they found and exploited such as *al-ʿAnqāʾ*, *al-Sandabad*, *Iram Dhāt al-ʿImād*, although important, their use was limited to the idea of quest of happiness, truth, and 'symbolic treasures', and they were not adequate to cover the other important aspects of contemporary Arab experience. Instinctively, the poets discovered that it was impossible to create new myths, a realisation which Yeats, the greatest of the modern European poets to try to use myth as a basis of his work, discovered early. Yeats says that 'a mere intellectual revolution cannot bring back the old celebration of life, but can only bring about something more deliberate... more systematised, more external, more self-conscious, as must be at a second coming'.[14] So it was with the contemporary Arab poets. They turned to history, creating their archetypes from the immense store of historical and semi-historical material. They might have had in mind Saint John Perse's application of time in his poetry. In his Nobel Prize address in 1960 he said, 'In spite of himself, the poet is also tied to historical events. Nothing in the drama of his time is alien to him'. The philosophy of Bergson concerning time, the element which helps us to become aware of our spiritual life, and Proust's magnificent treatment of memory and the recapturing of lost time, then James Joyce's experiment in Ulysses, and his description of the 'amorphous quality of inner experience, the boundlessness of the stream of time by which the soul is borne along',[15] all these may have exerted their influence on the more sophisticated poets, either directly or indirectly through the works of such writers as Lawrence Durrell who came to be well known in sophisticated literary circles in the Arab world at the outset of the 'sixties. We find such poets as al-Bayyātī, Adonis and Ṣalāḥ ʿAbd al-Ṣabūr resorting to historical archetypes particularly in Arab history. Adonis, profoundly influenced by Perse, has worked hard towards finding a common denominator for Arab existence, has tried to discover the correct coefficient for contemporary problems in Arab history so as to arrive at a mythic sense of race, and to root modern experience in a continuous history stemming from basic (according to him) repetitive equivalents in the past. The firm line of communal action he creates is directed by the deep disillusion of a contemporary Arab who has suffered the experiences of 1948 and, later, of 1967.[16] His vision grew darker with the years, particularly after 1967, as did that of other *avant-garde* poets. These poets have had too many shocking experiences since 1948 to be able to sustain an integrated, positive, vision of progress and rebirth. Even a poet like al-Bayyātī, whose faith in the inevitable victory of man's struggle guided his work for many years, joined such poets as Nizār Qabbānī, Adonis and others in a flood of national self-rejection after the June 1967 war.[17] In seeking to relate the past to the present they looked for pitfalls (or what they termed pitfalls) in Arab history, choosing a mistake for its universality, and for having appeared persistently in the nation's history. This is then given as a witness of what is happening now, so that man as heir to the past, is very much the heir of this past's wickedness and malignancy.

The emphasis in all this poetry lies in the continuum of experience as an integral part of a race. The accent is to re-interpret Arab history in such a way as to give example and warning to modern Arabs. Historical events are being intensified in some poems, deflected in others, accelerated, neglected, or inverted to fit this basic aim.

The use of the national archetype has proved to have a greater immediacy in Arabic poetry than the use of myth. Both have a unifying effect with general human experience, but the former also particularises certain aspects of the national experience, which enhances its effectiveness, giving an added strength and a warmer appeal. Moreover, both poet and reader have a greater emotional involvement with the national archetype than with a myth, and it is because of this emotional involvement that the use of the historical archetype demands a great adherence to the real, or at least to the legendary qualifications of the personage. The allusions by both Qabbānī and al-Bāyyātī to Harūn al-Rashīd as a symbol of lust and tyranny are, therefore an artistic mistake, since Harūn al-Rashīd's image is one of benevolent splendour firmly related to the most golden epoch of Arab history.[18]

al-Bayyātī has shown a growing interest in the use of the archetype. A poet's universal vision, al-Bayyātī explains, depends on three things: an objective understanding of the paradoxes of existence, a discovery of the logic of history and a dynamic involvement with the events of his own time.[19] From the appearance of his second collection *Abārīq Muhashshama* (1954), al-Bayyātī showed a cosmic sense, and sought to unify human struggle everywhere. As a Marxist, he forged links with famous left-wing poets such as Nazim Hikmat, Pablo Neruda, Mayakovski, Lorca, Aragon and Éluard. Even at the zenith of Arab Nationalism in the 'fifties, he showed a genuine preoccupation with the struggle for freedom all over the world. The broad cosmic outlook which, at the beginning preoccupied itself more with contemporary times, has persisted in his poetry, but has been greatly enriched by a growing historical sense that has been developing deeper in him, simultaneously as it did with various other major poets in the Arab world. Myths, historical events and recorded stories of bygone days are incorporated into the texture of many of his poems seeking unity with present day experiences. Historical figures are often developed into archetypes, and some are vested with qualities that surpass their basic historical descriptions in order to make their material rich enough for the creation of the archetype. However, al-Bayyātī, in what seems to be a very diligent search for historical material, sometimes toys with his findings too drastically for success. It is true that mythic or historical material can be embellished, and reinterpreted by the poet who might deliberately regroup and reformulate it according to a new outlook in order to suit his subject matter; however, some important authentic relationship with the origin of the material (whether myth or history) must be preserved in order to give the poem a spiritual force and to integrate the various details without too much artificiality and deliberation. The poet must be able to reconcile the basic idea of his poem with an aspect of the borrowed material important enough to merit its adoption, finding a philosophical equation, a common denominator that harmonises the theme of the poem with its symbolisation.

al-Bayyātī, despite his many successful and interesting attempts, does not always do that. He sometimes has an inadequate way of using historical or mythical material. This is well exemplified by the way he treated the story of the poet Dīk al-Jinn al-Ḥimṣi, a contemporary of Abū Nuwās: Dīk al-Jinn's jealous and cruel murder of his beloved is woven into the story of a 'heroic figure' shunning the temptations of the metropolis, Baghdad, with its golden treasures, limelight and court splendour, in favour of personal and artistic freedom.[20] Another example of his inadequate use of the archetype is his exploitation of the figure of ʻĀ'isha as related to history. As he explains in the appendix to his collection, *Al-Mawt fī'l-Ḥayāt*, ʻĀ'isha 'was a young woman whom the Persian poet, ʻUmar al-Khayyām greatly loved, but she died of the plague and al-Khayyām never mentioned her in any of his poems'. In al-Bayyātī's poetry (for she appears in several poems in three of his collections), she is a 'mythical woman', the personal and collective symbol of eternal and unique love, an elusive spirit that appears in countless visions and at all times, that dies and returns again to the world. His allusion to eternal beauty and love itself is a symbol, for in several instances this love exemplifies the fire of the revolution which will give life and happiness to the world. It is a revolution that can only be kindled by the heart's perpetual flame, a reminder of Muhammad Iqbal's philosophy of ʻIshq. al-Bayyātī would have done better had he contented himself with creating his symbol out of pure imagination or out of fresh personal experience, and allowed it to emerge as a 'type', by making it more distinctive and representative, or as a symbol, which admits a certain amount of ambiguity. As it is, the archetype is not authentic, but is grotesquely extended and re-fabricated out of all proportion to the original simplicity of the story.

Perhaps the most positive poem that takes inspiration from the past as a time of great national bliss is Muḥammad ʻAbd al-Ḥayy's long poem, 'al-ʻAwda ilā Sinnāri (Khartoum,1973). It is a poem that seeks harmony in present day Soudan between the two main races constituting its inhabitants, the Arabs and the Africans. The archetypal pattern in this poem is the old Sudanese kingdom of Sinñar (1509-1821) which had succeeded in unifying the people and transcending the contradictions of racial differences which the poet feels are again in conflict now. A mythical sense of continuity of race and racial experience pervades this poem. The poet's design shines with the will to attain a harmonious unity, to transcend the incongruities that have penetrated the spirit of modern man in his country, and have thus denied him the power of renovating man's experiences in their decisive climaxes. In its quest for unity and harmony, it is reminiscent of Saint-John Perse's poem, 'Amers' (1957) with its concept of *alliance*, a concept of universal harmony which stands in opposition to violence.

In its application of a mythical approach, in its imagery, its use of language, its rhythmic variations, the poem comes from the heart of the modern tradition of Arabic poetry. However, its absolute homage to ancestral achievements and its passionate fusion of retrospective experience with its prospective potentialities, are completely outside this tradition. Modern Arabic poetry pulses with the will to destroy, to dissolve and to change the present world by dislocating it from its ancestral roots. This poem preserves the past in its splendour, in fact seeks to rejuvenate the past. If contemporary Arabic poetry is the witness of pain and anguish, this poem is the witness of happiness and celebration.

Stopped Time

There is movement and dynamism in the invocation of the past and in prophesying the future; as for the present, so long as it is related to change and to the future, it also remains charged with life. It is only in the experience of the most intense emotions that time is stopped. Both the 1948 debacle and the 1967 war produced some examples of utter despair forcing on poets the feeling of a time stopped beyond times. In his long poem on the 1967 war, *Hādhā huwa Ismī*, Adonis has spasmodic allusions to a stoppage of time and space: 'Are my people a river without an outlet?' he asks, exclaiming: 'I have no more any past nor any present', for history seems to have dwindled into insignificance and degradation. 'This history lives in the lap of a whore... desires the rottenness of earth, walks in a worm. Go back (addressing himself) to your cave and lower your eyes'. Or again: 'I saw history in a black banner, walking like a forest; I did not write the date'.[21] However, the suspension of time is not sustained throughout the long poem which greatly varies in its attitude. Despite the tone of despair, degradation and abuse, the poem ends on a powerfully optimistic and glorious note, drastically out of harmony with the tone and mood of the whole.

al Bayyātī in his poem, 'Bukā'iyya ilā Shams Ḥuzairān'[22] written on the 1967 war, also fluctuates in his attitude. After such images of stopped time: 'We are dead... we are the generation of gratuitous death', or: 'We never died, we were never born', he forces a few lines of strength that point to a movement of life, a basic motif in his former poetry: 'My wounds are the mouth of Job... my pains are the blood that seeks revenge'.

Most poets, it seems, were watching their words, particularly after the heated criticism which the abusive language and complete rejection of past and present Qabbānī's war poems produced. However, the general mood in the Arab world just after the war was one of stopped time, a natural reaction after a terrible ordeal. A feeling of complete deadness was in the air, as the following lines demonstrate:[23]

> Have you heard of my death,
> the viper cup?
> death in love with itself?
> yes, you've heard...
> Your undertaker saw me buried
> as they stretched him by my side.

To recapture the impression of stopped time is a realisation of an acute experience: a dilemma, a tragedy, a great happiness; and it is because of this that its mood cannot last, whether the poet, facing an unbearable ordeal exclaims 'I live at zero point ... these times are not mine',[24] whether he, experiencing a moment of great happiness, calls, as Fadwā Ṭūqān did; 'This moment has no past, nor future... it is a flower of transient splendour..... let's hold on to it before the crossing, oh my love',[25] or whether he expresses his anguish as M. Badawi does, at the impossibility of capturing the precious moments that life yields, the glorious moments 'that fly away, perhaps without return.'[26]

Timelessness

Avant-garde Arabic poetry is not metaphysical in nature, and is not concerned, on the whole, with the timeless and the eternal. In less sophisticated examples in modern poetry there can be found some kind of metaphysical vision that takes strength from the fact that God is eternal and that, perhaps, the martyrs that die are eternally alive in heaven. However, *avant-garde* poetry strictly avoids any such references, and the death of heroes is life for future generations. If God is absent, if heaven has no presence in the vision of most *avant-garde* poets, then the qualities of timelessness and changelessness are absent.

The few poets who have contemplated the metaphysical aspect of life in their verses have done so only in individual poems and not as a permanent attitude in their poetry. Early in the 'fifties, M.M. Badawi touched on the theme of eternity, and his poem, 'al-Tilāl', (The Hills) posed an agnostic question of marked poignancy. Heaven is symbolised by the 'Hills' supposed to be overlooking the 'Valley' of life. The poet's search for an answer as to the real presence of the hereafter and the eternal emerges only in negative terms: no one has ever discovered the secret of the Hills, and no one has really seen them, although many 'Ambassadors', all varying in the colours they wear and the opinions they convey, have claimed that they had come from there. The only perpetual presence is the 'mute Lake' stretching around the Valley like a frame. It is the symbol of death, and when during the night the wind blows, and the thunder echoes the curses of the Lake, and tongues of fire break loose, people go to the shore in groups, each group with their Ambassador, singing the song of the Hills. In the morning, when the Lake is calm again, and life comes back to the market place, people speak of nothing else but the Hills. Yet, the poet reminds us with a hint of sarcasm, no one knows anything about the Hills, about the secrets behind the 'Iron Curtain'.[27]

In 1966 Fadwā Ṭūqān wrote her poem 'Amām al-Bāb al-Mughlaq' which describes her experience of anguish at the realisation that the full knowledge of God is forbidden to her. The poem reveals a psychic conflict between two states of being: one which asserts her deep conviction of the existence of God (somewhere behind 'the closed door'), and the other the incapacity of her heart to feel again the surge of love for this God. Love used to fill her heart with 'joy and wonder' during the days of purity and innocence, before her 'young plant' was burnt by God's 'poisoned winds'. It was God who changed, leaving her 'alone in the deserts of the night,... the ground forever shifting under her feet, revolving without an axis'. Her wish to return to God is meant to bring comfort to the problems of her existence and do away with doubts and contradictions. The poem ends on a statement of utter, existentialist despair. Seeing nothing but walls of darkness in front of her, she exclaims: 'In vain, no echo, no sound. Go back addressing herself , nothing here but loneliness, silence and the shadow of death'.[28]

Al-Sayyāb's communication with God came in his later years, when he faced serious illness and imminent death. His attitude shows little contemplation, but is mostly a prayer for a cure, built on exclamations of pain and hope, sometimes mixed with anger at God, sometimes with Islamic submission, and sometimes with a heart-breaking confidence in a cure. His approach to the religious theme, coming at such a critical time in his life, is understandable, but it does not seem mature, or emotionally satisfying.

This period, in fact, marks the lowest development of religious poetry in Arabic, and in *avant-garde* poetry, there is very little attempt at a revitalisation of religious themes among Moslem poets. Christian poets such as Yūsuf al-Khāl and Tawfīq Ṣāyigh have expressed deeper religious sentiments than others, adding a contribution to the Christian tradition in modern Arabic literature, but the question of religion is never limited to religious orthodoxy with either of them. The emphasis of the period is on other things and it can be said that contemporary poets are, on the whole, without metaphysical worries. It is not that they scorn religion, but that they are heedless of its presence.

The climate of contemporary Arabic poetry, on the whole, has been one of violence. If a critic were to anticipate the poetic currents in the coming few years, he would say that the rejection of both past and present will probably continue. The attainments of man in the past, and especially in the Arab past, will continue to be magnified and celebrated, but always his attainments *in spite of* the world. Again the image of the lone hero will be invoked and dramatized in ever renewed terms.

However, the motif of violence which carries the will to destroy, can only do so in order to build again. Poetry would be meaningless, and the whole role of the poet would be futile if all that is left in the world after a poem is ruin. It is precisely because of this that poetry has to be futuristic, to stand for future life and human greatness. *Avant-garde* art is a movement forward, a refusal to be stuck forever in the present. If contemporary Arabic poetry comes from this precise moment in history, a moment which is still benumbed with shock and sorrow, or resonant with anger and rejection, it will transcend this moment and will speak for the future which alone can embody life and continuity.

Salmā Khaḍrā' Jayyūsī

1. In fact, Arab poets have experimented with myths since the second decade of this century. However, their concept of the use of myth in poetry was not always clear, and was sometimes faulty. See the present writer's thesis, *Trends and Movements in Contemporary Arabic Poetry*, (1970), School of Oriental and African Studies, University of London, Vol. II, p. 1052.

2. In 1954, for example, al-Sayyāb, who was still in his Marxist phase, wrote in *al-Ādāb* saying that the new poetry came to crush romantic sentimentality, classical rigidity and rhetoric, and the poetry of the ivory towers. See the June number, p. 69. In 1957, Yūsuf al-Khāl who was to become editor of *Shi'r* magazine from 1958, gave a lecture at *al-Nadwa al-Lubnāniyya* in which he clearly demonstrated the above mentioned conditions for the new poetry which he dubbed 'modern poetry', a name adopted since by poets and critics. See 'Mustaqbal al-Shi'r al-Lubnānī', *Muḥāḍarāt al-Nadwa*, Beirut, May, 1957, pp. 367 - 84.

3. *Bayādir al-Jū'*, Beirut, 1962.

4. *Principles of Literary Criticism*, 1934, pp. 246 - 7.

5. *The Death of Tragedy*, London, 1961, p. 8.

6. Jean Anouilh, *Antigone*, trans. L. Galantière, 1951.

7. The present writer's poem, 'Bilā Judhūr', (1958), is probably a correct example of a concrete delineation of the tragic situation of the uprooted individual and the dispersed family, picturing the alienation, the heartbreak, and the growing resentment of the Palestinian refugees whose memory of a happy, concordant past is fading away under the unbearable pressures of a shocking present. See *al-'Awda min al-Nab' al-Ḥālim*, Beirut, 1960.

8. *al-Faraḥ Laisa Mihnatī*, Beirut, 1973, pp. 106 - 17.

9. 'Kalimāt 'an al-'Udwān, *'Ughniyāt al-Thaura wa'l-Ghaḍab*, Beirut, n.d., p. 89.

10. 'Fī Khamsa Ḥuzairān', *Dīwān Samīḥ al-Qāsim*, Beirut, 1973, p. 428.

11. *'Ammān fī Ailūl*, Dār al-Fārābī, 1970, p. 3.

12. 'Yaumiyyāt Jurḥ Filasṭīnī', *Dīwān Maḥmūd Darwīsh*, Beirut, 1973.

13. 'Fī 'l-Maghrib al-'Arabī', *Unshūdat al-Maṭar*, in *Dīwān Badr Shākir al-Sayyab*, Beirut, 1971, p. 395.

14. *Wheels and Butterflies*, New York, 1935, pp. 65 - 6.

15. Arnold Hauser, *The Social History of Art*, trans. by author and Stanley Godman, Vol. IV, London, 1972, p. 226.

16. Another poet, the Pakistani Muḥammad Iqbāl, standing in the Cordoba Mosque in the thirties, was able to see in the great monument the eternal hand of Love *('Ishq)* guided by the spirit of God. He could sense a completely different mythic sense of race, not his own, a race that was the creator of miracles, whose 'glances civilised East and West'. His great poem on the Cordoba Mosque is guided by a positive spirit that seeks union with the Islamic world, and firmly believes in the imminent rebirth of the spirit of Islam and, in fact, in the perpetual strength and vitality of the 'caravan of 'Ishq' throughout the world, a cosmic vision that portrays a deep faith in man and in life.

17. See for example 'Hādhā huwa Ismī', by Adonis, *al-Āthār al-Kāmila*, II, Beirut, 1971, pp. 613-43; see also Qabbānī's poem, 'Hawāmish 'alā Daftar al-Naksa', which he wrote directly after the war, and other poems; see also similar poems by al-Bayyātī such as 'Bukā'iyya ilā Shams Ḥuzairān', ''Uyūn al Kilāb al-Mayyita', 'al-Murtaziqa' and other poems in *'Uyūn al-Kilāb al-Mayyita*, Beirut, 1969. For a criticism of this attitude, see Iḥsān 'Abbās, 'Asābī' Huzairān wa 'l-Adab al-Thaurī', al-Ādāb, May, 1970; see also Ghālī Shukrī, 'Ab'ād al-Buṭūla fī Shi'r al-Muqāwama al-'Arabiyya, *Adab al-Muqāwama* , Cairo, 1970, pp. 398-407.

18. For example by Qabbānī, see *Yaumiyyāt Imra'a lā Mubāliya*, Beirut, 1973, p. 90; and for al-Bayyātī see 'al-Murtaziqa', p. 36.

19. *Tajribatī al-Shi'riyya*, Beirut, 1971, p. 36.

20. 'Dīk al-Jinn', *al-Maut fī'l-Ḥayāt*, Beirut, 1968, pp. 56-64.

21. 'Hādha huwa Ismī', pp. 634, 635 and 633 respectively.

22. *'Uyūn al-Kilāb al-Mayyita*, p. 30 *et seq*.

23. From a poem by the present writer, entitled 'Summer: 1967', *Shu'ūn Filisṭīniyya*, No. 1, Winter, 1971, Trans. by Suneet Chopra.

24. From a recent poem by the present writer entitled, 'The Climb in Zero Point'.

25. 'Laḥẓa', *Amām al-Bāb al-Mughlaq*, Beirut, 1967, pp. 34-5.

26. 'Hādhī hiya 'l-Laḥẓa', *Rasā'il min London*, Alexandria, 1956.

27. *Ibid.*, pp. 41-6.

28. 'Amām al-Bāb al-Mughlaq', op. cit., p. 72.

al-Sayyāb - A Study of his Poetry

There is general agreement that al-Sayyāb (1926-64) was one of the best Arabic poets of this century, and that his untimely death was a great loss to Arabic literature.

His development of Arabic prosody, his individual use of mythology, his superb imagery, his political poetry - in all of which he was an important innovator - have been sufficiently studied and I will not dwell on them here. It is my aim in this paper to consider only certain aspects of al-Sayyāb's writing. In particular, I should like to comment briefly on the various periods of his literary development; on certain points of his poetic technique which I believe demonstrate the high quality of his artistic ability; and to discuss the relationship between innovation and tradition in his poetry. I shall try to show in regard to the last point that in his writing he drew upon the vast resources of Arabic literature and culture, and not just on the imagery of non-Arab cultures, as is often supposed.

The earliest poetry of al-Sayyāb, up to about 1952 (namely his two *dīwāns*, *Azhār dhābila* (1947) and *Asāṭīr* (1950), and a few poems thereafter) is personal and, from a classificatory point of view, Romantic. The poetry of this period shows the influence of the poetry of the Apollo and *Mahjar* poets, but also that he drew directly on the poetry of Shelley and Keats.[1]

It is interesting that in Iraq the course of the development of modern poetry was abrupt in comparison with that of Egypt, where Romantic poetry developed through Muṭrān and Shukrī to the Apollo school and was well established in the 1930s and 40s, before the change to the new poetry.

In Iraq the Romantic period was very short. The new poets started in imitation of the existing Romantic schools and themselves, quite suddenly, abandoned the Romantic style, and in response to the changing situation after the war al-Sayyāb and al-Bayyātī[2] created the basis of the neo-classical school in Iraq with a new poetry which was to sweep aside the already moribund Romantic school.

This sudden shift and the high quality and relevance of the verse composed by al-Sayyāb after this time point to the poverty of the Romantic school and the need for it to be superseded.

The period after 1952 and until he was struck down by his fatal illness is the one in which his output showed his genius for re-forming and re-shaping Arabic poetry, and it is the work of this period which commands the highest respect of the critics as a new kind of non-personal social poetry both in theme and form. Nevertheless, the style of his neo-classical period did not attract all of his readers equally, since it contained many elements which seemed to them to be alien.

In this period the influence of T. S. Eliot becomes prominent for the first time, in his prosody, in his mythological imagery, and when he represents Iraqi society as a waste land waiting for the rain of revolution, a rain which, when it first came, did not alter for him the parched condition of the land. ʿAshtār, when she appeared, carried no basket of flowers, but a basket of stones with which she pelted every wife.[3] And of the resurrected god, Adonis, he says that he came with a clenched and menacing fist, reaping with his sickle blood and bones.[4] Despite political disappointments however, he, unlike Eliot, remains hopeful for the future.[5]

If we are to discuss the concept of the waste land here, however, we must turn to the differences as well as to the similarities with Eliot's thinking. A recent London thesis (Bullāṭa, 1969) says, 'some influence of Eliot can be surmised ... though perhaps not his cultural depth or politico-religious attitude ... al-Sayyāb's understanding of the "Waste Land" as a satire rather than a vision of a particular historical and cultural situation shows the limitations of his appreciation of T. S. Eliot ...'[6] The fact is, however, that al-Sayyāb re-created the image of the waste land in his own terms, or perhaps better, in terms of the needs of his own society. Eliot saw the West as a society in decline. al-Sayyāb was working in a society full of problems but full of hope; and even if the hope was to be frustrated he was still a writer in an emergent society, not one obsessed by the self-destructive tendencies that Eliot saw in his own society, nor, like him, haunted by the vision of a disintegrating civilisation. While Eliot saw loss and fragmentation in the changes overtaking European civilisation, for al-Sayyāb social change represented the rise of a more just society in the Arab world. The difference is finely pin-pointed in the contrast between their different imagery of hope. In Eliot's poem the image is that of hope tentatively salvaged out of the extremity of despair ('These fragments I have shored against my ruins'),[7] contrasting vividly with the positive and confident image that appears in al-Sayyāb's work: the disjointed limbs of Tammūz are re-united for his resurrection[8] (one of the symbols he chooses for the rebirth of society).

Let us now turn to the discussion of some less general aspects of his style during this period, and firstly to his exploitation of mythological themes and symbols.

Some writers give the impression that his mythological imagery was imported.[9] This is not so. The key *motifs* (ʻAshtār and Tammūz for instance) are based on early Babylonian and Syrian culture which still subsists in the consciousness of the Arabs of Iraq and Syria in the same way that the myth of Osiris subsists in the minds of Egyptians. Furthermore, most of the Biblical figures and images are also part of general Arab culture and only in his treatment of the Messiah figure does he take an interpretation different from that of Islam, and of this figure it can be said that poetic necessity requires a tragic hero who accepts suffering and is resurrected.

Even where he goes outside the Middle Eastern milieu and uses the imagery of Greek mythology, he is in this only exploiting a tradition which had already been established by the Apollo poets. In the 1930s Abū Shādī's works were full of this kind of mythological reference and his approach was taken up by other members of the school, to the extent that even al-Shābbī, who had no direct access to foreign culture, began to refer to such mythological figures as Prometheus Unbound.[10]

The difference between al-Sayyāb and the Apollo poets is that in his poetry the references are not superficial, but assimilated totally into his poetic purposes. Abū Shādī, for example, uses myths as a subject for a poem just as he uses pictures or romantic stories. This technique differs radically from that of al-Sayyāb, who fuses a myth into his poem, using it as an image that combines with other images and other elements to give the total effect. Nevertheless, credit must be given to Abū Shādī because, if nothing else, he introduced mythological references and used them extensively, making foreign names and mythology acceptable to many readers in a society which had no comparable previous experience of it.

Another writer suggests that al-Sayyāb's use of unfamiliar

mythological themes is in order to display 'cultural muscle' and not an essential part of his poetry and his thought. Yet another suggests that myths were deliberately imposed on his poems to give them a show of originality and innovation.[11]

This is a superficial and xenophobic judgement. Many of the mythological themes used by al-Sayyāb arose from inner necessity, or at least were particularly appropriate to the circumstances of his life. For instance the theme of Persephone taken into the underworld clearly struck deeply into his consciousness as a reflection of the death of his beloved Wafīqa in his early youth (cf. for example 'Ḥadā'iq Wafīqa' and Persephone's gardens).[12]

Basically the same is true of the images and themes which he adopts from the Middle East, namely that they correspond to his inner necessity. In the period of his illness, for example, he speaks of himself as Job, and as a Lazarus hoping for a saviour, desperately yearning for a cure:

> His son's eyes ... dream of the return of the crippled father from out of the depth of the tomb. 'Is he dead?' And the Messiah would call, after removing the stone, 'Arise, Lazarus!'[13]

Other mythological themes correspond closely to the popular beliefs of the people. The chilling gaze of the Medusa, for example, is another representation of the *jinniyya* whose fiery eyes have the power to stun those who behold her. Such presentation of familiar themes in a new garb shows a further aspect of the poet's genius for transforming and renewing archetypal beliefs buried deep in the unconscious mind of the masses.

I have spoken briefly of the illness which dominated his third period, which covers roughly the last four years of his life, and which is recorded in the last three published collections of his poems. Though there is undoubtedly a return in this period to a very personal note, this was dictated by his illness and is in no way a return to his Romantic period, and he loses none of the mastery of style which he gained in his middle period. The poetry of this last period is of a high degree of intensity and must be counted amongst the best poetry in modern Arabic.

However, even at the worst crisis of his illness, he showed his commitment to themes outside his personal predicament, and talked of the conditions in his country and of his hopes for it.[14] The personal note, however, was in a vein which has always been acceptable to Arab readers and the poetry of this period is well-loved and transcends in poetic value and appeal the cryptic, but more rational poetry of some of his contemporaries.

A striking feature of al-Sayyāb's poetry is that it is suffused with emotion. This sets him apart from the dry and cryptic poetry referred to above. In 'Waṣīyya min Muḥtaḍar' ('Testimony of a Dying Man') (which is an obvious allusion to the situation and statement of Abū Bakr when he gave his last testimony to the Muslim community, appointing ʿUmar to be his successor), al-Sayyāb says: 'I am dying: dead people don't tell lies: I disbelieve in meanings if they spring from any source but the heart'.[15] It is the complexity and richness of his feelings that lead him to employ a number of techniques that, together with other features of his poetry, serve to express his genius. We shall now proceed to discuss a few of these techniques.

The first is a stylistic feature of some interest in the poetry of al-Sayyāb's later periods, namely the 'interrupted sentence'.

Although the 'interrupted sentence' occurs in *Jāhilī* poetry it passed out of use in later times. One example from al-Nābigha al-Dhubyānī, however, is quite striking:

Famā 'l-furātu 'idhā jāshat ghawāribuhū
    Tarmī 'awādhiyyuhu 'l-ʿibrayni bi'l-zabadī
Yamudduhū kullu wādin mutraʿin lajibin
    Fīhī rukāmun min al-yanbūti wa'l-khaḍadī
Yaẓallu min khawfihi 'l-mallaḥu muʿtaṣiman
    Bi'l-khayzurānati baʿda 'l-ayni wa'l-najadī
Yawman bi-aṭyaba minhū sayba nāfilatin.[16]

The 'interrupted sentence' here is a good example of a sentence, whose ending is postponed until a number of subsidiary clauses (in this case mainly *ḥāl* clauses) have been introduced, bringing successive batches of imagery which contribute to a total effect that would otherwise not be realizeable. al-Sayyāb uses this technique to excellent effect, though there is little doubt that his master in this was not al-Nābigha, but the English poets.

There are many examples of this technique, which is new in modern Arabic poetry, in his poem 'Shanāshīl ibnat al-Jalbī', which begins:

'*I remember* of the village winter -
in which light / seeps through the clouds
like tunes / escaping through the holes of a

musical instrument to the notes of which
the darkness quivered to the music / *one morning*
many ... (how many years ago)
well, why should I care to count?'[17]

In these lines the basic proposition is introduced, followed by an interpolated comment on part of it, followed by a further comment on part of the interpolation, again followed by a comment on the one part of the preceding image, all before the introduction of the thing remembered. It is clear that the postponement of the object *(ṣabāḥan)* is intentional, since it would not have been difficult to compose the verse other than as an 'interrupted sentence', but he accomplishes more than one thing by putting the verse together in this way. He makes it carry the maximum load of imagery and gives it more immediacy and reality and brings it closer to the rhythms of everyday speech, in which clause tends to be interpolated into clause and sentences remain at times unfinished, as indeed the sentence in this verse of al-Sayyāb is unfinished.

This technique, with its piling up of ideas and interpolations, reminiscent of the style of spoken language, is clearly better suited to free verse than to the thoughtful and measured lines of the older poetry. The old, long metres are no constraint to certain kinds of noble exaltation, but they can be a constraint on spontaneity.

It is not out of a desire to attribute everything that is successful in al-Sayyāb to Eliot to note in this connection the fact that Eliot too had incorporated the use of the spoken idiom into his poetic technique.

In al-Sayyāb's later works the interrupted sentence is used frequently, but I choose one short example to bring to your notice from 'al-Maʿbad al-Gharīq':

Wa ḥaddatha-wa huwa yahmisu jāḥiẓa 'l-ʿaynayni, murtaʿidan
Yaʿubbu 'l-khamra - shaykhun: ʿan dujan ḍāfin wa 'adghālī
Talāmaḥa wasṭahā qamaru 'l-buḥayrati yalthimu 'l-ʿamadā
Yamassu 'l-bāba min janabāti dhāka 'l-maʿbadi 'l-khālī
Ṭawāhu 'l-mā'u fī ghalasi 'l-buḥayrati bayna aḥrāshin
mubaʿtharatin wa-'adghālī.[18]

And there spoke - whispering, eyes bulging, trembling,
gulping his wine - *an old man,* about an encompassing
darkness and dense undergrowth
amidst which the moon shimmered on the lake, kissing pillars, -
touching the door at the side of that empty temple

> which the water covered in the shadows of the lake
> amongst scattered undergrowth and forests.

I would like to draw attention to the 'interrupted sentence' beginning with 'There spoke' (*wa-ḥaddatha*) and ending with 'an old man' (*shaykhun*), but further to note that this 'interrupted sentence' is only the beginning of what I would like to call an 'extended sentence' - namely a sentence which has virtually ended, to which addition after addition is made, each contributing to the density of the imagery. It is the virtue of al-Sayyāb that he knows when to end such an 'extended sentence' before the structure collapses from its own weight. This kind of sentence is new in modern Arabic, rare in Classical Arabic,[19] but relatively frequent in European writing.

The interrupted and extended sentence enables him to pile up details in building up towards the complexity he desires. This accumulation of details is used in another technique which al-Sayyāb employed to great effect and which later came to be widely used in modern Arabic poetry: this was his dramatic scene-setting in the introduction to a poem. This is common enough in novels and short stories and, indeed, in European narrative poetry, but he was one of the first to employ it extensively in Arabic, and certainly one of the most successful. As examples of this technique we might consider the following lines from 'al-Maʻbad al-Gharīq':

> The horses of the wind neigh and the sunset touches the masts
> with bloodstained light, and the windows of the inn in the
>   harbour
> Have lamplights flickering their booths
> The company of drinkers gathered, linked to the bottle by a
>   cord of fear,
> Straining their ears for the tumultuous waves beyond the
>   tavern windows[20]

He then goes on to describe the trembling old man with bulging eyes who tells the story.

Another point of technique which seems small in itself, but which is used to great effect by al-Sayyāb, is concerned with his use of verbs,[21] a particularly important technique in a language in which most words are of verbal origin. Here al-Sayyāb virtually reverses the recent trend towards a decrease in the frequency of occurrence of verbs which is related to the increasing Europeanisation of the Arabic language: I do not mean, of course, borrowed words, but borrowed syntax.

Firstly, al-Sayyāb uses verbs in preference to nouns in a way that gives immediacy and increases the dramatic effect. In the lines quoted above and also in the succeeding four lines, the predicate, the clauses of concomitant action, and the adjective constructions, are all put into verbal forms. There we have the verbs:

taṣhalu, yalmasu, tarāqaṣu, jamma'a, yamuddu, ḥaddatha, yahmisu, ya'ubbu, talāmaḥa, yalthimu, yamassu, ṭawāhu, etc.

Such verbal structures create a dramatic effect which would not have been achieved had nominal structures been used.

The lines quoted above also lead to the consideration of another feature, and one which is also expressive of intense emotion, namely the high frequency of occurrence of intensive verbs or rather of verbs which are intensive either in terms of grammatical form or of semantic content. For example we have:

yatafattaḥu, tafajjara, taṭaffa'a, tahazza'a

as well as other verbs of the same intensive form in the succeeding lines.[22] Elsewhere in his *dīwān* we find such lines as the following ones, which are remarkable also for their Qur'anic references:

Wa fattaḥati 'l-samā'u li-ghaythihā 'l-midrāri bāban ba'da bābī;
Wa ji'ta yā maṭar, tafajjarat tanuththuka 'l-samā'[23]

which are taken directly from

Fa fatḥnā 'abwāba 'l-samā'i bi-mā'in munhamir, wa fajjarnā 'l-arḍa 'uyūnan

and

wa 'arsalnā 'l-samā'a 'alayhim midrāran.[24]

Notice also al-Sayyāb's lines:

... tanaffasati 'l-ṣaḥrā'u qur'ānā

tanaffasat 'inda 'nḥisāri l-layli 'ashtāru [25]

both of which echo the Qur'ānic verse:

Wa'l-ṣubḥi 'idhā tanaffas.[26]

Since it is the task of a poet to imbue each word with as much suggestive content as possible, I have no doubt that this summoning of the linguistic power of the Qur'anic verse is deliberate, but indirect in that a more specifically Qur'anic reference would stamp his lines too strongly with associations other than those he was striving after.

In a similar way he makes more extensive use than other poets of quadriliteral verbs, which as a class are formally intensive and enable him to express intensity of feeling. One should note, for instance, the profusion of such verbs as:

taraqraqa, lamlama, zalzala, bar'ama, yudaghdighu, yudandinu[27]

There are, indeed, occasions when one wonders whether the important point is not rather the doubling of the consonant or syllable, since apparently as part of his overall pattern he makes use of verbs such as:

majja, madda, nazẓa, imtadda, nadda, radda

and so on, which are not formally intensive though they have certain of the characteristics of intensive verbs. Thus:

Wa lawlā zawjatī wa mizājuhā 'l-fawwāru lam tanhadda 'a'ṣābī
Wa lam tartadda mithla 'l-khayṭi rijlī dūnamā quwwah
Wa lam yartajja ẓahrī fa huwa yasḥabunī 'ilā huwwah ...[28]

Certainly the high frequency of occurrence is not demanded by metrical criteria and we are compelled to conclude that the poet by using them deliberately gives force and energy to his verses.

We might look at some lines which contain verbs which are semantically intensive:

Yanhamir,
Yahṭilu 'l-maṭar
Alhatha 'l-jadāwila 'l-jafāf
Yasūṭuni 'l-'aṭash
Wa ghalghala fī qarārati 'arḍina wahaju[29]

As a final example I should like to draw your attention to the lines in which he describes the painful progress of the crippled Ḥamīd:

Fa 'ayyu 'nsiḥāqin wa 'ayyu 'nkisār yashi''āni min'aynihi[30]

in which he uses verbal nouns which are intensive in meaning.

Before we leave the subject of his extensive use of verbs, one feature can be noticed in his use of tense, namely his movement between perfect and imperfect tense to change the dramatic tension - using the imperfect to give a sense of immediacy of the action. Some of these usages are suggestive of *Iltifāt* in Arabic *balāgha*. In this, as in other respects, there are in Arabic ancient usages which he has renewed partly, perhaps, because his inclinations have been confirmed by similar usage in European poetry.

Another point of technique which gives immediacy to his style are paratactic constructions which are not unknown in older Arabic. al-Sayyāb's intention is to increase the pace of his narrative by his use of asyndetic structures, as for example:

Ṣaḥā min nawmihi ... ṣaḥā Tammūz, ʻāda li-bābil

and also

Ta'ūbu 'ilāhatu 'l-dami, khubzu bābila, shamsu 'āzār[31]

or we might compare al-Sayyāb's lines:

Law yūmiḍu fī ʻirqī nūrun, fa-yuḍī'a liya 'l-dunyā

law 'anhaḍu law 'aḥyā, law 'usqā, 'āhi law 'usqā![32]

with Eliot's lines:

If there were water
And no rocks
If there were rocks
And also water
And water
A spring
A pool among the rock
If there were the sound of water only[33]

This omission of the conjunction is one of the features which go to make up the eagerness and intensity of al-Sayyāb's lines, which are so characteristic of his verse.

Equally characteristic of his eagerness and his desire to give his poetry immediacy is his omission of the introduction of direct speech by any word such as *qāla* and it may be pointed out that this is a prominent feature of the Qur'ān. Badr al-Dīn al-Zarkashī says under *ḥadhf al-qawl* , 'so frequently is it omitted in the Qur'ān that its absence is just as much part of the style of the Qur'ān as its inclusion'.[34] It can perhaps be assumed that al-Sayyāb first encountered this in European poetry and as a result resurrected the Qur'ānic traditional form, but it would not be safe to assume that the influences were all European since one example from al-Sayyāb seems to echo quite clearly Qur'ānic usage, namely:

> The wind blew, propelling me across seas to night, ice and the unknown ... then the two drowning ones resort to a board, cling to it, and raise their supplication, 'Save us Lord of Heavens'.[35]

The Qur'ānic verse is:

> *Ḥattā 'idhā kuntum fī'l-fulki wa jarayna bihim birīḥin ṭayyibatin wa fariḥū bihā jā'athā rīḥun 'āṣifun wa jā'humu 'l-mauju min kulli makānin wa ẓannū 'annahum 'uḥīṭa bihim da'awu 'l-lāha mukhliṣīna lahu 'l-dīna: la'in 'anjaytanā min hādhihi lanakūnanna mina 'l-shākirīn.*[36]

In the Qur'ān the omission of *qāla* gives immediacy and dramatic effect:

> *Wa'l-malā'ikatu yadkhulūna 'alayhim min kulli bāb: salāmun 'alaykum bimā ṣabartum*

> *Wa tatalaqqahum 'l-malā'ikatu: hādha yawmukumu 'l-ladhī kuntum tū'adūn*

> *Wa yawma yu'raḍu 'l-ladhīna kafarū 'ala 'l-nāri: 'alaysa hādhā bi'l-ḥaqqi*

> *'Ana 'unabbi'ukum bi-ta'wīlihi fa 'arsilūn: yūsufu 'ayyuha 'l-ṣiddīqu 'aftinā*

> *Wa 'idh yarfa'u ibrāhīmu 'l-qawā'ida mina'l-bayti wa 'ismā'īlu: rabbanā taqabbal minnā*

> *Wa nazzalnā 'alaykumu 'l-manna wa 'l-salwā: kulū*[37]

Examples from al-Sayyāb are very numerous and I give only a few instances:

> 'To shake the throne of God, "My Lord, I am crippled", and the angel's eye would look at me, "Is there any heartbroken person who does not bewail his affliction to God?"'

> 'We were there - our noisy grandfather laughing or singing ...

and his peasants waiting in expectation, "Send us your rain, O Lord!".'

'She was moved by a mother's love and weeping "Oh my son you are far away from home".'

'If only you would light candles in the "simple", dusty village mosque. They would send forth a thread of light hung with tears. If only you would implore God at the call to *maghrib* prayer, "Dear God, be kind to my young child. Cut not short his father's life and spare him, dear Lord, that end".'

'Whenever a day passes and the cold night comes, I find myself counting what money is left in my pocket: "Can this little bit buy the cure?".'[38]

The Tammūz school, amongst whose members al-Sayyāb was counted, was criticized for overusing non-Islamic myths and symbols, though we showed earlier that al-Sayyāb's usage was dictated by a kind of psychological necessity. What I believe it is necessary to add is that al-Sayyāb, unlike others of the Tammūz school, certainly did not agree with them in their *rafḍ* (rejection) of the Islamic tradition. Although he uses Greek, Christian and Syrian imagery, the instances of this are in fact outweighed by his use of Islamic and Arabic imagery and symbols.

There is no question of this tendency being conventional or a desire for orthodoxy, because in the process of employing Islamic symbols and imagery he recreates his material skilfully and makes his readers look afresh at it, breaking down in them the compartmentalization in their minds and putting religious elements into a new poetic context. Thus he uses for poetic purposes the elements of *ṣakhrat al-mi'rāj, al-burāq, al-mi'dhana, ghār ḥirā, Ya'jūj wa Ma'jūj, Yūsuf wa Zulaykha, Ṭūfān Nūḥ, Qābīl wa Hābīl, Abraha wa 'aṣḥāb al-fīl, Al-mann wa'l-salwā, Iram dhāt al-'imād, Thamūd* and many others.[39] He uses the symbols of *Muḥammad al-yatīm, al-Anṣār, al-Ka'ba 'l-maḥzūna, Ayyūb, 'adhān al-fajr, nafkh al-ṣūr, al-nushūr* and many others.[40]

It can be further reasonably postulated that the theme of rain and the invocation of rain in 'Unshūdat al-Maṭar' is taken from the desert environment as exemplified in pre-Islamic and Islamic poetry and in Islamic tradition by *ṣalāt al-istisqā'*.

The importance of this element in his poetry is further emphasised by a point already referred to: namely the expressions that clearly echo Qur'ānic ones. Other examples are also to be found - examples, moreover, that strongly suggest that his usage of Qur'ānic expressions was not random and coincidental, but the result of a deliberate search in the pages of the Qur'ān for linguistic inspiration. Compare, for instance:

hawā'un kullu 'ashwāqī[41]	with	*Wa 'af'idatuhum hawā'*[42]
and		
tasiḥḥu min dumū'ihā'l-thiqāl[43]	with	*wa yunshi'u 'l-saḥāba 'l-thiqāl*[44]
and		
ghāḍa 'l-mughīrūna, yaghīḍu 'l-mā'u[45]	with	*wa ghīḍa 'l-mā'u*[46]
and		
law awda'a 'l-Lāhu 'iyyāhā amanatahū[47]	with	*'Inna 'araḍna 'l-'amānata 'ala 'l-samāwāti wa 'l-'arḍi wa 'l-jibāl*[48]
and		
ramāhu 'asfal sāfilīn[49]	with	*radadnāhu 'asfal sāfilīn*[50]
and,		
'innahu 'l-ruṭabu tasāqaṭa fī yadi 'l-'adhrā'i[51]	with	*tasāqaṭ 'alayki ruṭaban janiyya*[52]

And, finally, an obvious source for

warā'a Makkata fi 'l-ṣayāṣi and *ta'lū min ṣayāṣina*[53]	is	*min ṣayāṣīhim* in the Qur'ān.[54]

Similarly, al-Sayyāb will deliberately use a line or a metre to invoke the poetry of the past for dramatic comparison and other purposes. Thus the beginning of ''Unshūdat al-Maṭar'[55] echoes the form of the *qaṣīda* in that it begins with an equivalent to the *nasīb* but with a far different effect and with no hint of conventionalism, indeed giving the reader an element of shock when the poet's true intention dawns upon him. Compare also the famous line by 'Alī b. al-Jahm (3rd cent. A.H.):

> Beautiful as the wild cow's eyes, the women's eyes
> between *al-Ruṣāfa* and *al-Jisr* kindle love from whence
> I know and whence know not

against al-Sayyab's line:

> Beautiful as the wild cow's eyes, the women's eyes
> between *al-Ruṣafā* and *al-Jisr* are bullet-holes
> variegating the face of the moon.[56]

In his long poem on *Bur Sa'īd* he suddenly shifts into conventional metre *(basīṭ)* and mono-rhyme[57] to echo Abū Tammām's poem on *'Ammūriyya,* but only by suggestion. Only a word here or there, and his choice of metre and rhyme, directly recall Abū Ṭammām's poem. This particular example seemed to some of his readers to be a lapse into conventionalism and in this they did not understand his intention and purpose.

We have already remarked that in Iraq the Romantic Period was very short. This meant that Iraqi poetry remained longer with the traditional style, while with the Egyptian and *Mahjar* romantic poets this style became diluted. When al-Sayyāb was coming to poetic consciousness the literary atmosphere in Iraq was different from that dominated by the romantic style.[58] Moreover, during his formative years al-Sayyāb had a very sound grounding in classical Arabic. The society in which he lived was a conservative one, more overtly attached to the Arab past and less exposed to foreign culture than that of Cairo or Beirut at the same period. His cultural environment and his attitude to the past enabled him to appreciate and assimilate the classical heritage - as his poetry clearly shows.

Yet despite al-Sayyāb's grounding in classical Arabic, he was capable of creatively breaking away from it: his conservative background enabled him to retain the strengths of the past and yet at the same time he was capable of absorbing the European poetical tradition. He had the ability to harness those different elements in his work in a creative and integrative process. This shows a remarkable flexibility of mind and real power of cohesion. Like men of true genius he had the capacity for drawing richly upon, and using a tradition, without at the same time being bound by it. He did not lose himself totally in the Classical Tradition like many traditionalist poets, neither did he abandon himself, like some of his contemporaries, to a quasi-modernist attempt to break completely with the past. His poetry consequently reflects the strengths of traditional poetry while revealing the vigour of creative innovation.

Eliot said, 'No poet, no artist of any art, has his complete meaning alone. His significance, his appreciation, is the appreciation of his relation to the dead poets and artists'.[59]

Al-Sayyāb said, 'In my opinion, mature revolution is one kind of development. It is a review of the literary heritage, discarding what is bad in it and going forward with what is good in it. To revolt against the past merely because it is the past is madness and regression, for how can we live when we have lost our past?'.[60]

M.A.S. ʿAbd al-Ḥalīm

For the purpose of convenient reference, all quotations from al-Sayyāb's works have been taken from *Dīwān Badr Shākir al-Sayyāb*, (Beirut, 1971), referred to here as '*Dīwān*'.

1. See L. ʻAwaḍ, *Al-thawra wa'l-'adab* (Cairo, 1967), pp. 39-48.

2. One should note, of course, that Nāzik al-Malā'ika was one of the leading figures in reforming Arabic prosody; see her book *Qaḍāyā 'l-shiʻr al-muʻāṣir* (Beirut, 1962).

3. *Dīwān*, p. 473.

4. *Ibid.*, p. 466.

5. *Ibid.*, p. 485.

6. I.J. Boullāṭa, *Badr Shākir al-Sayyāb: The Man and his Poetry*, Ph.D. thesis, pp. 256-7.

7. T.S. Eliot, *Collected Poems* (London, 1963), p. 79.

8. *Dīwān*, p. 485.

9. See ʻAbd al-Jabbār Dawūd al-Baṣrī, *Badr Shākir al-Sayyāb* (Baghdād, 1966), p. 44.

10. Abū 'l-Qāsim al-Shābbī, *Aghānī 'l-Ḥayāh* (Cairo, 1955), p. 179.

11. Referred to in J. al-Khayyāṭ, *The Development of Modern Iraqi Poetry*, Ph.D. thesis (Cambridge, 1966), p. 255.

12. *Dīwān*, pp. 125, 131.

13. *Ibid.*, pp. 705-6.

14. *Ibid.*, pp. 181, 197, 309, 320.

15. *Ibid.*, p. 283.

16. *Dīwān al-Nābigha 'l-Dhubyānī* (Beirut, al-Maktaba 'l-ahliyya, n.d.) p. 24.

17. *Dīwān*, p. 597.

18. *Ibid.*, pp. 176-7.

19. Ibn al-Rūmī is renowned for squeezing the last drop out of a theme and sometimes in this process employs extended sentences.

20. *Dīwān*, p. 176; see also pp. 21, 543.

21. For the profusion of verbs in al-Sayyāb's style see, for instance, *Dīwān*, p. 491.

22. See also *Dīwān*, pp. 463-4.

23. *Ibid.*, pp. 598, 464.

24. *Qur'ān*, LIV, 12-3; VI, 7.

25. *Dīwān*, pp. 494, 627.

26. *Qur'ān*, XXCI, 18.

27. See also *Dīwān*, p. 491.

28. *Ibid.*, p. 687.

29. *Ibid.*, pp. 481, 626, 467, 491.

30. *Ibid.*, p. 699.

31. *Ibid.*, pp. 486-7.

32. *Ibid.*, pp. 410-1.

33. *Collected Poems*, pp. 76-7.

34. *al-Burhān fī 'ulūm al-Qur'ān* (Cairo, 1958), III, p. 196.

35. *Dīwān*, p. 684.

36. *Qur'ān*, X, 23.

37. *Ibid.*, XIII, 23-4; XXI, 103; XLVI, 34; XII, 45-6; II, 127; XX, 80-1.

38. *Dīwān*, pp. 713; 597-8; 616; 700; 287-8.

39. *Ibid.*, pp. 119, 468, 394, 425, 529, 215, 197, 215, 368, 396, 373, 602, 477.

40. *Ibid.*, pp. 467, 402, 396, 248, 402, 501, 392.

41. *Ibid.*, p. 601.

42. *Qur'ān*, XIV, 43.

43. *Dīwān*, p. 475.

44. *Qur'ān*, XIII, 12.

45. *Dīwān*, pp. 505, 488.

46. *Qur'ān*, XI, 44.

47. *Dīwān*, p. 359.

48. *Qur'ān* XXXIII, 72.

49. *Dīwān*, p. 369.

50. *Qur'ān*, XCV, 5.

51. *Dīwān*, p. 598.

52. *Qur'ān*, XIX, 25.

53. *Dīwān*, pp. 400, 402.

54. *Qur'ān*, XXXIII, 26.

55. *Dīwān*, pp. 474-5.

56. *Ibid.*, p. 450; for another example see *Op.cit.*, p. 409.

57. *Ibid.*, pp. 498-501.

58. This is not to say, of course, that al-Sayyāb was not influenced by these romantic poets - as indeed I earlier remarked that he was.

59. *Selected Prose* (London, 1963), p. 23.

60. ʻAbd al-Jabbār Dāwūd al-Baṣrī, *Badr Shākir al-Sayyāb*, p. 86.

Social Values Reflected in Egyptian Popular Ballads

My subject needs to be approached with much circumspection. The whole of Arabic popular literature has suffered not only from neglect, but also from contempt; and now that a handful of scholars have turned their attention to it, some significant issues are being obscured rather than clarified by premature theorising, in which selected facts are made to fit into a preformed frame of literary or social reference. Yet the more closely one looks at this literature with its great diversity and many ramifications, the more difficult it becomes to formulate its distinctive features or delimit its true territory.

In the hope of establishing a reasonably firm foothold, and because I am all too aware of my handicap in trying to study such a subject from a distance, I have limited myself severely to a comparatively small but easily definable *genre* within popular literature, namely the narrative told entirely in song or verse, to the exclusion even of such epic cycles as the Hilālī stories that are partly in prose.

The evidence I have come across regarding the origination and transmission of the texts is far from clear-cut or uniform. For the art is indeed practised by men and women who conform with the conventional image of the wandering minstrel carrying songs part remembered and part improvised from one rural festival to another. But there are also men of some education and possibly city-based who are better at composing pen in hand than they are at singing; these may sell their compositions directly to singers (one of them, Azhar-trained, has been known to deliver an *ijāza* in time-honoured fashion to whomever memorised 200 quires of his work), or they may publish them in cheaply printed booklets. Yet if - as does happen - their names are held in reverence by the itinerant singers and some of their compositions are remembered a generation after their death, is it not arbitrary to exclude them from the canon of popular literature? It is reasonable to assume that the heart of this literature is in the countryside rather than the city, but how strongly is the contrast to be made? The itinerant singers who travel from one *mūlid* to another do not give the city a miss. Indeed the most popular - or the greediest - of them find it rewarding to give regular performances throughout Ramaḍān in cafés or specially erected pavilions in the vicinity of the Ḥusaynī mosque in Cairo. But there they may find themselves next to a State-sponsored group using the same art-forms to put forth political propaganda. The more fortunate of the popular singers may themselves receive State patronage. They may also be invited to cut a record or appear on television where they have to adapt to unaccustomed conditions if only to fit in with a strict time-table. What do they take back to the country-side from these city experiences? Without a wealth of material recorded over a long period, how are we to judge the nature of the changes that are brought about? And if the changes are significant, how are we - without prejudging what may be important issues - to determine whether they amount to a new development in a living art or the corruption of a once pure tradition?

There are issues here that affect the admissibility of some texts as social documents representative of the way of thinking of one social group or another - more issues, in fact, than we can examine in detail here. For my part, I find that nothing concerning popular literature comes closer to being definable than the kind of audience it attracts: villagers of any status, but also town people who have had either a traditional type of education, or very little formal education at all; the hall-mark of the overwhelming majority of them is the wearing of the *gallabiyya*. My inclination is therefore to accept as genuinely popular any composition, no matter what its provenance may be, that proves acceptable to such an audience by remaining current for, say, a generation. This criterion has the disadvantage (among others) that it debars us from making any but the most provisional assessments of the contemporary scene. It may also be radically unacceptable to other participants in this colloquium, so I shall make a point of indicating which of the texts I refer to do *not* come from the lips of provincial singers. Finally, it need scarcely be said that no one individual - least of all one who is no longer resident in Egypt - can claim to have anything like a comprehensive view of a literature which is largely oral and on which much fundamental work is yet to be done.

With these many reservations in mind, let me turn to the ballads I happen to know, and set out as objectively as possible the standards that they - and they alone - reveal as governing social relationships. We shall have to read between the lines, for there is very little explicit moralising or philosophising in these stories. I have come across a fable in an undated litho-graphed booklet in which a bird caught in a net pleads with the hunter to be spared, promising to give him in return three valuable gems. When he is released, he tells him that the three gems are the letters *ṭā mīm ʿayn*, which spell out 'greed'; and very valuable they are since it is to the hunter's greed that the bird owes its life. But fables are remarkably rare in this type of composition. By far the commonest are embroideries on Qur'anic stories, legends concerning the Prophet and his Companions, and stories of local saints. Not so numerous but apparently at least as popular are chronicles of contemporary emotive events, such as honour crimes or vendettas. In stories with a religious tinge, the obvious moral is often drawn that God's will is not flouted with impunity. In contemporary ones, when the hero's fortunes are at a low ebb there are equally conventional reflections on the fickleness of fate and the instability of life. But for the most part, the point is made by the story itself and the artistry of the story-teller.

Let us start with what is expected of the individual before moving to wider and wider circles of involvement.

The behaviour most commonly celebrated is that of the man of honour and unlimited physical courage, ready to spring into instant action to avenge a wrong done to him or his, pursuing his purpose with unflinching determination and utterly reckless of the cost. L-Adham esh-Sharqāwī has only to hear that his uncle has been murdered - the reason is not even disclosed - and he embarks on a series of revenge killings that pit him against the authorities and end in his death. In the very popular story of 'Shafīqah we Metwallī' or 'el-ḥādsah l-Girgawiyyah', the moment Metwallī is taunted with having a sister who has become a prostitute, he must set out to hunt her down and butcher her. In 'Bardanōha', which tells of a vendetta between Muslims and Copts that came to a head in 1942, we see the scorn with which compromise is regarded when the Muslim *ʿumda* instead of avenging his cousin's death obtains £300 compensation for him and offers the money to the victim's daughter.

> The girl took it and said, 'ʿUmda, may you live!
> And you, my father's uncle, may you live!
> And you my father's son!
> Here is your money thrown on the ground.
> May all the men live on!
> Because you have become women, shall I sell him
> to eat bread?'

It is then the victim's maternal uncle, not a fellow-villager but a beduin, who exacts a multiple revenge, for he has no compunction about shooting not only several members of the guilty family but also their chauffeur and an innocent by-stander.

There are comparatively few stories with love as the central theme. In these, both male and female beauty are admiringly described. Not surprisingly, there are manifestations of the universal double standard, for a man is sometimes shown boasting of his prowess as a seducer. But resistance to sexual temptation on the man's part is respected if not always expected. This is hardly surprising in the story of Joseph, as published by Muṣṭafā ʻAgāg, which follows the Qur'anic narrative but also adds that Joseph eventually married Putiphar's wife after she was widowed, and had several children by her. It is equally obvious in the contemporary story of 'Ḥasan we Naʻīma'. Here it is Naʻīma who is said to have fallen in love with Ḥasan, and when her father refuses to marry her to him she goes to his house unbidden; but though she remains there for a fortnight, Ḥasan is careful to spend his time in a café that all may see he is not with her, and when her father comes for her Ḥasan calls in a police officer and a doctor to certify that she is still a virgin. Certainly of a woman nothing less than the strictest chastity is expected. Thus in the story of the saintly Gharīb, as his widowed mother is sailing from the Ḥijāz back to Egypt, she rouses the lust of the ship's captain but she lets him carry out the threat of throwing her child into the sea rather than submit to him. In fact, the sex-drive features in these ballads more commonly as a threat to honour, than in its own right.

Most of the ballads are thus concerned with elemental human forces operating within a framework of long-established and virtually unquestioned priorities. Not one of the stories hinges on an inner conflict, on a choice between two honourable obligations or two painful courses of action. It seems to be assumed that in any situation the right course will be immediately and glaringly obvious to the hero, to the narrator, to the audience, to any right-thinking, noble-minded person. In stories with a contemporary setting especially, the character of the wise counsellor, the elderly spiritual mentor, is noticeably absent. Suspense and tension are created entirely by the obstructions that bar the hero's path and make the pursuit of the right course costly.

But the consensus thus implied is a consensus of opinion only. To judge by these ballads, it was only in the halcyon days of the Prophet and his Companions that men vied with one another in noble and generous behaviour. Our own times are out of joint, and it is anyone's cursed spite to find himself in a position demanding that he set it right. It is very much part of the hero's image that he should safeguard his interests and honour himself by his own valour. He may espouse the cause of the weak and oppressed - as Muṣṭafā Kāmil does when he springs to the defence of the victims of Danshawāy; but he himself never appeals to any constituted authority - not, say, to a council of elders or to any organ of the State; indeed it does not greatly trouble him if he falls foul of such authorities as did l-Adham esh-Sharqāwī and Metwallī. For if, as we have seen, it is assumed that what is Right is self-evident, it is not inconsistent also to assume that it is open to anybody to see to it that the Right is made to triumph.

It is also in keeping with this black-and-white view that anyone who refuses to conform with the unwritten code places himself entirely beyond the pale; and the hero who has appointed himself judge, jury and executioner can treat him and even those incidentally associated with them with unmitigated ferocity. There is no limit to the number of unbelievers that ʿAlī or Ḍirār may put to the sword. In a printed story, we are told of a beduin who bred a camel specially to take him to see the Prophet- but on his way to Medina he has the misguided kindness to share his mount with three villains described as 'Christian Jews' one of whom claims the camel as his own and produces the other two as witnesses, so that the Prophet is about to judge in his favour when the camel speaks out the truth; for what is no more than an attempted fraud, the Prophet orders the three Christian Jews to be burnt. L-Adham esh Sharqāwī takes not one life but several in revenge for his uncle's murder, and his method is to tear his victim apart with his bare hands. As for Metwallī, when he has traced his sister to a brothel he not only slaughters her but in one version cuts her up and throws the pieces from the balcony for the street dogs to eat.

It remains to be said that it is not only to violent confrontation that the hero may resort. He is also admired for successful ruses and dissimulation, even in circumstances that might have been considered undignified. Thus l-Adham esh-Sharqāwī in dealing with the police uses ambiguous phrases that mislead without actually telling a literal untruth, and he dresses now as a woman and now as a European. Similarly the police officer who tracks down the murderers in 'Ḥasan we Naʿīma' goes to great lengths to disguise himself as a woman, epilating himself and carrying about everywhere an infant that he has borrowed from an orphanage.

Treachery, on the other hand, is the most heinous mark of villainy. It is almost a convention of the modern stories that although the prime motive of dark and evil plots may be revenge or envy, they involve suborning close relatives of the victim. Ḥasan in 'Ḥasan we Naʿīma' and Ḥesēn in the story of 'Bardanōha' are both led to their death by cousins who have yielded to money bribes.

It will already be apparent that these ballads focus on individuals, and tend to speak of good or evil forces in terms of the moral qualities or failings of these individuals; but it will be no less apparent that the most binding obligations by which the individual is tested arise from blood relationships. If a connecting link is needed, it probably lies in the strong belief not only that qualities are transmitted from generation to generation by dint both of upbringing and of heredity, but also that children may be tainted by their parents' sins. So it is that in 'Bardanōha' Ḥesēn is described as 'having been brought up by his father and having drunk of his mother's milk', whereas the kinsmen who betray him draw the comment: 'By God, one who connives at his cousin's murder must have a mother who strayed.' So it is also that none of the stories of 'honour crimes' are concerned with a cuckolded husband: when a woman errs, it is her father and her brothers who are shamed. Part of Metwallī's dialogue with the judge who asks him why he has killed his sister is instructive in this respect:

> He answered: If you had a tree whose root had cracked a house,
> Which cast its fruit outside, but had its roots in the house,
> Its use outside, but bringing shame to the girl -
> Would you, I wonder, cut off the roots, or remain disgraced in your decision?
> He said: I should hasten, Metwallī, and fetch a saw;
> I'd fetch an able carpenter with his axe drawn.
> He said: This is why the crime was committed and the shame incurred.

One story, that of 'Ḥasan we Na'īma', has a number of features that run counter to the general trend, and as such deserve a closer look. The facts on which the story is based are these: Ḥasan was a professional popular singer. Na'īma fell in love with him, and - at least in her father's eyes - compromised herself with him. With the connivance of his son, the father had the young man killed - and this is in itself a most unusual departure from the rule that it is in the woman's blood that family honour has to be washed. Finally, the murderers were tracked down by the police, and imprisoned. Needless to say, the story is handled in different manners by different balladmongers. One version, a printed one, ends rather cynically:

> So Na'īma was left alone in the house.
> Her menfolk had perished all because of her -
> For a woman can lay a town to ruins and she alone survive,
> Boasting: 'By guile against the best of men I have prevailed
> (For Iblīs has tempted her and she has spread evil about her)-
> Ḥasan is gone, I shall surely love another.'
> His mother is grieved and weeps over him alone

But his loved one cares nothing for him.
Consider the omens and what they forecast, deluded one:
Excellent homes are ruined that once were prosperous.
What shall I write, and what shall I say, o listener?
All our misfortunes come to us from women.

But another version treats the lovers much more sympathetically, deriving its effects from the pathos of their situation. Certainly Ḥasan is represented, as I have already mentioned, as strictly honourable in his intentions, refusing to take advantage of Na'īma's virtual offer of herself. But her brazenness is also passed off without a hint of disapproval. Even more startling is her triumph at the end, for when a zealous police officer has discovered the identity of the murderers,

Na'īma thrilled with joy and said: 'Thank God I have found a real man in the Government!'
He took her to the Prosecution to tell the story of Ḥasan the Singer,
And when she had told the story before the examining magistrate,
He was pleased with Na'īma and asked, 'What sentence shall we pass on the wanted men?
Ten years for each?' She ripped her shirts and the magistrate stopped and said:
'Don't be upset - you pass whatever sentence you think fit.'

At the trial, she heightens the emotional tension by producing the severed head of her lover, ensures that heavy sentences are passed on her menfolk, and again at her suggestion the judge arranges for her to live thereafter under the protection of Ḥasan's father.

It can only add to one's puzzlement to note that the illiberal version comes from the pen of a Cairene writer, and the one that pits daughter against father from the lips of an Upper Egyptian singer. Have we here the first drum-rolls of a women's liberation movement deep in the Egyptian countryside? Or was prejudice turned round in this one case because the murder victim was himself a singer, whose offer of marriage was superciliously turned down precisely because he belonged to that despised confraternity? Is it simply that the artist realised how more effectively his story could be told if sympathies were heavily engaged on the side of the star-crossed victims? At all events, one must note that there is among the common people a sufficient fund of basic human compassion to make it possible for the story of a wayward and tragic love to be presented in this unconventional fashion.

One has to peer unexpectedly hard to catch glimpses of the wider community of which the family is a part. It is a far from egalitarian society. There are frequent references to the power of money to corrupt, to turn the heads of young girls and to buy the services of unprincipled men ready to lead their kinsmen into a death-trap. There is also a clear sense of grievance in 'Bardanōha' where it is asserted that the Government appointed a headman over the Copts and another over the Muslims, yet gave the Copt much greater allowances than it did to his Muslim colleague. But except in such an obvious case involving direct remuneration, it is in keeping with the tendency we have already noted of reducing issues to matters of personal morality that the power of money is seen as a temptation for the honourable individual to resist - as did the daughter of the murder victim in 'Bardanōha' - rather than as a tool or gauge of social justice.

In fact, three types of men are spoken of without recrimination as enjoying positions of prestige or privilege. The first is the landowner, apparently not only because he is wealthy but also because he is a stable member of the community. It is surely significant that the wandering minstrels themselves, whose rootlessness exposes them to contempt, seem to accept the prejudice as a matter of course. Thus in 'Ḥasan we Naʿīma' when the girl's father tries to trace her to the singer's native village of Bahnasā l-Gharrah

> A regular watchman met him outside the village,
> And he said: 'Come, watchman, lead me to the singer's house.'
> The watchman flared at him saying: 'Watch your tongue, Uncle.
> He is no singer. His father has 45 acres to his name
> And his father is headman of Bahnasā l-Gharrah.'

Lineage is also deemed worthy of special regard, and ought to set one above menial labour. In the ballad of 'Gharīb' we are told the story of the saint's father, a descendant of the Prophet, in the following terms:

> The sharīf's wealth was stolen - such is the judgement of
> Fate, what a shame!
> So he said to himself: 'Idleness has weakened my body and
> made me powerless.
> I must seek any means to live by and eat.
> Poverty is an ill thing, a condition that confuses the
> clear-minded.'
> So he took up with some people who had no basis and no
> standing.
> They made him carry stones. They were gypsies, of course.
> They demeaned a venerable sharīf whose ancestry and
> appearance went back to the Prophet.

Finally, the ungrudging admiration with which the bold and fearsome strong-arm man is regarded seems to stretch into an equally ungrudging acceptance that he is entitled to what he grabs for himself. In 'Bardanōha', Ḥesēn of whom it has already been said that he had the qualities expected of a sound upbringing in a good family,

> Became notorious, recruiting watchmen by force,
> And when notorious he returned to the village and exacted a toll from it.

To lead him into an ambush, his cousins suggest a raid on the cereals-yard - which, like poaching or tax-evasion in some British milieus, seems to be regarded as a sport rather than a crime. He does raise an objection:

> He said: 'We have reached a higher status than to go stealing cereals.
> I have in there eighty ardebs out of our own crop.
> If it is greed that moves you, what is there is no small thing, but plenty.'

But having thus established that it is not greed that drives him, he has only to be taunted with being afraid and he readily embarks on the adventure.

All this may be seen as passive recognition of conditions that have obtained in the countryside for hundreds of years. As for the big city, it looms only in the distance, as it were, exerting the kind of attraction that sophistication has perhaps always held for country folk. A singer recorded in an oasis in the Western desert who admitted that he had never travelled to the Nile valley nevertheless had a stock of ready-made lines in which Cairo street-names were used as rhyme words; and in his version of the Metwallī story, the hero - ostensibly ogling girls, although really searching for his sister - calls out to one of them, promising her 'sweetmeats from Groppi'. Sometimes, even titbits of Western lore percolate in unexpected places. In yet another version of the same story, the prostitute is shown entertaining her brother who is in disguise, and she pours out for him *wiskī ʿalā ʾuṭār*. I was puzzled by this *ʾuṭār*, but the singer explained to me that 'drink' came in three qualities: the best was in triangular bottles and was called *Inzī*, the middle quality was in square bottles and was called *Īg*, and the cheapest and worst came in round bottles and was called *ʾuṭar*! Clearly all this is in the nature of name-dropping; it indicates that there is some prestige in being able to claim acquaintance with city life, but of the penetration of urban or modernistic values there are very few signs indeed.

The agencies of the modern State feature as hazards rather than positive forces in the life of the people catered for by this literature. It is all too clear that the law of the land carries moral weight only insofar as it coincides with the traditional *mores*. A police officer may be praised if he furthers the action along desired lines as in 'Ḥasan we Naʿīma', although here too the praise is in terms of his personal qualities and almost with a hint of surprise - 'Thank God I've found a man in the Government,' is Naʿīma's cry. But where there is a clash the fact may be distorted - e.g., Metwallī's judge is said to have praised him, released him, and confirmed him in his Army rank, whereas in reality he was imprisoned - or else the authority of the State is treated as if to fall foul of it was inconvenient rather than reprehensible. L-Adham esh-Sharqāwī is neither shamed nor broken by being sent to prison; on the contrary he defiantly carries on with his vendetta within the prison, dismembering yet another of his enemies under the nose of the authorities; then

> The Government came asking: 'Why did you do this, Adham?'
> He replied: 'What a dead loss of a government you are! What did you do when my uncle was killed?
> And here I have killed, o Government, while I was in your own gaol!'

In 'Bardanōha' there is even a hint that those who are prepared to drag the authorities into other people's feuds almost deserve what is coming to them, for when the revenge killings against the family of the Coptic *ʿumda* have taken place,

> A hundred pities for the ill-luck of a peasant by the canal, returning from his field.
> He said: 'I saw you, who were shooting at the *ʿumda*.'
> Maḥmūd replied: 'Man, you were going about your business; what concern have you with shēkh or *ʿumda?*'
> He made straight for him and fired a single shot,
> And Ḥesēn's uncle made straight for his head with the rifle butt,
> Saying: 'If you have children orphaned, let the *ʿumda* settle your account.'

Of course that same ballad makes open accusations of massive Government partiality to the Copts, for not only is the Coptic *ʿumda* shown to have had preferential treatment from the start, but after his murder Makram ʿEbēd, who was Minister of Finance at the time, is said to have presented to the King a plea for exemplary punishment.

> The King took the request and referred it to the master of exalted knowledge,

His Majesty the King referred it to the Head of Islam.
And the Head of Islam referred it to Naḥḥās.
When Naḥḥās looked at the papers and saw Makram ʻEbēd's signature, calamity was set in motion
There was a Christian working in Naḥḥās's office, who interfered in criminal investigations.
Naḥḥās said to him: 'Off to Banī Mazār, to the police station.
I want you to multiply the numbers of the accused; then will you be high in my favour.'

On the subject of government, one last detail may detain us for a moment. When l-Adham esh Sharqāwī was busy outwitting the Government, we are told that at one point

He dressed as a European, and by another road he met them.
In Arabic and French, in every tongue he spoke to them.

Is it too facetious to see in this the merest hint that to the masses the machinery of government remains something of a foreign institution?

One must even raise the question: how deeply has nationalism struck root in the Egyptian countryside? In his pioneer work on the whole of popular literature, Aḥmad Rushdī Ṣāliḥ recognizes that this is a movement that was born in the city and only later moved to the rural areas. But how far has it actually spread? When speaking to my informants, I generally refrained from asking them leading questions in the hope that they would reveal their own priorities. Not one ballad with a clearly nationalistic theme was volunteered. As a last resort, I did question the singer Abū Dirāʻ about this matter, although wary of the genuineness of the material he might offer me since he performs a great deal in the city and receives a regular stipend from the State as an army entertainer. He told me he had himself composed a ballad celebrating the events of the 1956 Suez war; but he did not get very far with the recording as neither he nor any member of his company could remember how it ended. Clearly, whatever vogue it may once have had, it had dropped out of the author's repertoire and did not meet the test of lasting popularity. By contrast, the events of Danshawāy had touched such a live nerve in the consciousness of the people that ballads about it were in circulation a good fifty years after the event.

One version of this, ascribed to the extremely prolific Azharist I have already named, ʻAgāg, is a rather wordy composition that inveighs against the English for their ruthlessness and for treating the village 'as if it was their property', specifically against Cromer 'who came asking for excessive compensation', and against 'a Christian judge who deserves beating with a shoe'. Its last line is something of an anti-climax:

> This is indeed something that brings tears to the inhabitants
> and sons of the Fatherland

but it is notable for its use of the word *waṭan*.

Another much more spirited anonymous version starts:

> After judgement had been passed by Governor, sergeant and
> Pasha -
> Galleons piloted by Cromer, at war with mankind -
> Now do the English act like Pharaohs who once were only
> riff-raff.

But then, after dwelling on the helpless plight of the villagers it describes the emergence of Muṣṭafā Kāmil not as a nationalist leader but as 'the pillar of the faith' whose career is cut short when:

> So clever were the Christians they poured poison in his shoe.

Such nationalist sentiment as may be detected here seems at least overlaid with religious consciousness. Taken by and large, the corpus of texts available gives overwhelming evidence that religion retains by far the greatest claim on the allegiance of the masses. Ballads with a religious theme outnumber all others by an incalculably wide margin. Indeed one could trace in them almost the entire history and destiny of mankind as understood in popular Islam, from the creation of Adam to the Day of Judgment.

There is, however, one unexpected feature of these ballads that ought to make us pause at this point. It is that whereas the religious stories abound in miracles and wonders, those with a contemporary theme are uncompromisingly earth-bound. They are interspersed with invocations and references to the will of God, but apart from an occasional rather faint premonition that something dreadful is about to happen, there is never the slightest supernatural intervention. There is not even a role for the shēkh as spiritual guide or father confessor. Can it be that the Egyptian man-in-the-field, who is so beset by hard realities in his daily life, likes to dream dreams that he projects into another age or environment, but that in dealing with the here and now he keeps his feet firmly on the ground? Can it be that in facing an immediate crisis his gut reaction - like that of many others with greater pretensions to sophistication - is to 'praise the Lord and pass the ammunition'?

Perhaps it is not for us here to determine how deeply his devotion runs, or how effective it is in directing his actions. What is clear is that the community he recognizes as his own is the Islamic brotherhood, and that any non-Muslim is therefore an outsider. In the language of these ballads, the words Nuṣrānī, Yahūdī, and Kāfir are virtually synonymous; they may be strung together or used interchangeably. In the story of Abraham, for example, the patriarch's enemies and persecutors are called Naṣārā, and this once again by ʿAgāg who, as a man of some education, must have known that his use of the word was, to say the least, anachronistic. There are, of course, many issues in which religious and national loyalties coincide or reinforce each other. 'Bardanōha' shows all too painfully that they may also clash. And when they do, it is the religious label that the balladmongers and their public prefer to wear.

P. J. Cachia

The material in this paper is to be incorporated in a forthcoming book. It is drawn entirely from oral sources, or from cheaply printed, anonymous and undated booklets.

Innovation in the Egyptian Short Story

This study cannot treat fully, either on the methodological level or in their historical aspect, all the questions and problems which its ambitious title provokes. The assimilation of all the movements of innovation in the history of the Egyptian short story would require a fairly sizeable volume, if not several volumes. In other words, it demands a rewriting of the whole development of this literary *genre* from the point of view of its ambition to break new ground, either in form or in content, and its desire to change and modify the traits of its artistic structure to be able to digest the constant alterations in social and cultural sensitivity. That is true because the history of the Egyptian short story is the history of its perpetual search for change, renewal, metamorphosis, and modifications. From the moment of its birth, this literary form has accomplished a deep exploration of the consciousness of the Egyptian personality, in order to create a mature embodiment of its fluctuating feelings. The Egyptian short story sought to proceed along two main lines: the first was to authenticate this new literary form through creating several ties between this new-comer and the social and cultural life of the Egyptian, whose anxieties and dreams it tries to express. The second was to try out this new literary *genre* in the field of social and individual reality, in order to achieve a certain distinction from the original form, which came from the West. In other words, it had to give a local taste to this form, to put paid to any accusation about its alienation from Arabic literary life.

Because the rewriting of the entire history of the Egyptian short story is not this study's concern, it will only concentrate on the innovations of the 'sixties, and on the roots of those movements in the early similar attempts of the late 'forties. First, an attempt to define what this study means by 'innovation' would save it from the ambiguity of generalization. Every good and genuine work which has been added at any time to the legacy of the Egyptian short story is a new work, but it is not necessarily true that every new work is novel and contains innovations. The endeavour to clear up the meanings of this quite simple but vague word 'innovation' would carry us into a region where all the problems of literary style, structure, and aesthetics lie in wait.

However we still need such a definition: in broad and general terms, this study means by the term 'innovation' any attempt to add and create an unprecented group of features, either in structure or in content, which has not appeared before in a crystallized form in the Eqyptian short story. Sometimes this definition fits single short stories, but what concerns this study is the existence of numerous works by one writer or more, adopting an attempt to innovate until it forms an artistic trend which plays a major or minor role in the development of the Egyptian short story. Ignoring these single works does not mean that they are insignificant - some of them are very significant indeed - but only that they do not concern this limited study.

Although the full history of the Egyptian short story cannot be told in any reasonable detail in the span of a single paper a brief survey sketching out the development of this literary *genre* and showing its main landmarks is necessary. This is not only because of the lack of reliable studies in the field, but also because a brief survey will provide this talk with a historical background which will save its treatment of the innovation movement from indulging in abstractions and generalizations, and it will specify the position of the innovatory trends in the broad scheme of the Egyptian short story, which stretches from the second decade of this century until the present day. Originally one notices that mature patterns of the short story in Egypt (and fictional forms of literature in general) appeared at the same time as the emergence of the Egyptian nationalist movement; they became interwoven with its desire to express itself as a movement belonging to the modern age and through its terms. The national renaissance witnessed the birth of mature new literary *genres* in Arabic literature. The years of the second decade of this century which ended with the modest success of Egyptian nationalism expressed in the 1919 revolution, and then in the constitution of 1923, were the same years which saw the appearance of the early works of the Egyptian pioneers of the short story, such as Ṣāliḥ Ḥamdī Ḥammād, Muḥammad Luṭfī Gum‘a, Muḥammad Taymūr, ‘Īsā ‘Ibaid, Shiḥāta ‘Ibaid, Ḥassan Maḥmūd, Maḥmūd Ṭāher Lāshīn, Sa‘īd ‘Abdū, and Aḥmed Khayrī Sa‘īd. Just as Egyptian nationalism used elements of western thought blended with elements of classical traditional culture in its attempt to express itself in this phase, so the early beginnings of the Egyptian short story emphasised the importance of the genuine marriage between the inherited traditional elements, (especially as found in some patterns of the Arabic *Maqāmāt* and didactic tales), and the western short story. This primitive marriage and this mixture of elements left its mark on these early works. This mark was typified by didacticism and a certain incoherence in structure, and also reflected the strong links between the short story and questions concerning the national character. Those who study the works of the talented pioneer Maḥmūd Lāshīn and his associates - who called themselves

Gamā'at al-Madrasa al-Ḥadītha (Group of the Modern School) - will recognise their attempt to accomplish in their stories a special kind of social survey of the problems of Egyptian society and the Egyptian personality in this period. They tried to root this new art in Egyptian culture and society, and to reach through their works the reader who was unaccustomed to this form of art. For the reader could more easily accept this new form if he found that it reflected his vision, and treated his own familiar events and problems.

While Maḥmūd Ṭāher Lāshīn, Aḥmed Khayrī Sa'id, Maḥmūd Taymūr, and most of the Group of the Modern School tried to express in their works the life of Egyptian society, Yaḥyā Ḥaqqī - a member of this school - discovered that the nature of the short story made it more relevant to questions of the individual personality, than to those of social problems. He sought to express through his short stories the interests and anxieties of this individual personality, which was suffering in Egypt at that epoch from the contradiction between its reality and its ambition. Yaḥyā Ḥaqqī's stories depicted the eagerness of the Egyptian character to form a new future, and the strain from which it suffered in the process of trying to realise it. Maḥmūd al-Badawī, Nagīb Maḥfūẓ and others continued at different levels of maturity the approach of Ḥaqqī in their works. If the stories of the pioneer Group of the Modern School reflected the strong belief of the Egyptian character in its capacities and potentialities during the era of the 1919 revolution and the 1923 constitution, the works of this second group of writers described the dilemma, grief, and disillusionment which this character felt after the signing of the independence treaty of 1936.

A few years after the Second World War, a new generation of short story writers appeared. These writers separated, in a general way, into four groups representing four artistic trends:

(i) The sentimental and melodramatic trend as reflected in the works of Maḥmūd Kāmil, Amīn Yūsif Ghurāb, Yūsif al-Sibā'ī, Yūsif Gūhar, and Ibrāhīm al-Wirdānī, which tried to create an escapist attitude from the real problems of the community, a refuge from the suffering and disillusionment, from which the common reader could derive comfort.

(ii) The romantic trend whose writers, such as Sa'ad Makkāwī, Ṣalāḥ Dhuhnī, Ibrāhīm al-Maṣrī, and 'Abdel-Raḥmān al-Khamīsī were distinguished by poetic sensitivity, which reflected the romantic aspirations of the Egyptian to overcome his gloomy present. The romanticism of this trend mingled in certain stories with some realistic elements.

(iii) The realistic trend which sought to continue the true line of the Egyptian short story in the light of the achievements of Lāshīn, Ḥaqqī, and al-Badawī in their expression of the social reality and the several dimensions of the national personality in that phase. This trend is represented in the works of Yūsif Idrīs, Shukrī ʻAyyād, Ṣalāḥ Ḥāfiẓ, ʻAbdel-Ghaffār Makkāwī, ʻAbdel-Raḥmān al-Sharqāwī, and many others. The writers of this trend were very conscious of the several dimensions of the historical moment in which they lived and wrote, and the specific nature of the Egyptian personality at this time. This trend reached its acme and dominated the whole scheme of the Egyptian short story in the first half of the 'fifties.

(iv) The experimental trend, containing a blend of symbolic, expressionistic and surrealistic traits, appeared in the late 'forties and early 'fifties; although this trend was very weak in comparison to the strength of the realistic trend, it nevertheless paved the way for the innovative movement of the 'sixties. This trend is represented in some works of Yūsif al-Shārūnī, Fatḥī Ghānim, Edward al-Kharrāṭ ʻAbbās Aḥmed, and Badr al-Dīb. Despite its experimental nature, some of the masterpieces of this trend succeeded in expressing vital aspects of the problems of the Egyptian character in the autocratic years of the 'forties.

After this short historical background, we shall concentrate on the features of the last two of the four trends by which this study classified the works of the generation known in Egyptian criticsm as the ''Forties Generation'. This is the generation whose cultural formation occurred in the late 'thirties and early 'forties, who expressed its vision in the last half of the 'forties, and then reached the peak of its influence in the 'fifties. Ironically, by the 'sixties most of them declined artistically or fell off into silence and repetition, becoming at the same time the pillars of the formal literary establishment, dominating most of the cultural activities in the country. The importance of studying the last two trends is due to several reasons:

(i) Because the effect of the first two trends was limited and mainly negative, especially the sentimental and the melodramatic.

(ii) The contribution of the realistic and experimental trends was signigicant in the development of the Egyptian short story, making it capable of expressing the various dimensions of the present and the future of the Egyptian character in the late 'forties and early 'fifties.

(iii) Most of the innovations, either in structure or in content, appeared through the achievement of these two trends.

(iv) The young writers in the 'sixties were moved and influenced to a great extent - positively or negatively - by these two trends, and sought to place their own interpretation of the historical moment and the new sensitivity in opposition to the realistic and experimental trends.

(v) These two trends produced in their works two different solutions to the crisis of the Egyptian short story in the 'forties.

In fact these trends appeared, in the historical sense, later than the first two. When they appeared, or more precisely, when their most prominent exponents Yūsif Idrīs and Yūsif al-Shārūnī, began their work, the Egyptian short story was in a state of crisis. This was because the most valuable works of Yaḥyā Ḥaqqī and Maḥmūd al-Badawī had been published years earlier, and Nagīb Maḥfūẓ had abandoned the short story and had specialized exclusively on the novel, whilst Ṣalāḥ Dhuhnī and Yūsif Gūhar had fallen into silence. Moreover, wartime conditions created an atmosphere of social disintegration, which was propitious for the blossoming of these sentimental and melodramatic stories on a wide scale. This encouraged the writers to produce more and more in the shortest time. Without any doubt, this quantity was achieved at the expense of quality, and the interest in technical and social elements. The wartime circumstances and the political vacuum which followed the complete loss of confidence in political parties after the incident of 4th February 1942, helped to spread these works amongst the reader with the speed of an infectious disease, thereby causing a great break in the continuity of the development of the Egyptian short story. In fact, it continued to suffer from this crisis until the appearance of Idrīs' and al-Shārūnī's works at the end of the 'forties, when both of them tried to save the short story from this crisis, but in different ways.

Yūsif Idrīs presented the first realistic solution to the crisis, starting from his belief that the trend of escapist dreams had distorted the correct path of the Egyptian short story. To end the alienation between the short story and reality, it was vital to adopt the vision of the Egyptian character and its style of expression. The Egyptian personality during this period had begun to overtake the state of depression and frustration which followed the war, as it advanced along the path which culminated in the abolition of the 1936 treaty, the beginning of the armed struggle in the canal region, and the ending of the monarchy and the occupation. At that stage, the Egyptian personality began to reassert its control over its destiny, after it had suffered a post-war semi-dictatorship from the palace, and the exploitation of the occupation.

During this period Yūsif Idrīs began to understand the real depth of the Egyptian personality as he adopted the vision and approach of its most typical, and authentic characters - the *Felāḥeen*. He began through their customs, way of life, rituals, and traditions, to present new artistic realms. He adopted their love of story telling and their special style of narration, returning to folkloric roots different from the roots of the classical Arabic tradition on which the pioneers of the Egyptian short story had relied. He was thus able to depict new realms, new questions, new themes, and new social groups from the village and the city, which had not previously been treated in the Egyptian short story. Yūsif Idrīs expressed in his stories the striving of the Egyptian personality to face the external world, because all the enemies and problems of the Egyptian personality were at this time external ones. It seemed that this style and this solution was the true answer to the crisis of the Egyptian short story.

A great number of writers followed or supported Yūsif Idrīs in his path, the most talented, sensitive, and least productive of them being Shukrī ʻAyyād. One group in their attempt to imitate reality and to achieve a higher degree of resemblance to it, forced their fictional material into preconceived stylistic patterns of false reality. Many of them were preoccupied with ready-made notions, if not fallacies, about reality and forced their stories to prove them. The work of these authors had a negative effect on the development of this trend, in particular those who called themselves the socialist realists, such as Muḥammed Ṣidqī, Ibrāhīm ʻAbdel-Ḥalīm, and Fatḥī al-Ramlī. However, during this period the significance of Yūsif Idrīs and the other gifted writers who followed him lies in their discovery of the essence of both the characteristic types and questions of this phase. They were also innovators in structure and technical style. They therefore relied on description which concentrates on the embodiment of the time and the place of fictional action, in a manner which crystallizes notion, vitality, and dramatic sense. During this phase, they did not pay much attention to character analysis because of the external orientation of the Egyptian character. They therefore concentrated on many social and political problems, through which the ambition of the Egyptian personality appears to defeat its gloomy present and to conquer all the causes of its problems. Indeed, Idrīs's particularly fertile and creative talent was the vital element which made this solution widely acceptable. He wrote a collection of short stories almost every year during the first five years following the publication of his first collection *Arkhaṣ Layālī* (The Cheapest Nights) in 1954.[1] The solution offered by Idrīs seemed to be the only correct and possible one for some time, and the Egyptian short story adopted it wholeheartedly.

However, there was another solution proposed by the writing of the experimental trend, and one which was to recede into the shadows for a long period. This was perhaps because the talent of the writers who proposed it was not equal to that of Idrīs in depth and breadth, or because this trend expressed a limited phase in the life of the Egyptian personality. Perhaps some of its writers went too far in their experiments, or perhaps the faith of its exponents in themselves was relatively weak. In any event it was only a matter of time before this trend gained great importance, that is when its discoveries and accomplishments appeared in the 'sixties. Despite the fact that some of this trend's experiments were eccentric and sterile, its achievements in general revitalized the Egyptian short story, and as far as innovation is concerned, they were of great importance. These innovations echoed different individual and social motives and stimuli, presenting a partial fragmentation of the questions of Egyptian society, in which the writer's attention focused upon the individual and his relationship to his fellows. This concentration on the individual, usually alienated from his society, filled with his own dreams and visions, yielded a tremendous gain in fictional power.

Many factors were involved in the birth of this experimental trend. There was a general state of social frustration after the false promises of independence made during the Second World War had evaporated; then the crucial crisis of the Egyptian short story in the early 'forties had created amongst the young writers of this age a strong impulse to save it from the abyss of melodrama and sentimentality; there existed also a general mood of anxiety and grief amongst intellectuals during their feverish search for adequate means to express themselves, in the face of the heavy fist of the post-war autocratic governments. Apart from these factors, there were others of a literary and cultural nature. It is accepted amongst Egyptian scholars and critics that by the end of the 'thirties, most of the new literary forms - the play, the novel, the short story - had gone beyond the stage of birth, reached a certain degree of maturity, gained a reasonable base in the reading public, and started to fulfil their ambitions for evolution and innovation. Because all these new literary genres were influenced by each other, what happened in one field affected the others. The desire for innovation appeared first in the drama, after Tawfīq al-Ḥakīm had produced some allegorical and symbolic elements in some of his works known as the rational plays, such as *Ahl al-Kahf (The People of the Cave)* in 1934 and *Scheherazade* in 1936.

Two other important works appeared and played a major role in promoting the spirit of innovation and rebellion against old forms and concepts. These were *al-Kitāb al-Manbūdh (The Discarded Book)* by Anwār Kāmil in 1936, and *Mafraq al-Ṭuruq (The Cross-Roads)* by Bishr Fāris in 1938. The first is a scatological work in the form of episodic dialogues between a man and a woman discussing in a shocking, obscene, and frank way sexual digressions in every episode. The second is a symbolic play and in its important preface underlines the significance of symbolism and the abstract in literature, and emphasises the importance of expressing interior reality.[2] Four years after the publication of *The Cross-Roads*, Bishr Fāris practised his symbolic attitude in short story form in his book *Sū'Tafāhum (Misunderstanding)* in 1942. He attacked in this book's preface the reliance entirely on narrative and action in the short story, and called for the necessity of transforming the short story into a group of poetic and symbolic flashes.[3] In 1940, Anwar Kāmil, the author of *The Discarded Book*, established his *avant-garde* magazine *al-Taṭawwur* (Evolution) to express the thought and the notions of the *avant-garde* group of artists who called themselves *Gamā'at al-Fann wa'l-Ḥurriyya* ('The Association of Art and Freedom'). In the same year, Ramsīs Yūnān - a leading member of the Association of Art and Freedom - became the editor-in-chief of the well-known periodical *al-Magalla al-Gadīda (The New Magazine)* after Salāma Mūsā had left its editorship. For four years, until it ceased publication in 1944, this magazine made an influential call for change and innovation in art and thought. In 1948 the necessity for innovation and change tried to express itself again through the new magazine *al-Bashīr (The Announcer)* which published in its first issue the revolutionary manifesto of this young generation.[4] A few years before the appearance of *al-Bashīr*, Ṭāhā Ḥusain's famous magazine *al-Kātib al-Miṣrī (The Egyptian Writer)* participated a great deal in the cultural formation of the *Bashīr* group, when it introduced them to the valuable writings of some of the western masters of modernity, such as James Joyce, Franz Kafka, T.S. Eliot, Jean-Paul Sartre, Albert Camus, and others. Although the writers of the experimental trend echoed important aspects of local reality, they were influenced by post-First World War western culture, not only through translation, but mainly through first-hand contact. In fact some of those writers wrote their work originally in French, such as George Ḥinain and Albert Quṣayrī.[5] In the critical writings of some members of this group, one can realise how they appreciated the achievements of European culture in literature, art, music, thought and criticsm, and how they benefited from the advance of both human and pure science.[6] Finally, one should not forget that those writers were, to a certain extent, suffering from the horror of the shock of the first two atomic bombs on Hiroshima and Nagasaki.

Against this moving cultural background and through its means, the experimental writers created much innovation and added considerably to several artistic fields. One of the important features of this movement was its broad ambition to affect all the Egyptian fine and verbal arts, and to change both the structure and the content of all art. Amongst the members of these movements there were painters, musicians, sculptors, novelists, poets, translators, critics, and, of course, short story writers.[7]

The principal innovators in the field of the short story were Yūsif al-Shārūnī, Faṭhī Ghānim, Edward al-Kharrāṭ, Badr al-Dīb, ʿAbbās Aḥmed, Bahīj Naṣṣār, and Aḥmed ʿAbbās Ṣāliḥ In fact, al-Shārūnī, Ghānim and al-Karrāṭ produced the most outstanding examples of this experimental trend. al-Shārūnī's first collection, *al-ʿUshshāq al-Khamsa (The Five Lovers)* appeared in the same year as Idrīs's first collection, 1954. However while Idrīs was to publish six collections by the end of the 'fifties, al-Shārūnī's second did not appear until 1960, and another nine years were to pass before the appearance of his third.[8] Edward al-Kharrāṭ's short stories also were few and far between: after he rewrote most of the stories he had written in the 'forties and published them in his first collection, *Ḥīṭān ʿĀliyya (High Walls)* in 1958, he waited fourteen years before he published his second *Sāʿāt al-Kibriyāʾ (The Hours of Haughtiness)* in 1972. Furthermore, Faṭhī Ghānim was not able to publish in his first short story collection *Tajriba Ḥubb (Experience of Love)* in 1958 any of his experimental stories, which only appeared after a long period of hesitation in his second book *Sūr Ḥadīd Mudabbab (Pointed Iron Fence)* in 1964, after the new generation of the 'sixties had already proposed its own new visions and notions. Faṭhī Ghānim was thus encouraged to publish his experimental stories of which he had been originally ashamed.

Due to the fact that the works of the outstanding writers of this trend were few and far between, and because some writers were hesitant and did not take their experimental adventure seriously, this trend remained far from influential for the first ten years or so, until the arrival of the young generation of the short story writers, known in criticism as the generation of the 'sixties. Nevertheless, the achievements of the experimental adventure of the 'forties were extremely important from several points of view. It did not only refresh the Egyptian short story and develop it, but also expressed the spirit of rebellion in the Egyptian character against those who dominated its present. Because they were expressing their views against the authorities under heavy censorship, the result was that every being in many of their stories, men, women, birds, beasts, landscape, objects and society, are only symbols and metaphors. Nothing is studied by itself, the mind is a dark well, no surface, only depth. Many stories investigated the several dimensions of the feeling of ambiguous fears and loss of security. The short story writer used, in addition to the main plot, a group of sub-plots to widen the horizon of his theme, without losing the advantages of dealing with the individual and fathoming his interior vision. The use of sub-plots provided some of these stories with a vital comparative vision,[9] investigating various dimensions of reality, and placing individual cases in the general scheme of the community. The writer also blended the different levels of illusion and reality, because of his recognition that man could not endure much reality at that time, when most elements of reality were against his freedom and his dreams.

In order to mingle these different levels in a refined and suggestive way, they paid great attention to their language and emphasised the function of the interior monologue in the structure of the story. The writers of this trend paid much attention also to the usage of different tenses, to describe various levels and phases of the action. In the narrative they would change the tense of the action from the past to the present, and sometimes to the future, without caring about the succession of the action in external reality, giving the reader a sense of immediacy and continuity, and in order to fulfil the apocalyptic role of the artist. Thus the stories of this movement became more poetic and suggestive than those of other trends.

This type of work was far from influential and widespread for ten years or more, during which time the realistic trend reached its peak and started to suffer from a decline by the beginning of the 'sixties. Yet, it was only natural that the experimental trend should remain in the shadow during this period because the historical moment, suddenly, surpassed its potential with the revolution of 1952. During the first years of the revolution, the Egyptian character looked forward to a new era, and thought that it had been rescued from the fear and loss of its sense of security in the 'forties. Therefore, because the general climate was one of the externalization and hope of fulfilling the frustrated dreams of the 'forties, most of the writers of the 'fifties followed in the wake of the trend set by Yūsif Idrīs, but a great number were falling into the abyss of artificial imitation of the works of this prominent writer.

By the time the 'sixties arrived, it was clear that the years of fear and lack of security had returned in a severer version, and that the Egyptian short story was involved in another crisis. Y. Idrīs, after having produced annual collections, had ceased writing short stories for a period of six years, during which he concentrated on the drama and the novel. Moreover, Y. al-Shārūnī had for many years refrained from publishing short stories even in periodicals, turning his energies to critism. S. ʻAyyād similarly stopped writing in this *genre*, A. al-Sharqāwī turned to the novel, then to the poetic drama, F. Ghānim to the novel, while B. al-Dīb and ʻAbbās Aḥmed stopped writing altogether. It was apparent that the short story had come to a halt and that a new phase in the history of the Egyptian personality has been reached. The reign of externalization and the discussion of the social, economic, and political problems finished with the end of the 'fifties. A new type of contradiction had made its appearance with the generation whose cultural formation had taken place in the 'fifties and in the early part of the 'sixties. It attempted to express itself through literature, and was on the point of crystallizing its vision and features towards the end of the 'sixties. The work of the new 'generation of the 'sixties' was one of the decisive elements in the solution of the crisis of the short story, as the reader regained his confidence in the capacity of the short story for the expression to help him to understand this confused world.

Perhaps the nature of the historical moment and the new character which the 'sixties crystallized, made the short story the most suitable form for these years. Simultaneously, with the early appearance of the works of this new generation, Najīb Maḥfūẓ, Y. Idrīs, Y. al-Shārūnī, and E. al-Kharrāṭ resumed short-story writing. But it was for Maḥfūẓ and Idrīs in particular, a return of a new kind, bringing another style from that of their beginnings in the same field. During the 'sixties Sulaymān Fayyāḍ, Abū'l-Ma'āṭī Abū'l-Najā, Bahā' Ṭāhir, 'Abdel-Ḥakīm Qāsim, Ibrāhīm Aṣlān, Muḥammad al-Busāṭī, Yaḥyā al-Ṭāhir 'Abdulla, Muḥammad Ḥāfiẓ Rajab, Gamāl al-Ghiṭānī, and others stand out from the numerous writers of this generation in the field of the short story. To understand the features and the nature of their vision which restore our faith in the Egyptian short story, one needs to have a general look at their achievements, especially from the point of view of innovation.

It seems at first sight that social aspects are much more prevalent in the works of the last generation than in the works of the younger one, because the younger generation emphasises the development of moods of language, and the evolution of types of form and aspects of structure, features which most Egyptian literature had previously neglected. But a searching look at the works of this generation and the cultural and political milieu in which they formed and expressed their vision, would prove this accusation irrelevant. To reveal the truth of the demagogic and autocratic Egypt of the 'sixties; to test its possibilities and dramatize its perversion; to put writing to the test against a life of ambiguous fears and confused action, and that life against the necessities of the mind; to try to create oneself as a myth and to try at the same time to be an immediate physical force; to stagger openly between wisdom and foolishness, lucidity and dementia; to risk and to play safe; to fall and to be resurrected; to be a conscious, exemplary, half-clownish, half-grave and naked public destiny; to tackle the serious problems of society sincerely and to deceive the censorship; to throw the ego against the impersonal rubrics of the age; to try to move and shake the times while representing an unappeasable nostalgia for the artist's indifference to temporality; to be Narcissus and to be Prometheus; to be a cloud of discontent that bumps the stagnant heavens into motion.[10] This has what being a young Egyptian writer in the 'sixties meant. Or in other words, the tongue of a whole generation has been prohibited from any genuine political activity, and surrounded by deformed values and fallacies. This generation has grown up in a paternal society, in the fullest and worst sense of the word, where the governor and his corrupted bureaucratic establishment considered themselves the only possible substitute for all political and social systems and organisations. When this unfortunate generation started to express its rebellious visions, it conflicted not only with the heavy fist of censorship, but also with the reluctance of the previous generation who dominated the literary establishment and benefited from it, in a literary and economic manner. This dual resistance to the new generation of writers did not prevent them from expressing their revolutionary visions, but merely affected the clarity and simplicity of their works, and pushed them to explore new means of expression. The result was sophistication of structure, and much innovation, in both form and themes. In fact, it is difficult to classify this generation according to schools, trends, and categories, and to study the radical changes in its vision, or to compare it with its counterpart in the preceding generation. Most of those writers have published no more than one or two collections of short stories, and they are still in the stage of development and promises. However I shall try to discuss some of their features and tendencies.

Originally, one finds that their favourite human character was that of the frustrated man incapable of fulfilling his desires and dreams, suffering from contradictions and vague fears; one who felt the loss of his faith, sense of security and balance in the face of these radical illogical changes in the scale of social and ethnic values. This character is the opposite to that which was expressed in the stories of the 'fifties, because he is not external and powerful, and not prepared to struggle with the outside world in order to achieve his ambitions and dreams. He is an internal character filled with fear and frustrations, sulking in silence with his anxieties, and suffering from the state of purgatory between innocence and guilt. The sophisticated nature of this character was reflected in the form and structure of the stories. Any attempt to classify these works according to trends would find that the only possible classification is to separate them, not on the basis of literary schools, but rather on that of structural styles. One can find, under each style, expressionistic, realistic, and symbolistic stories, and in some stories the elements of these different literary schools are interwoven and mixed together. It is hard to find in these works a story which would fit completely into a known literary school without having elements or traits from another. Thus classification according to styles is a good means of showing the innovation of these writings in the 'sixties. In brief, the main types were as follows:-

(i) The first used symbols, legends, fragmentations of history and folkloric tales, starting most often from fantasy to create a dream world in which writers could take problems which they could not treat directly, since they fell into the arena of social and political taboos. This style helped the writer to express his opinion indirectly but frankly, to create a dream world, in which he deals with the contradictions in society and prophesies the future. This style is crystallized in the works of S. Fayyāḍ, Maḥfūẓ, ʻAbdel-Raḥmān, M.H. Rajab, and M. al-Busāṭī, and influenced by the climate and the tools of Kafka, Camus, and Faulkner.

(ii) The second style depends on description and the direct line between the eye and the subject, trying to express indirectly its rejection of the broken line which had become the rule in every other field. This style distinguished stark reality without any attention to the interior, to prove how internal anxieties and frustrations could dominate the surface and appear to the observer. It benefited from the significant achievement of Ernest Hemingway in the short story and from the discoveries of the psychological school of behaviourism. This style has been represented in the writings of B. Ṭāhir, S. Fayyāḍ, I. Aṣlān, and Ghālib Halasā.

(iii) The third style used words in a more poetic fashion, to express the stream of consciousness of the depressed and frustrated character, and to make the story full of suggestion and inspiration. This style concretizes the interior monologue of this character, suffering from the gloomy present and loss of sense of security. It is indebted to Joyce, Virginia Woolf, and Marcel Proust. Its best achievements appeared in the early works of Y.T. ʻAbdulla, M.H. Rajab, and G. al-Ghiṭānī, and also in the works of Aḥmed Hāshim al-Sharīf, ʻAbdulla Khayrat, and M. Mabrūk.

(iv) The style of the comparative vision of reality, which relies on the relativity of the truth to raise strong doubts about what seem to be the stable pillars of the present regime, and to shed strong light upon the neglected true scale of social and ethical values which lie in the shadow of the present false one. This style used to divide the main plot of the story into several sub-plots and project each sub-plot to different levels of reality to underline numerous levels of meaning in the same story, and to assert that what appears on the demagogic surface is not the only truth, or moreover not the truth at all. In other words, this style was an artistic attempt to call for an absolute revision of all that appeared as stable facts in society. It was influenced by the works of John Dos Passos and the Gestalt psychologists, and crystallized mainly in the short stories of ʻAbdel-Ḥakīm Qāsim, then the more recent works of Y.T. ʻAbdulla, Muḥammed al-Mansī Qandīl, and Majīd Ṭubyā.

(v) The style of the stream of trivial experience and stress on the inanimate, which resorted to the treatment of trivial details, believing reality to be embodied in every one of its particles. It emphasises the inanimate aspect to underline the contradictions between the solidity of objects and the weakness of human character. It describes in concrete terms how man has become alienated from his surrounding milieu, benefiting in this description from the accomplishments of the French *Nouveau Roman* and the American short story writer J.D. Salinger. It has been represented by the works of I. Aṣlān, M. al-Busāṭī, and Muḥammad Mustajāb.

(vi) The style of the new version of semi-didactic tales; it depends on the rich heritage of this *genre* in Arabic literature, and profits from ancient traditional methods of treating those contradictions of cold deaf reality which require a loud voice. Or it uses the language and the atmosphere of classical historical texts to draw comparisons between the past and present, or to assert the resemblance between what happens in the present, and the decadent periods of the past. This style is represented in the recent works of G. al-Ghiṭānī and in the tales of Ṣabrī Mūsā.

(vii) Finally the style of the poetic echoes of the realistic trend and the Chekhovian short story, which attempted to develop the technical accomplishments of the Egyptian short story after the manner of Y. Ḥaqqī and al-Badawī. It emphasises poetic symbols, linguistic elements, well-analysed character, and smooth narrative. This style is embodied in the works of Abū'l-Ma'āṭī Abū'l-Naja, 'Abdulla Khayrat, and Muḥammad Rūmaysh.

These various styles reflect multiple interpretations of objective reality and embody the essence of this historical moment as the new generation has seen it. It reiterates that literature has been a basic means of understanding social and political life in Egypt in the last decade, without sacrificing any of the elements of structure and form, or losing any of its significance as pure art.

Ṣabry Ḥāfeẓ

1. After his first collection, Y. Idrīs published *Jumhūrīya Faraḥāt (Faraḥāt's Republic)* 1956, *A Laysa Kadhālika (Isn't It so)* 1957, *al-Baṭal (The Hero)* 1957, *Ḥāditha Sharaf (An Incident of Honour)* 1958, and *Ākhira Dunyā (End of the World)* 1961.

2. See the introduction to *Mafraq al-Ṭuruq* by Bishr Fāris, supplement to *al-Muqtaṭaf*, March 1938.

3. See the preface to *Sū'Tafāhum* by Bishr Fāris, Dār al-Ma'ārif 1942.

4. For the Manifesto of the Experimental movement, see the first number of *al-Bashīr*, 2nd October 1948.

5. At the same time there was in Alexandria another replica of the Cairene experimental group, but it was influenced mainly by English culture. One of its members, the poet Muḥammad Munīr Ramzī, wrote some of his poems originally in English. The principal short story writers of this Alexandrian group were E. al-Kharrāṭ, and Alfred Faraj. However, there was some contact between the Cairene group and its Alexandrian counterpart when 'Abbās Aḥmad moved to Alexandria and stayed there for a certain period.

6. See Ramsīs Yūnān's critical essays in *al-Magalla al-Gadīda* during its last four years.

7. Amongst the members of this group were: Anwar Kāmil, Fo'ād Kāmil, Kāmil Salīb, Ramsīs Yūnān, 'Adel Kāmil, Kāmil Zuhīrī, Albert Qoṣayrī, George Ḥinīn, Fatḥī Ghānim, Yūsif al-Shārūnī, Majdī Wahba, Maḥmūd Amīn al-'ālim, and others.

8. His second collection *Risāla ilā Imra'a (Letter to a woman)* 1960 and his third *al-Zaḥām (The Crowd)* 1969 included some stories prior to the first collection, and a few new ones.

9. As in the stories *Dunyā* and *Ma'a al-Salāma* by F. Ghānim, and *al-'Ushshāq al-Khamsa, Maṣra' 'Abbās al-Ḥilw, Ziṭa Ṣāni' al-'Āhāt* and *al-Wabā'* by Y. al-Shārūnī.

10. I derived this long sentence from the similar one by Richard Gilman in his book, *The Confusion of Realms*, p. 81, after some alterations to suit the context.

Najīb Maḥfūẓ's Short Stories

Although Najīb Maḥfūẓ is known above all as a novelist, he began his literary career by writing short stories and articles while in his first year at university, in 1930. At this time, the popularity of the short story as a *genre* was at its height, and it is not surprising therefore that the young writer should make his first efforts in this form, especially considering the difficulty of publishing during this period. Indeed, almost the only way of seeing one's writings in print was to persuade a periodical to publish them, in serial form if necessary. This method of publication naturally favoured short stories and articles rather than longer works.

By 1944, Maḥfūẓ had published more than seventy short stories on various subjects. However, because most of these stories appeared in periodicals and were never published as collections in book form, they have been overlooked by the critics, who misleadingly usually refer to this early phase of Maḥfūẓ's writing as 'historical' because of the three historical novels he wrote during this period. His first collection of short stories, *Hams al-Junūn*, was published in 1938, and contains 28 stories, about half of what he had already published in periodicals. These stories can be discussed most conveniently in two main groups. The first consists of stories which clearly betray the influence of what is called in Egypt the school of Muḥammad Taymūr, or the Modern School of the Short Story, which came into being in the late 1910s and flourished in the 1920s. The principal writers of this school were Muḥammad and Maḥmūd Taymūr, ʻĪsā and Shihāta ʻUbayd, Maḥmūd Ṭāhir Lāshīn, and Ībrāhīm al-Miṣrī. The writer's purpose, which was given impetus by the national revolt of 1919 against the occupying British, was to give expression to the Egyptian personality in a specifically Egyptian, and more realistic, type of literature. Therefore the themes they dealt with were frequently common family problems, such as polygamy, the marriage of young girls to old men, adultery, drunkenness, and the compelling by law of a wife to remain in the home of a husband she hates. Another characteristic was their attention to local colour. Maḥmūd Taymūr, in particular, delighted in depicting characters from the Egyptian lower classes. As might be expected in short-story writing at this early stage of its development in Egypt, the authors frequently relied upon unlikely coincidences or unusual incidents to give their stories a striking or unexpected ending.

Maḥfūẓ began writing in 1930, and most of the stories he wrote at this time indicate that he took stories of this school as models for his own. His stories have the same type of social theme, for instance, in *al-Sharīda*. A husband's neglect of his wife drives her to take a lover; in *Thaman al-Sa'āda*, an elderly man shuts his eyes to his young wife's love affairs, hoping to keep her with him; *Nakth al-Umūma* is the story of a middle-aged woman who desperately tries to maintain the illusion that she is still young, and in *al-Zayf*, a woman goes out of her way to have an affair with a man, simply because she thinks, mistakenly, that he is the most celebrated poet of the time, and she wants to boast of her connection with him. When her mistake is revealed, she becomes an object of ridicule. We also find in Maḥfūẓ's stories descriptions of lower-class characters, such as Filfil, in the story of that name, an apprentice waiter in a cafe; Ja'da, an ex-convict in *Naḥnu Rijāl*, and Ḥasan Shalḍam, a traditional comedian, in *Ḥayāt Muharrij*.

Certain stories display even more striking similarities with earlier stories by writers of Taymūr's school. For example, Maḥfūẓ's *Kayduhunna* is about a man married to a woman 25 years younger, who takes a lover, and although her husband suspects, and attempts to surprise her with her lover, she is too clever for him. This plot closely resembles that of Maḥmūd Ṭāhir Lāshīn's *Qarār al-Hāwiya*, in which a poorly-educated petty official marries a rich upper-class woman, who is involved in an affair with her cousin, and successfully foils her husband's attempt to catch her. Again, there is Lāshīn's story *Walākinnahā'l-Ḥayāt*, in which a desolate widow, dedicated to her husband's memory, is consoled by the lawyer employed to clear up her husband's estate, and in the end, one understands that they will marry; this story is closely echoed by Maḥfūẓ's *Iṣlāḥ al-Qubūr*, which describes a widow who goes regularly to visit her recently deceased husband's grave; she is seen by a man whose house she passes on her way to the cemetery, and finally he asks for her hand in marriage. Although she is shocked at first, she soon yields, and the money which she was going to spend on improvements to her husband's grave is spent instead on her trousseau.

It is not surprising that Maḥfūẓ, when he first started to write, should have been influenced by the popular Egyptian writers of the day, especially as his acquaintance with Western literature was only beginning at this time; what is more surprising is that while critics have tried to show that Maḥfūẓ was influenced by writers of the older generation such as Ṭāhā Ḥusayn, al-ʻAqqād and Salāma Mūsā, they have overlooked the influence of the younger generation, and Maḥmūd Ṭāhir Lāshīn in particular.

The second group of short stories in *Hams al-Junūn* gives indications of Maḥfūẓ's growing belief in socialism, although he had not yet discovered how best to express his views in literary form, and indeed his ideas of socialism do not yet seem to have crystallized. In one story, *al-Jūʻ*, he appears to suggest that reform could be achieved by the capitalist upper classes, if they were prepared to make the effort. A factory worker who has lost an arm in a factory accident and cannot support his family on the miserable pension allotted to him is about to commit suicide, when he chances to be saved by the factory owner's son, who promises him a new job and gives him some money, while reflecting that the money he loses gambling every night could support many such families. On the other hand, the message of *al-Waraqa al-Muhlika* is that any help rendered by the upper classes to the poor is destructive. In this story, a rich man gives ten pounds to a poor singer; the money makes him change his way of life; he becomes a gangster and is eventually hanged for murder. A search for his accomplices leads the police to destroy the slum homes of his former neighbours. Although Maḥfūẓ's attitude varies in these stories, it is clear that he is attempting to pass judgement on aspects of social injustice, whereas in his later works he is content to describe appalling social conditions objectively without comment.

From the artistic point of view, the stories in *Hams al-Junūn* are mediocre. Their principal defects are the improbable situations and coincidences, the contrived effects and the unexpected endings, although it should be remembered that these were common faults in short stories of that period. Sometimes Maḥfūẓ expresses his social criticism much too directly, without any subtlety, and many of the stories are mere narratives, superficial, and lacking any deep significance; indeed some sound almost like summaries of novels. At the same time, Maḥfūẓ's language in these stories is often too pompous and rhetorical, and he slips frequently into the use of clichés. However, these were Maḥfūẓ's first literary efforts, and should not be judged too harshly.

There is one story in this collection which stands out above the rest. Called *Badhlat al-Asīr*, it describes how Jaḥsha, who goes daily to Zagazig station to sell cigarettes, loves a servant girl, but she prefers a chauffeur who wears a suit and shoes. One day a train carrying Italian prisoners of war stops at the station. Jaḥsha barters his cigarettes first for a prisoner's uniform jacket, and then for a pair of trousers, which he puts on. At the last moment he remembers that he needs a pair of shoes, but the train has already begun to move off. The British military guard orders him to board the train, thinking, in the dusk, that he is one of the Italian prisoners. Jaḥsha does not understand what the guard is saying, and, upset about not getting any shoes, turns to go. The guard thinks his prisoner is escaping, and shoots him dead. This story contains the qualities that the others lack, and I am certain that it was written much later, especially as its setting seems to be the Second World War, when many Italian prisoners were being transported to Cairo. It may have been included only in later editions of *Hams al-Junūn*, but I have been unable to check this as yet.

Contrary to popular belief, after *Hams al-Junūn*, Maḥfūẓ continued to publish short stories in periodicals as frequently as before, until about 1942, when he began to concentrate on the publication of his novels. The stories which appeared during this period, although more than twenty in number, have not been published as a collection, and unfortunately I have not had the opportunity to study them.

After 1942 only a few sporadic stories were published. But in the early nineteen-sixties Maḥfūẓ produced another batch of short stories, which appeared in the newspaper *al-Ahrām*, and were then published under the title *Dunyā Allāh* in 1963. Since the publication of *Hams al-Junūn*, a quarter of a century had passed, during which Maḥfūẓ had established himself as the most important novelist in Egypt, perhaps in the Arab world. At the same time, the standard of short-story writing in general had improved immensely, thanks to the efforts of such writers as Yaḥyā Ḥaqqī Maḥmūd al-Badawī, and Ṣalāḥ Dhuhnī in the nineteen-forties, and Yūsuf Idrīs, Yūsuf Shārūnī and Fatḥī Ghānim in the 'fifties. As one might expect, there is a considerable difference between the stories of *Hams al-Junūn* and those of *Dunyā Allāh*. The stories of the first collection are quickly read and quickly forgotten: the book seems a mass of insignificant detail, whereas the stories of *Dunyā Allāh* are mature, realistic, and therefore convincing. The basic reason for this important change is that Maḥfūẓ has managed to embody his social and metaphysical message in situations and actions which are entirely true-to-life. Even those stories which are symbolic - and symbolism is a new dimension which was lacking in *Hams al-Junūn* - have a valid meaning when taken literally. Therefore these stories compel the reader to take them seriously and to ponder on their message. In addition to this, Maḥfūẓ's message is clearly thought out, so that the reader easily grasps his attitude to life at this stage. The book contains fourteen stories which can be divided into two groups, those with social and those with metaphysical themes. Maḥfūẓ's preference for this type of theme is seen also in his novels: his realistic novels of the 'forties and 'fifties dealt with social themes, while his concern with metaphysics had its beginnings in the second part of the *Trilogy* (1957). with the intellectual crisis of Kamāl, and occupied an increasingly important place in his work from that time until 1967.

In *Dunyā Allāh* we find the social and the metaphysical side by side. Maḥfūẓ's social criticism takes various forms. In the title story, Maḥfūẓ condemns a society which denies to the poor even the simplest of pleasures. The poor and elderly ʻAmm Ibrāhīm, whose long life has been devoid of any pleasure, has one dream: to go to Alexandria, and see the sea. To achieve this dream he steals the monthly pay packet of some office workers whom he knows will be able to manage without the money. He enjoys several days of pure bliss, before he is found by the police and arrested. The reader has to sympathise with ʻAmm Ibrāhīm, in spite of his one crime, which one feels was justified. A similar impression is given by *Ḥanẓal wa'l-ʻaskarī*. Ḥanẓal, a drug addict lying in the street in a stupor, dreams that this time when he is picked up by the police, he is treated kindly, sent to the hospital and cured, and then given a little shop and a wife, so that he can start a new life. He asks for his friends to be given the same kind of help. He is just dreaming that his new wife is caressing his neck when the caress begins to feel rather rough; he regains consciousness to find that, not his wife's hand, but a policeman's boot is on his neck, and he is dragged off to the police station. In *al-Jāmiʻ fī l-Darb*, Maḥfūẓ ridicules hypocrisy, flattery, and the use of high-sounding slogans merely for personal gain. In this story, Maḥfūẓ shows that some prostitutes are more honest, more patriotic, and closer to God, than the Imām of the mosque in the street where they work. It would take too long to describe all the stories of this type, but there is one, more significant story, which deserves mention. This is *al-Jabbār*, which shows the despotism of a village headman, ʻAbd al-Jalīl al-Jabbār. A peasant, named Abū 'l-Khayr, is to be executed for a rape which al-Jabbār committed; his sole crime is that he witnessed the rape, unseen by al-Jabbār, but gave himself away by a cry of horror. The whole village realises that he is innocent, and also who the real criminal is, but they are helpless. It is clear that Maḥfūẓ's criticism is not aimed at despotism in the village alone, but has a much more general application. This type of political criticism is found increasingly in Maḥfūẓ's subsequent collections of short stories.

The metaphysical themes found in *Dunyā Allāh* are basically two: the problem of death, and the search for a religious faith. There are three stories on death. Two describe death's unpredictability and seeming irrationality. In *Ḥāditha*, a stranger is killed in a car accident, and a letter found in his pocket reveals that on this very day he had seen the realisation of his hopes: his daughters were married and his son had found a job. Therefore, he had decided to go to the country, where he had been looking forward to enjoying the rest of his days with his relatives round about him. *Maw'id* describes how a man named Jum'a feels that death must be near, when his application for a life insurance policy is rejected on medical grounds. He summons his brother from the country to commend to him the care of his wife and children. His brother is so distressed by the bad news, that when he leaves Jum'a, he does not look where he is going, and is knocked down by a car and killed. The third story is called *Ḍidd Majhūl*, the implication of which is, briefly, that death is a mindless criminal, and we have to ignore the murders he commits, if we are to be able to carry on living a normal life.

There are two stories which symbolise man's search for religious faith in order to cure his spiritual desolation. In *Za'balāwī*, a man learns that he has a disease which the doctors are unable to cure. He had been told that Za'balāwī can cure such diseases, and he searches for him in vain. At times he begins to doubt Za'balāwī's existence, but eventually, while in a drunken sleep in a tavern, he dreams that he is in a beautiful garden, and has reached a state of harmony and content. He awakes to find that Za'balāwī was with him and tried unsuccessfully to wake him up, but now he has disappeared again, and nobody knows where he went. The afflicted man is convinced by his mystic dream that he must continue his search for Za'balāwī. It is this theme, the search for God or a meaning to life, that Maḥfūẓ tackles again in his novels *al-Ṭarīq* and *al-Shaḥḥādh*. His message appears to be that God is necessary for human peace of mind, and can only be reached through a mystic experience of some kind.

We find the same idea in the story *Kalima fī 'l-Layl* which is about a high-ranking official who has been driven by ambition to devote himself to work all his life, even sacrificing human relationships. On the first day of his retirement, he does not know what to do with himself, and feels utterly lost. He wonders in misery how he can manage to endure his retirement. He prays as a matter of routine, but one day the meaning of the phrase *bismillāhi*, in the name of God, dawns on him. Out walking, he reflects that, all his life, his actions were performed in the name of ambition, greed, selfishness or hatred, but not a single action was done in the name of God. This realisation enables him to appreciate beauty around him, to which he had been blind before. On his return home, he tells his wife of his intention to start a new life. For the first time, he smiles a smile of pure happiness, unmixed with hypocrisy, gloating or cunning.

I have discussed *Dunyā Allāh* at some length because I consider this his best collection. Here Maḥfūẓ has succeeded in conveying his social message, as well as portraying man's deepest emotions through a great variety of situations. To achieve this, he has made use of dreams, the stream of consciousness, dramatic dialogue, symbolism, and expressive language which reaches, at moments, the level of poetry.

Two years after the publication of *Dunyā Allāh*, Maḥfūẓ's third collection *Bayt Sayyi' al-Sumʻa* appeared, and here again Maḥfūẓ continues his social criticism and his philosophical searchings. We find in this collection indications of the growing tendency towards political criticism, noted earlier. There are three stories in which the political meaning is very obvious, and a further two stories which could be taken as symbolising Egypt's political situation at that time. In *Sā'iq al-Qiṭār*, the engine-driver, in a fit of seeming madness, drives faster and faster, and refuses to stop the train at any of the stations. His fellow railway workers and the passengers implore him to stop because he is endangering their lives, but to no avail. As the train crashes, all this turns out to have been a nightmare dreamed by one of the passengers on the train. The political significance of the story, *al-Khawf*, is equally clear. The people living in the quarter of al-Farghāna are terrorised by two thugs: al-Aʻwar, the one-eyed, and Juʻrān, the scarab or dung-beetle. A young police officer rids them of these thugs, but gradually his behaviour towards the people becomes even more offensive that that of the thugs. The people wonder helplessly how the man who risked his life to bring them peace and security, can now treat them in this way.

A different type of social criticism is found in *Sūq al-Kantu*, the moral of which is that the different classes in Egypt steal from each other, but punishment only falls upon the poor, while the rich keep their ill-gotten wealth.

On the metaphysical or philosophical side, we notice the disappearance of stories about the search for God, maybe because Maḥfūẓ had exhausted this theme in his novels: he had just published *al-Ṭarīq* at this time, and *al-Shaḥḥādh* was on the point of publication.

On other aspects of human life, we find *Qubayl al-Raḥīl*, which illustrates how man's happiness can be based on an illusion, and how the least thing can destroy it. Feeling flat on his final day in Alexandria, before leaving for Upper Egypt, Barakāt picks up a rather attractive prostitute, significantly called Dunyā (life), and pays her £2 in advance for a night's services. After making love, they are both bored, then he notices her slipping the £2 into the dressing table drawer; he is surprised and she explains that she does not take payment when she enjoys herself. He immediately becomes filled with virile pride, and in his elation, he decides to be extravagant and have a proper night's enjoyment. First they go to a night club to dance, where he brawls with a man who arouses his jealousy. On the way home, he has a second punch-up with a man who annoys Dunyā on the crowded tram. They have a good meal in his room, and he is already planning how he can return to see her frequently. They spend a wonderful night together. In the morning, he finds her preparing to leave, and is shattered to see her retrieving her £2 from the dressing table. Enraged, he concludes that it was all a despicable trick; her rejoinder is 'But after all, it gave you real happiness, and I deserve some gratitude'.

We also find stories on the suffering inherent in human life, the best of which is *al-Qahwa al-Khāliya*, which presents a moving picture of the loneliness of an elderly man. His wife dies after forty years of happy married life. None of his friends are at the funeral to console him: they have all died. It is the friends of his son and son-in-law who attend as a matter of courtesy. He is too old to live on his own, and has to go to his son's house; he watches in desolation the destruction of what was his home, as his belongings are packed. His daughter-in-law welcomes him with a smile, he appreciates her kindness, but it strikes him that now he really has no home. He goes to the cafe where, in former years, he had always sat with his friends, and now he looks at the chairs where they used to sit, imagining their faces and gestures and recalling the discussions they had had together. The cafe is crowded, but he sits there wondering why it seems so empty.

This kind of situation, although it is not found frequently in *Bayt Sayyi' al-Sumʿa* reveals Maḥfūẓ's sensitive imagination and great skill at selecting the most expressive and significant details to describe human experience. In my opinion, it is the poetic depiction of such situations which is Maḥfūẓ's triumph in the field of the short story, for we rarely find such writing in the works of Maḥmūd Taymūr, or even Yūsuf Idrīs and Yaḥyā Haqqī.

Unfortunately, the stories of this collection are not all of this standard. There are two stories on death, but they deal with the same aspects of death as the stories in *Dunyā Allāh*, that is, its unexpectedness and its inevitability, and what is more, these stories are less successful than the corresponding ones in the earlier collection. Other stories, such as *Qaws Quzaḥ*, which contains criticism of the strictness of traditional methods of upbringing, and *Bayt Sayyi' al-Sumʿa*, the title story, about the changing values of Cairene society, are both superficial and unstimulating.

After the Arab-Israeli war of 1967, Maḥfūẓ published five collections: *Khammārat al-Qiṭṭ al-Aswad* (1968) *Taḥt al-Miẓalla* (1969), *Ḥikāya bilā Bidāya walā Nihāya* and *Shahr al-'Asal*, both in 1971, and *al-Jarīma* (1973).

The stories written after the war are noticeably different from those written earlier, both in technique and in content. This phase of Maḥfūẓ's writing can be termed political, because these later stories are almost entirely political and topical in content. This makes them more difficult for non-Egyptians to appreciate. But even Egyptian readers find these stories extremely obscure, because Maḥfūẓ relies so heavily on symbolism and the use of the absurd that, while the general message of a story may be grasped, the significance of details is sometimes not at all clear. Critics, on the whole, have avoided commenting on these later collections, and have hesitated to offer any interpretations.

In addition to this use of symbolism and the absurd, we find that Maḥfūẓ has increased his use of dramatic dialogue. The vast majority of these later stories are written almost entirely in dialogue. The first five stories of this type, which appeared in *Taḥt al-Miẓalla*, are actually called one-act plays, and are arranged on the page as such. Later stories are not called plays and are not so arranged, but nevertheless they consist of dialogue, apart from occasional lines of narrative which read rather like stage directions. A number of these 'theatrical stories', as Maḥfūẓ calls them, have been acted on the stage, in spite of the difficulties of interpretation which the producer faces.

The first of the post '67-war collections, *Khammārat al-Qiṭṭ al-Aswad*, is really transitional, as it contains a large proportion of stories written before the war. These 'pre-war' stories resemble those of the earlier collections, except that Maḥfūẓ has now almost abandoned the metaphysical, in order to concentrate on the social, and above all the political aspects of Egyptian life. From the artistic point of view, these stories are inferior to the best of *Dunyā Allāh* and *Bayt Sayyi' al-Sum'a*. As I have already given sufficient examples of this type of story, I shall discuss instead the title story from *Khammārat al-Qiṭṭ al-Aswad* which was written after the war, and gives an indication of the new trend in Maḥfūẓ's writing.

This story is somewhat obscure. The regular customers of the Black Cat Tavern suddenly notice a large and powerful stranger wearing black, who blocks the exit from the tavern. Threateningly, he refuses to let them leave, because he thinks they heard him reveal his 'secret' *(ḥikāya)*. They can't understand what he is talking about, and, finding themselves imprisoned, drink themselves stupid. They begin to come to after a while, but they can't remember who and where they are. They recall that there was talk of some secret, to which the black cat is the clue. Did not their ancestors worship the cat, who sat one day at the door of a prison cell and revealed the secret and made threats. But what is the secret? The cat was once a god, then he became just an ordinary cat, because he revealed the secret. Their discussion is interrupted by the shouting of the head waiter at the black-clothed stranger, who is now humbly and sadly clearing and wiping tables. This story appears to refer to the position of the Egyptian Government before and after the '67 defeat.

Maḥfūẓ's stories in the following four collections were all written after the '67 war, and are similar to the story I have just described. The stories can be divided into two main groups: those which criticise the Egyptians for their attitude of indifference towards their government's conduct, and those which comment on the Arab-Israeli situation.

In the title story of *Taḥt al-Miẓalla*, we find a crowd trying to shelter from the rain in a bus shelter. As they wait, they observe a thief fighting with his pursuers, a bad car crash in which several people die, a naked couple making love on top of one of the corpses, the burial of the couple alive with the crash victims, and an orgy of sex, murder and dancing, which takes place round the grave. A policeman is there but turns his back on all this. Eventually one of the men under the shelter shouts to draw the policeman's attention to what is going on. Instead, he comes over to the shelter, and asks for their identity cards. Declaring that their gathering is suspicious, he shoots them all dead. Clearly Maḥfūẓ wants to say to the Egyptian people: 'What is happening in reality is as absurd and as terrifying as this, yet you do not wish to get involved. This passive attitude will result in your destruction'.

al-Nawm conveys a similar message, but is directed more to the intellectuals, who waste their time in useless discussion, while their country is being destroyed by incompetent government.

The one-act plays in *Taḥt al-Miẓalla* are no different. An example is *Yumīt wa Yuḥyī*: on a platform at the back of the stage are lying a number of figures, either dead or asleep. In the foreground, a young man is insisting on avenging his defeat by a more powerful enemy, in spite of the pleas of his girl friend, who begs him not to fight. A giant enters and offers his help, but the fulfillment of the conditions he wishes to impose would produce consequences similar to those of defeat by the enemy. The young man rejects his proposal, and in a struggle, is pushed against the platform, thus shaking the sleeping figures into life. They slowly rise and fill the stage. The giant takes the opportunity of slipping off in the direction of the enemy; then the young man, at the head of the troops of figures, marches off with determination against the enemy. The reference to the political situation between Egypt and Israel is too obvious to require any comment; the giant might represent the United States or even Russia, and the girl perhaps peace.

The remaining two collections, *Ḥikāya bilā Bidāya walā Nihāya* and *Shahr al-ʻAsal* do not differ greatly as far as the subject matter is concerned, but the stories are longer: the first collection contains only five and the second seven stories. Also Maḥfūẓ more frequently suggests an outcome to the situations he presents. In the title story of *Ḥikāya bilā Bidāya walā Nihāya*, an outwardly pious Ṣūfī Shaykh called Maḥmūd who is revered by the common people, leads a private life of ease and corruption, in which he is joined by his close associates. The younger generation of the quarter notice his hypocrisy, and criticise him publicly. Finally Shaykh Maḥmūd decides to have their leader ʻAlī killed. ʻAlī's mother, to save his life, brings proof that he is actually Shaykh Maḥmūd's illegitimate son. This revelation is shattering to both ʻAlī and to Shaykh Maḥmūd, and the latter finally agrees to confess all his past crimes in public, and to begin a new life. The story alludes to the situation which existed between the government and the students, born after the 1952 revolution, and here Maḥfūz is suggesting a solution to the problem.

The title story in *Shahr al-ʻAsal* describes how a young couple enter their apartment to find some thugs hiding in it. The thugs lock the door to prevent them escaping, and when they try to call for help from the window, people in the street throw stones at them. After several fantastic complications, the wife manages to set fire to the kitchen, and in the ensuing confusion, she and her husband are able to attack the thugs with knives. The neighbours and the police now break in to control the fire and put an end to the fighting. Everything in the apartment is smashed and the couple are wounded, but the thugs are removed. Here again the Arab-Israeli problem is clearly intended, as is also the case in *Walīd al-ʻanā'*, in which a woman who has lost two babies succeeds in giving birth to a third, this time living, baby, after a difficult labour during which she is aided by modern equipment and experienced helpers. Four thugs arrive to shoot the baby, but the baby, in defence, strikes them all to the ground, killing them. To the Egyptian reader, the baby here represents a new generation, capable of defending itself against its enemies.

One can see from the outlines of these stories that they have very little meaning when taken literally, and the majority can be understood only at the symbolic level. Moreover, the symbolism is such that most of the stories are experienced on the level of riddles or crossword puzzles than of artistic and emotive allegories. In his enthusiasm to comment on contemporary events, it is not surprising that Maḥfūẓ should turn to the short story, rather than to the novel, which requires time and reflection. In these most recent collections, although Maḥfūẓ may be said to have perfected his techniques, the stories are so topical and so limited in application that it is questionable whether they have any lasting literary value. His political stories are, in my opinion, surpassed by those of Yūsuf Idrīs, whose stories are richer, and can often be read at both the symbolic and the literal levels with equal enjoyment.

To conclude: although Maḥfūẓ's principal contribution to literature is in the field of the novel, it cannot be denied that many of his metaphysical and social stories are first-class literary productions by any standard, and deserve world-wide recognition.

Ḥamdī Sakkout

Arabic Novels and Social Transformation

Novelists may object to the subjection of their works to sociological analysis even by fellow novelists. Similarly, social scientists may dismiss sociological analysis of literature as tender-minded speculation. The present author conceives of the novel as an alternative to, and a subject matter of, scientific study. In the first instance, novels present the whole man in depth as an integral part of society. As such, they reflect as well as re-create reality and portray the most intimate aspects of human behaviour. In the second instance, they are human products and could be subjected to rigorous study as a system as well as a rich source of information and insights.

The overall hypothesis of the present paper is that contemporary Arabic novels tend to be critical exploration into Arab society and not just a faithful reflection of the *status quo*. The prevailing climate of social and political crises has promoted a critical stance *vis-a-vis* society and its institutions. The trying challenges and events of the last quarter-century, including the Palestinian tragic uprootedness, the Egyptian Revolution of 1952, the tripartite invasion of Egypt in 1956, the Algerian Revolution, the 1967 June War, have shaped modern Arab literature and inspired it with new themes and forms of expression. While the Palestinian uprootedness and the 1967 defeat generated a mood of reflective criticism and self-confrontation, the Algerian Revolution and to some extent the Egyptian resistance of the 1956 invasion inspired enthusiasm and self-confidence. On the whole, however, the general inclination that permeated Arabic literature has been one of desperate search for a new order, and in the direction of restructuring and rearrangement of society, rather than reflection and maintaining or promoting the established order. In this sense, contemporary Arab novelists could be considered as creative critics of their society and not as partisans of the established order. Furthermore, disappointments with Arab governments, especially after the June War of 1967, has added to the intensity of such critical stances. Contemporary Arab writers have been pre-occupied with themes of struggle, revolution, liberation, emancipation, rebellion, alienation. A writer could not be part of Arab society and yet not concern himself with change. To be oblivious to tyranny, injustice, poverty, deprivation, victimization, repression, is insensitively proper. I would even say that writing about Arab society without concerning oneself with change is a sort of *engagement* in irrelevancies.

In short, the present paper argues that the theory of influence which sees writers as agents of social change, applies more accurately to contemporary Arab novelists than the theory of reflection, which sees writers as objective and detached observers holding a mirror to reality. Contemporary Arabic literature reflects reality, but by doing so it exposes its weaknesses and embodies its yearnings for a new order. This paper, however, is not meant to praise contemporary Arabic fiction. So far, the overwhelming trend has been to focus on the emotional reactions of Arabs to historical events, on their involvement in self-centred solutions, and on their attitudes of compliance and withdrawal.

Specifically, the present paper intends to explore contemporary Arabic novels for conceptions of social and political transformation. Judging by the roles of the major characters, episodes, images, concerns, and themes in recent novels, an attempt will be made to describe and evaluate these conceptions. To what extent are Arab novelists committed to change? What kind of change are they committed to? Are they seeking partial or total change? To what extent do they reject the traditional loyalties and cultures? What kind of solutions do their characters and protagonists seem to undergo in order to transcend their situations? How do they confront reality? What kind of activities are they engaged in?

In order to respond to these questions and several others, this paper seeks to examine a number of contemporary Arabic novels characterized by breadth of vision on Arab society and which represent diverse orientations toward social transformation. The theoretical scheme of analysis is based on the author's conception of alienation[1] and is further expounded in terms of three basic dimensions of behaviour.

Change occurs because of alienation from the established order, i.e., as a result of the encounter between reality and utopia, and the emergence of a significant gap between them. The gap between the Arab society as it exists in reality, and as it ought to be in order to confront trying challenges, has contributed to the emergence of acute awareness among Arab intellectuals of the urgency for basic changes. A mood of dissatisfaction with and rejection of the dominant conditions and value orientations has manifested itself in the works of such novelists as Najīb Maḥfūẓ, Jabrā I. Jabrā, Ghassān Kanafānī, Laylā Ba‘albakī, the present author, and a few others. Alienation manifests itself also in the feelings of despair, powerlessness, uprootedness, discontent, anxiety, boredom, resentment, anger. Man is quite often portrayed in several novels as being in conflict with his society, with others, and even with himself.

The above theoretical scheme of analysis is further expounded in terms of the following three specific dimensions:

The first dimension pertains to the degree Arabic novels embody an explicit commitment to social and cultural transformation. The determining condition here is whether or not the major characters in these novels (a) stand for social and cultural revolutionary change; (b) orient themselves to the future and not the past; and (c) reject the prevailing value orientations.

The second dimension is connected with the extent to which Arabic novels concern themselves with political issues. What are the reactions of their major characters to political events? Do they stand for political tranquillity or political upheaval and revolutionary change? How do they relate to the state and the existing régimes? In the process, do novelists subordinate politics to creative and critical thinking, or do they subordinate literature to politics?

The third dimension pertains to behavioural modes of confrontation of reality. If alienated, how do major characters resolve their alienation from society? Do they retreat from, comply with, or react against the social order? Do they engage in individual-centred solutions or do they become part of a general movement that is committed to revolutionary change?

On the basis of the above dimensions and conception of alienation, the following trends in contemporary Arabic novels could be identified:

I Novels of non-confrontation
II Novels of compliance
III Novels of regression
IV Novels of individual rebellion
V Novels of revolutionary change

I. Novels of Non-Confrontation

Non-confrontation of, or escape from, reality is portrayed most accurately and vividly in two recent novels: *Tharthara fawq al-Nīl*

(Chattering on the Nile) by Najīb Maḥfūẓ (1966), and *al-Safīna (The Ship)* by Jabrā I. Jabrā (1970). In spite of the wide divergence in their points of departure and artistic forms of expression, the two novels converge in portraying contemporary Arab man as constantly living in a state of escape from reality. Even the setting and mechanisms of non-confrontation are the same. In the former a floating cabin over the Nile and in the latter, a ship over the Mediterranean, provide calm resorts for desperate characters. Their mechanisms of escape include gossip (sometimes referred to as dialogue), oral aggression against society and themselves, sex, drug addiction, alcoholism, art, and myth-making.

The characters of *Chattering on the Nile* consciously isolate themselves and show not the least concern with their society, except as a source of their jokes. In fact, they lost the ability to enjoy jokes since their life itself 'became a boring joke'.[2] They do not seem to belong and while one of them asserts, 'we are not Egyptian nor Arab nor even human', another fellow explains 'that the ship moves without any need for our opinion or cooperation'.[3] During the first half of the day they work just to earn a living and amusingly observe fellow employees 'seriously trying to accomplish trivial tasks'.[4] They become lively only in leaving work and gathering in their floating cabin - the kingdom of their drug addiction. The only thing that is taken seriously is absurdity itself, and success for them is completely forgetting the world outside their cabin. Exchange with society is minimal and almost exclusively in one direction.

The characters of *Chattering on the Nile* are not typical of Maḥfūẓ's other works. No matter how hard they try to occupy themselves, they continue to be unoccupied 'for they are without a role ... just like an appendix'.[5]

al-Safīna by Jabrā provides a similar dim perspective on the world. Time is seen as a terrible thing that robs human life of its novelty and freshness. One of the characters puts it as follows: 'If I were a painter, I would have painted that (i.e., life) as a black blotch interrupted in two or three places by red spots. Time is the enemy'.[6] The scattered red spots stand for scarce moments of joy with women, arts, battles, illusions.

The characters of *al-Safīna* are in a state of desperate escape for a wide variety of reasons, generally including failure (a) in love, marriage, national battles, self-assertion, and/or other personal pre-occupations, and (b) in keeping silent in an age of injustice and domination. In the latter category, we find those who reject their society because it does not allow them to protest, demand, speak their mind, or insist on being human. Since silence is the only alternative apart from escape, hypocrisy and opportunities dominate the scene. One has to constantly swallow the lies of reporters, writers, politicians, and others. Thus, a character wonders: 'How can I ... read a paper, hear a speech ...? The word means its opposite, and the opposite means nothing. I lie to you and you lie to me, and the cleverest among us is the one who makes his lies sound most plausible ... I am fed up, bored, disgusted ... Let the liers marry one another; let the liers bury one another'.[7]

Being bound to a repressive and impoverished world, man escapes into illusions. One of the characters in *al-Safīna* reflects, 'no doubt who ever invented the flying carpet must have been like me: Never departed from his overcrowded, poor, dirty and smelly neighbourhood in Baghdad or Cairo'.[8] Under these circumstances, illusions must be a necessity. Hence, the slogan, 'destroy illusions ... and pleasure will vanish, and nothing would remain except salt'.[9]

Yet, escape into illusions does not provide a solution. The society continues to be repressive and impoverished, and its members continue to suffer from loneliness in the midst of others, and whenever their suffering re-emerges they try to suppress it by tranquilizers. Their alienation is never resolved. By the end of their illusory journey, they are not any less desperate. The illusion itself becomes another prison. Simply, the non-confrontation novel tells us that man, in escaping from reality, ends up by creating another depressing environment.

II. Novels of Compliance

Another common alternative for alienated Arabs is compliance. Because of the repressive nature of the society and the weakness of change-oriented movements, the great majority of the alienated find it more convenient to comply rather than to retreat from, or rebel against, the established order. Again, Maḥfūẓ's novels are most illustrative of this orientation of compliance. In fact, this orientation is much more pervasive in his works than that of non-confrontation or rebellion. The great majority of his characters, especially the powerless status seekers, try to transcend their conditions by complying publicly and not privately with the demands, expectations, and norms of the prevailing order. Simply, they try to resolve their alienation from the system by playing its game and accommodating themselves to its hardships.

In almost all his novels, man is portrayed as a passive being living in a world not of his own making. His destiny is shaped by events and changes which stand beyond his reach. Things occur to him, and his main pre-occupation is to adjust to his new situations. The characters of *The Quail and the Fall* are constantly and hopelessly trying to adjust to the 1952 revolution. They feel exiled and haunted, and no matter how hard they try to occupy themselves, they continue to be bored and unoccupied.

In the long run, they adjust to their powerlessness, marginality, and hardships. In *Chattering on the Nile*, a character comments, 'because we fear the police, the army, the English, the Americans, and the visible and the hidden, we end up by not fearing anything'.[10] Another character, Uthmān in *al-Shaḥḥādh (The Beggar)*, asserts, 'it has been proven that if we were to be thrown into hell, we would inevitably get used to it'.[11] These characters keep silent for 'nothing comes out of words except headache'[12] and avoid thinking for 'it might result in distress and high blood pressure'.[13] Furthermore they realize that 'it is ill-fate to attack a man of prestige'.[14] Yet, they keep alert and patiently wait for the right moment when their 'blow will be as strong as their long patience'.[15]

The poor in Maḥfūẓ's novels are tempted into playing the game of the system. Motivated by the middle class dream of success they struggle to improve their conditions but in vain. Because of lack of legitimate opportunities, they resort to opportunism and illegitimate means. The consequences, however, are always catastrophic for the 'roads are closed to the degree of suffocation'[16] and the prevailing conditions do not allow for vertical social mobility. The novel *al-Liṣṣ Wa'l-Kilāb (The Thief and the Dogs)* (1961) portrays the poor as living in a state of constant flight from the secret police only to fall into the trap. Anger against the system is suppressed or re-channelled and surrender becomes the only available alternative. The educated who speak for the poor climb the ladder of success and 'join the dogs'. Furthermore, whenever an attempt is made at revenge against the powerful, another poor innocent is victimized. Salwā in *The Quail and the Fall* may well represent Egypt, for she moves from the hands of the aristocrat ʻĪsā into the hands of the bourgeois Ḥassan. The poor continue to struggle in vain for they are Egypt but Egypt is not theirs. Just like the quails in *The Quail and the Fall*, the poor 'fall into a pre-destined destiny following a tiring journey'.[17] The style of Maḥfūẓ's writing itself is a perfect example of the behaviour of compliance. He is often characterized as an objective writer for he diversifies his characters and allows them to express themselves freely. Furthermore almost all shades and colours of political and social trends are represented in his novels. Here I wish to argue that Maḥfūẓ is critical of his society and its political system in a seemingly detached way. In order to play safe and keep his distance, he resorts to two other techniques besides diversifying his characters. First, his novels deal with past periods rather than the controversial present. Second, he resorts to what might be called mystifying symbolism in contrast to artistic symbolism. His story *Honeymoon* (1971)[18] is a good case in point. A newly wed couple (perhaps denoting Egypt's new generation) enter their new apartment (perhaps Egypt) to find it occupied by a strange tough, and brutal character who behaves as if the apartment were his own private property. In this story and other works by Maḥfūẓ, man is portrayed as (1) always followed by police, (2) uncertain of what is happening to him, (3) always involved in some kind of difficulty *(warṭa)*, (4) forced to comply and keep his distance, and (5) waiting for a new birth with the help of a real physician and not a midwife. In the above story a character reflects, 'we think and labour, we suggest premises, we try all premises, we collide against mistakes, we re-think and re-labour, we suggest new premises, and all the time we look around with alarm fearing arrest by police or death from members of the organization, and sooner or later we will fall in the trap'.[19]

In short, the Egyptian is portrayed in Maḥfūẓ's works as resorting to public compliance as a way out of his powerlessness. Those in power are deceived for they believe they are admired. In *Chattering on the Nile*, a character notes, 'it wasn't strange that Egyptians worshipped the Pharoah; the strange thing was that the Pharoah believed he was a God'.[20]

III. *Novels of Regression and Search for Roots*

Arab novelists have registered a variety of responses to the East-West encounter since the beginning of the 19th century. Here, two such responses will be identified and described in brief. The first response could be labelled as regression into the ancient past, and is most explicitly portrayed in the early works of Tawfīq al-Ḥakīm. The second response reveals a condition of uprootedness as a result of close and enduring exposure to Western ways of life, and the consequent search for roots in the intimate primary relations of childhood. This latter response is clearly revealed in the works of the Sudanese novelist al-Ṭayyib Ṣāliḥ.

In his two novels *'Awdat al-Rūḥ*, (1933) - dealing with the Egyptian 1919 uprising - and *'Uṣfūr min al-Sharq* (1938) - recounting his experiences in Europe - Tawfīq al-Ḥakīm resorts to a mechanism that serves both offensive and defensive purposes, i.e., it raises the morale of the Egyptians and calls on them to resist British rule as well as securing a haven against disturbing challenges. In these two novels, al-Ḥakīm regresses into the ancient Egyptian past and indulges in a superficial and reductionist argument that the East represents spiritualism or the heart, while the West represent materialism or the mind. This mechanism could have been intended to raise Egyptian morale, but it seems to be more of a defensive nature because it has helped to dismiss the Western challenge and to make for psychological security. In other words, the net result is insulating oneself against disturbing questions and seeking a panacea that provides easy responses to complex and trying challenges. Hence, the unjustified experience of psychological satisfaction in an age of anxiety.

Using the same concepts of Tawfīq al-Ḥakīm, the Sudanese novelist al-Ṭayyīb Ṣāliḥ tells us that 'his mind has captured the essence of Western civilization, but it had destroyed his heart'.[21] Thus, after a long time of enduring exposure to Western civilization and consequent uprootedness, the protagonist of al-Ṭayyīb Ṣāliḥ returns back into 'the warmth of life in the tribe'.[22] His tongue almost slipped to say the warmth of the womb. Back in the tribe, he contemplates some of the political and social changes that have taken place, but he is not interested in conducting an anthropological study. Here, he feels he is no more 'a feather in the wind; he is rather like that palm tree; a creature that has roots and goals'.[23] He further contemplates along the same line, 'According to the standards of the industrial European world, we are poor peasants, but when I embrace my grandfather I feel rich, as if I am a note in the heart-beats of the universe itself.[24] Simply, he is returning to his village seeking harmony, reconciliation with the universe, security, and peace of mind. The only source of worry for him is his children who might be infected by the germ of departure.[25]

On their return to village life, Ṣāliḥ's protagonists show some concern with political and social changes which take place normally and moderately, just like seasons.[26] Their main interest, however, lies in reminiscence (the word is repeated quite often), celebrating traditional occasions, and enjoying the warmth of intimate primary relations.

Novels of regression and search for roots show an alienation from both western culture and the present dominant social and political conditions in Arab society. By resorting to the ancient past and seeking warm traditional relations, the protagonists of al-Ḥakīm and Ṣāliḥ may reconcile themselves to their own personal situations, and experience peace of mind, but they do not seem to contribute much to the cause of socio-economic and political transformation by promoting a new consciousness.

IV. *Novels of Individual Rebellion*

Another orientation among contemporary Arab novelists is most typically represented by such socially alienated rebels as Jabrā I. Jabrā, Laylā Ba'albakī, Ghāda al-Sammān, Ṣin'alla Ibrāhīm, and others. The point of departure of these novelists is the individual ego and the posing of self-centred attempts at resolving the problem of human alienation. Their characters are pre-occupied with problems of social and cultural limitations on individual freedom. They resolve their alienation by social criticism and defiant rejection of prevailing value orientations. Thus, these characters are constantly in a state of tense clashes with society and its institutions. They show little political concern, and dissociate themselves from all political movements including revolutionary ones, especially when devoid of social and cultural revolutionary spirit.

The rebellion of Lena, the protagonist of Laylā Ba'albakī in *I Live* (1958), is rooted in her assertion of her individual freedom. Her point of departure is her ego and not the society. Thus, she contemplates the following analogy, 'I am a luxurious palace ... it has all that is needed for the sustenance and reproduction of life; it needs no help from the outside ... The surrounding wall is high and separated from the road by a moat. I am an independent world whose course of life is not influenced by any outside event which does not depart from my ego; from the problem of man in my ego'.[27] Being full of herself and almost totally engaged in nurturing her ego, she pays no attention 'to those strange creatures who slide on the outer surface of my life'.[28] Lena is most bothered by her family. She despises her father and his wealth, and shows a mixture of pity and disgust for her mother. Though she lives with her family, she keeps them outside the walls of her world. In short, her attitude is one of defiance.

Lena is not interested in politics. 'I simply confess that I do not have the mind to find a solution to the problem of Palestine, Kashmir, or Algeria. What worries me ... is how to walk with my shoes which raise me for the first time seven centimetres over the ground: Will they break as I rush into the street?'[29]

The individual also constitutes the point of departure in Jabrā's works. In his first novel *Ṣurākh fī Layl Ṭawīl* (1955), Jabrā clearly points out that his reason for writing novels was psychological relief, and that his characters represented different parts of his personality. Jabrā, however, is more aware of the complexity and dynamism of social life and its impact on the individual. Social class differences, for instance, are highly visible in his novels. In so far as taking account of social forces shaping human life, he stands half way between Baʿalbakī and Maḥfūẓ. Unlike the former, he diversifies his characters and treats them in a more comprehensive social context. Though as critical of social and cultural conditions, his characters are less defiant and self-centred. They show some interest in politics and some of them did engage in political struggle in times of difficulties. Yet, though he diversifies his characters, they tend to speak his own language and debate his own ideas. In this sense, he is less objective and detached than Maḥfūẓ.

The novels of rebellion dismiss themes that might be construed as political or ideological and pose them as conflicting with artistic standards. Such a claim assumes that artistic standards can be met in dealing with certain themes and not others. The fact of the matter, however, is that any theme can be presented in an artistic or non-artistic form. Simply, there is no theme that could not be presented in an artistic and creative form. The novels of rebellion focus on self-centred solutions or individual attempts at resolving one's alienation through defiance and creative social-cultural criticisms. Their characters are seeking exits from despair, irrelevance, anxiety, boredom. The call for disengagement of literature from politics undermines the role of novelists in creating a new consciousness, and consequently, as agents of change. By confining themselves to cultural criticism and artistic recreation of reality, they do not seem to realise that basic transformation of society can take place by changing the prevailing socio-economic and political structures and not by mere creation of the counter-culture.

Rebellion in the above sense is mostly a sort of oral aggression against society; it is a struggle on stage through which artists experience catharsis. But conditions making for the alienation of man continue to dominate.

V. Novels of Revolutionary Change

Novels of revolutionary change have not been written yet; they are rather in a state of becoming. Nevertheless, a few novels could be thought of as showing the way in that direction by (1) shifting the focus from ego-centred problems and personal salvation, to the realm of the society as a whole and societal salvation, and (2) aiming at a social, cultural, and political revolution, i.e., supplementing the entire fabric of society. They share with novels of rebellion the tendency to reject the prevailing culture and particularly its value orientations, to place a special value on artistic presentation and speak a new language, to explore the inner world of the individual, and to portray man as an alienated being. However, novels of revolutionary change differ from those of rebellion by their intense emphasis on societal salvation, political issues, processes of exploitation and oppression, and identification with underprivileged groups and strata.

On the other hand, novelists of revolutionary change share with other Arab committed writers their societal concerns, but differ from them by their intense emphasis on their own autonomy, rejection of the prevailing culture, critical reflexion, complexity of human behaviour, artistic presentation, and bridging the gap between what is public and what is private. Here, reference is being made to a group of Arab writers who think of themselves as committed, but who voice the message of certain regimes against others. They practice dualism, (i.e. what they confess in public is different from what they confess in private); they are integrated in the prevailing culture; they lack critical reflection and see Arab defeats as accidental; and finally, they simplify issues and focus on daily political events showing a mood of optimism, anger, intolerance, closed-mindedness, and suspicion.

The revolutionary orientation has not taken shape yet in Arabic fiction, but the novels of Ghassān Kanafānī and the present author could be examined as attempts in that direction.[30] Here, I will confine myself to the works of the former. Ghassān Kanafānī was concerned with changing the fate of the Palestinians through writing as well as through action, and saw his fate as inseparable from that of his people. As a result of such identification with his people, their concerns and sufferings became his own. His novels and short stories record the voice of the stateless and uprooted Palestinians, especially the deprived masses who paid most dearly for the successive defeats.

Kanafānī's novel, *Rijāl Taḥt al-Shams (Men Under the Sun)* (1963), portrays the Palestinians as trapped and threatened with death. Three characters try to smuggle their way through Kuwait hidden in a truck water tank. At the borders, the driver is delayed and the three Palestinians suffocate to death. After 1967, a new Palestinian mood emerges and death follows a different course. One of Kanafānī's protagonists, Umm Saʻad proclaims a fresh start: 'so far war started on the radio and ended on the radio'. The first task of the Palestinian after 1967 was to free himself from the big prison. Thus, Umm Saʻad asserts, 'Don't you realize we live in prison? What are we doing in the camp besides walking inside that strange prison? Prisons are of different types ... The camp is a prison, your house is a prison, the newspaper is a prison, and the radio is a prison ... Our life is a prison and the last twenty years is a prison'.[31]

The way out of prison for her sons lies in becoming commandos. Suddenly it dawns on the Palestinian refugees that instead of shovelling mud in their camps, they had better stop the rain. Shovelling the mud represents compliance and accommodation to their miserable condition, but stopping the rain is a radical transformation of reality. While ʿAbd al-Jawwād in the Maḥfūẓ trilogy tried to prevent his son from participating in demonstrations for Egyptian independence, Umm Saʿad became most proud that her sons joined the resistance movement. She is delighted to 'give birth, while Palestine takes away'. Socially Umm Saʿad is also transformed for she replaces the old religious charm *(Ḥijāb)* which she had worn since childhood with a machine-gun bullet. Her husband, Abū Saʿad is also transformed for instead of losing his temper, he began to show affection for his wife and himself. Before, he was 'crushed under poverty, gambling, the ration card, the tin roof, and the government boot ...', but on the departure of his sons to join the resistance movement, his spirit was returned to him, 'life started to have a taste'.

Novels of revolutionary change invalidate the hypothesis that literature reflects reality, and confirms the hypothesis of influence or the creation of new awareness towards transcendance and a restructuring of existing arrangements. Such novels invalidate also the hypothesis that there is a conflict between art and political commitment. Literature can subordinate politics to creative and reflective thinking, and undertake the task of promoting a new consciousness.

Ḥalīm Barakāt

1. Ḥalīm Barakāt, 'Alienation: A process of Encounter Between Utopia and Reality', *The British Journal of Sociology*, Vol.XX., No.1, March 1969, pp. 1-10; 'al-Ightirāb wa'l-Thawra fī'l-Ḥayāt al-'Arabiyya' (Alienation and Revolution in Arab Society), *Mawāqif*, Vol.1, No.5, 1969, pp. 18-44.

2. Najīb Maḥfūẓ, *Tharthara fawq al-Nīl*, Maktaba Miṣr, 2nd edition, 1967, p. 28.

3. *Ibid.*, p. 60.

4. *Ibid.*, p. 5.

5. Najīb Maḥfūẓ, *al-Sammān wa'l-Kharīf*, Maktaba Miṣr, fourth edition, 1967, p. 89.

6. Jabrā I. Jabrā, *al-Safīna*, Beirut; al-Nahār press, 1970, p.22.

7. *Ibid.*, p. 130.

8. *Ibid.*, p. 24.

9. *Ibid.*, p. 84.

10. Najīb Maḥfūẓ, *Tharthara fawq al-Nīl*, *op.cit.*, p. 37.

11. *Ibid.*, *al Shaḥḥādh*, Maktaba Miṣr, second edition, 1967, p. 146.

12. *Ibid.*, *al-Liṣṣ wa'al-Kilāb*, Maktaba Miṣr, fourth edition.

13. *Ibid.*, *Tharthara fawq al Nīl*, *op.cit.*, p. 60.

14. *Ibid.*, *al-Liṣṣ wa'al-Kilāb*, *op.cit.*, p. 154.

15. *Ibid.*, p. 8.

16. *Ibid.*, *al-Ṭarīq*, Maktaba Miṣr, second edition, 1965, p. 123.

17. *Ibid.*, *The Quail and the Fall*, *op.cit.*, p. 84.

18. *Ibid.*, *Honeymoon*, trans. and published in *Arab World*, Vol. XVII, August-September 1971 originally published by Dār Miṣr, 1971.

19. *Ibid.*

20. *Ibid.*, *Tharthara fawq al-Nīl*, *op.cit.*, p.25.

21. Al-Ṭayyib Ṣāliḥ, 'Mawsim al-Hijra ilā 'l-Shamāl', *Ḥiwār*, No.24/25, 1966, p. 21.

22. *Ibid.*, p. 5.

23. *Ibid.*, p. 5.

24. *Ibid.*, p. 41.

25. *Ibid.*, p. 38.

26. For Ṣāliḥ's neutral observations on change, see *Bander Shāh, Ḍaw' al-Bayt*, Beirut: Dār al-ʻAwda, 1971, pp. 43-46, 61-64, and 88-93.

27. Laylā Baʻalbakī, *Ana Aḥyā*, Beirut: Dār Majallat Shiʻr, 1958, p.45.

28. *Ibid.*, p. 226.

29. *Ibid.*, p. 46.

30. Several critics have associated Ghassān Kanafānī and the present author together. For references on both authors see: Ghālī Shukrī, 'Ma'sāt Falasṭīn fī 'l-Riwāya al-ʻArabiyya', *al-Magalla*, Vol.7 No.79 - July, 1963: George Sfeir, 'Contemporary Arabic Novel', *Daedalus*, Fall, 1966; *T. J. Le Gassick*, 'Some Recent War-Related Arabic Fiction', *The Middle East Journal*, Autumn 1971; S. J. Altoma, 'Socio-political Themes in the Contemporary Arabic Novel', in H. E. Lewald (ed.), *The Cry of Home: Cultural Nationalism and the Modern Writer*, University of Tennessee Press, 1972.

31. Ghassān Kanafānī, *Umm Saʻad*, Beirut: Dār al-ʻAwda, 1969, p. 21.

An Analysis of al-Ḥubb taḥt al-Maṭar (Love in the Rain) - a Novel by Najīb Maḥfūẓ

Najīb Maḥfūẓ' latest novel, *al-Ḥubb taḥt al-Maṭar*, was publish in book form in 1973, after partial serialization, beginning in December 1972 in the only three issues of *al-Shabbāb (Youth)* magazine produced by the Arab Socialist Union. It has proved a controversial work and is intriguing for both its content and form. Written with even greater incisiveness than his novels of the earl and mid-sixties, there is none of the camouflage within allegory and symbolism apparent in many of his stories of more recent years In this novel Maḥfūẓ certainly fulfills the expectations of his extensive readership for a vivid and critical representation of life in contemporary Egypt. His characters express, in their actions, reported thoughts and in dialogue, frank and powerful comments on the recent mood in their country.

A short work, of 196 small, well-spaced pages mostly of dialogue it is divided into the extraordinarily large number of 45 numbered chapters. The interest-focus moves cyclically from scene to scene, each changing in locale and characters. The cast is also surprisingly large. No less than 20 individuals are given speaking roles In only one other novel has Maḥfūẓ attempted so ambitious a scope, in *Zuqāq al-Midaqq* written thirty years earlier. A comparison is interesting. In that novel there were 10 chapters less and only a dozen speaking characters, although it is perhaps three times as large in word-count. Most of his other novels - the *Thulāthiyya* excepted, of course - have had a clearly dominant central interest in one major figure around whom the plot movement and rest of the cast revolve. Though one character here sees himself in such a pivotal role, he clearly does not dominate the writer's interest.

This novel, then, has no central plot development; rather, the scenes portray a medley of incidents involving the constantly interchanging cast of characters. Each group moves through its own plot; these may be summarised in the order of their introduction. Marzūq and ʻAliyyāt, about to complete their university studies, walk in Cairo's crowded streets discussing their nation's current extreme malaise and their own marriage plans. We meet them next so forty pages and ten scenes later as the engaged couple are parting in a train for Upper Egypt, where Marzūq has been assigned to teach

ʻAliyyāt has been appointed to the Cairo Ministry for Social Affairs and immediate marriage is impossible. Their farewell conversation is interrupted, however, by a stranger who introduces himself as Muḥammad Rashwān the film producer. He insists that Marzūq become the hero of a new film he is making on the heroism of the Egyptian front-line troops. Marzūq, guilty at his deferment from military service due to family responsibilities and eager to serve his nation's cause by raising morale, agrees immediately.

Over the next chapters his co-star in the film, Fitna Nāḍir, the mistress of both an Arabian sheikh Yazīd (who never appears in the novel) and another producer Aḥmad Raḍwān, falls in love with Marzūq who gradually abandons ʻAliyyāt. His marriage to Fitna is not prevented by a mysterious attack on him which leaves his face damaged and his film career ruined. Conflicts over their career possibilities soon develop, however, and Marzūq decides at last to pursue his original goals of a teaching career and marriage to ʻAliyyāt. But by now she has herself progressed through a series of unhappy romantic involvements, including an aborted pregnancy and determined approaches from a procuress, Samrāʼ Wagdī, a lesbian who is strangled by ʻAliyyāt's father. Yet, as is often the case with Maḥfūẓ's most disaster-ridden characters, her future looks secure at the novel's end in her likely marriage to Ḥāmid, Sālim ʻAlī's brother.

Another plot revolves around this Sālim ʻAlī, a prominent lawyer who is romantically involved with Munā Zahrān, a friend of ʻAliyyāt. But, unable to accept her independent desire for a separate career as an actress, they part and he promptly marries a prostitute! Munā, meanwhile, realizes that the interest of the film director Muḥammad Rashwān in her was purely sexual. They come to blows and her brother, ʻAlī Zahrān, a doctor, soon avenges her by ambushing the dissolute director and killing him with one blow! This scandal introduces Ḥasan Ḥammūda, a prominent, middle-aged bachelor trial-lawyer who is engaged to defend the doctor. Munā's subsequent romance with him soon fades, however, and she marries Sālim ʻAlī who has reconciled himself to her independence of spirit and has abandoned his wife, the former bar girl.

Still another plot centres on Ibrāhīm, the front-line soldier brother of ʻAliyyāt and lover of Sanniyya, sister of Marzūq. Ibrāhīm and Sanniyya become acquainted when he comes to Cairo on leave and decide to marry. Early in the novel we learn that Ibrāhīm is severely wounded in skirmishes with the enemy but his marriage to the patriotic and faithful Sanniyya does take place as planned; thereafter they fade from the novel's central stage.

These, then, are the novel's principal characters and incidents and they are all brought together through the agency of Ḥusnī Ḥijāzī, who himself recognizes with some regret his pivotal role. On one occasion, as he sits in his usual seat in the coffee-house witnessing Samrā' Wagdī's dramatic arrival so soon to lead to the tragedy for which he was ultimately to blame, it occurs to him that he is:

> 'The millstone crushing a group of people for whom he has all his life felt only friendship.'

Ḥusnī Ḥijāzī appears early in the novel, in the second scene, emerging from his white Mercedes to enter the *Inshirāḥ* coffee-house where we also meet ʻAmm ʻAbduh who is the waiter and father of Ibrāhīm and ʻAliyyāt, and ʻAshmāwī the aged shoe-shine. We soon learn that Ḥusnī is a middle-aged bachelor film photographer at whose artistic flat on Sharīf Street in central Cairo two of the novel's three young women have lost their innocence. Introduced to him by Samrā' Wagdī, they have there viewed pornographic movies, drunk cocktails at his bar and accepted the presents that have helped them through college. No dramatic events or developments affect Ḥusnī personally through the progress of the novel, but due to his continuing friendship with its major figures he is constantly seen advising them and commenting on their problems as well as on those of society at large.

The events of the novel extend over an indeterminate period from some time following the June war defeat of 1967. There is a reference on the last pages to Egyptian acceptance of American cease-fire proposals, presumably those offered in mid-1970. It clearly covers part of that period of intense frustration, apprehension and disillusionment of the inter-bellum period in Cairo. Although many of the comments and situations would have remained appropriate up to the Autumn of 1972, by which time the manuscript had unsuccessfully been offered to *al-Ahrām* for daily serialization, there is no reference to the death of President Nasser in September 1970, which would have been expected to influence the thoughts and conversation of the characters.

The novel's chief claim to our attention does seem to rest on the significance of the impression it gives of life in Cairo under the stresses of the inter-war period. Maḥfūẓ' presentation of a complicated set of interconnected plots in so short a novel as this seems designed both to suggest and underline the apparent turmoil of recent years as the social-political-ideological structure of Nasser's Egypt underwent such rapid changes concurrent with all the tensions of actual and threatened warfare. The majority of the characters in this novel vacillate constantly in their personal relationships and in their views of morality, just as they do in their relationships to their nation and its problems.

One essential point is reiterated through the dialogue and reported thoughts of many characters. This is that one's personal difficulties are totally insignificant compared with those of the nation and world at large. Already on the second page we find the overall sense of pervasive crisis underlined and yet treated with utter cynicism. The passage reads:

> 'But where is the world heading?' asked ʻAliyyāt.
> This was the question he collided with everywhere and all the time. Where indeed. War or peace? And the storm of rumours?
> 'Who cares where!' replied Marzūq. (p. 6)

The chapter ends with Marzūq's comment in response to ʻAliyyāt's forecast of future difficulties in their relationship:

> 'I believe they're not even worth mentioning when compared with those of the world at large!' (p. 8)

Somewhat later we find Ḥusnī Ḥijāzī attempting to cheer Munā by saying:

> 'Do you know how I cure the depression I sometimes feel? I think of all those thousands of men killed and what the future probably hides. At once my own discontent seems insignificant to me ...' (p. 84)

Yet again later Fitna the actress discusses the uncertainties of the film industry, and is reminded by Ibrāhīm the producer:

> 'You must remember that our problems are trivial when measured against the disasters pouring down on our nation!' (p. 150)

The basic reasons for this pervasive distress are also reiterated throughout the course of the novel, both in dialogue and in reported thoughts. The crushing defeat of the Arabs in the 1967 war with Israel is referred to often and without euphemism as the 'hazīmat yūniya', the 'June defeat'. Ḥusnī, asked why he has laughed at a certain comment, replies:

> 'Believe me, I've never once laughed from my heart since the 5th of June!'

The point is repeated from another perspective, a few pages later when ʻAshmāwī the old shoe-shine angrily comments:

> 'When I see someone laughing I feel like spitting in his face!' (p. 90)

It is left to Ḥasan Ḥammūda, the lawyer, to express the ultimate sense of pessimism regarding the conflict with Israel. In a conversation discussing class conflicts, international alignments, and the effects of the Israeli air raids on Egypt, he bursts out:

> 'The problem is that we're a defeated nation but refuse to acknowledge our defeat!' (p. 146)

In contrast to this defeatism, however, several of Maḥfūẓ' characters express the conviction found in so many Arabic works of fiction written in this period, that the military reverses had beneficial effects too. Dr. ʻAlī Zahrān comments, for example:

> 'The defeat shook us to the core.'

But his sister Munā replied:

> 'And enlightened us too!' (p. 73)

The café group consisting of ʻAmm ʻAbduh Badrān, his son Ibrāhīm and his wife, ʻAshmāwī the shoe-shine and Ḥusnī the photographer, express constant stoicism along with their distress, and faith and determination that their country will ultimately prevail. In one conversation ʻAshmāwī insists:

> 'But God will give us victory in the end ...'
> 'Better add: "If God wills"', cautioned Ḥusnī Ḥijāzī.
> 'All depends on His will,' agreed ʻAshmāwī and continued:
> 'We must defeat them or else say goodbye to peace on earth.'

Ḥusnī asked him:

> 'But what if the situation ends in a peaceful solution?'
> '"Aʻūdhu bi-Allāh!", God forbid it!' shouted the bleary-eyed old man. (p. 33)

Here, moreover, as in so much other recent Arabic fiction we find the expression of admiration for the Palestinian guerrillas and an optimism that their cause will prevail. At one point the *fedā'is* are credited by one character as being the 'miracle of this period'. (p. 132) The novel ends by drawing attention to the contrast between their selfless dedication and the selfish triviality of others. The final scene has Ḥasan Ḥammūda the reactionary lawyer drinking away his personal cares while Abū Naṣr, a Palestinian Resistance leader just then introduced, expresses his convictions and an almost mystical view of the long-range struggle ahead.

That there is a 'generation gap' problem in the characters' differing views of the situation is also emphasised. The father of ʻAlī and Munā is distressed at his children's lack of patriotism and disillusionment, but Munā:

> '... was amazed how the June 5 defeat had dramatically revived and restored his patriotism, whereas she had become completely disillusioned and impelled towards a total change in her outlook. And this had happened to ʻAliyyāt, Sanniyya and others too, as well as to her brother.' (p. 50)

The classes are shown to differ, as do the generations, in their view of the current situation. The lower class characters of the café circle express a stoic willingness for self-sacrifice and some trust and acceptance for their government's posture, despite ʻAshmāwī's disbelief that young men from rich families are sent, like the poor, to fight at the front. (p. 42) The professional class of inherited wealth, however, ʻAlī Zahrān the doctor, Sālim ʻAlī the jurist and Ḥasan Ḥammūda the trial lawyer, express degrees of cynicism. The 'intellectuals', represented by Ḥusnī Ḥijāzī and his film industry friends express an ambivalent scepticism of the current policies of the government of the country they nevertheless clearly love so much.

Scene 26 provides a good illustration of Maḥfūẓ' delineation of the intensity of feeling generated by the class problem. Set in the villa of the leftist journalist Ṣafwat Murjān and his independently wealthy wife, the concluding passage of conversation following dinner reads as follows:

> 'What's the current news then?' asked Ḥasan Ḥammūda.
> 'Oh, nothing new, but things are improving I think' replied Ṣafwat, a man whose opinions always carried some weight.
> 'But how can you say that, for God's sake?' Ḥasan demanded.
> Ṣafwat laughed heartily, replying: 'I forgot I was talking to a man who sides with the Israeli army against that of Egypt.'
> 'Is that truly how you view my position?' asked Ḥasan somewhat bitterly.
> 'It's a matter of patriotism more than anything.'
> 'How patriotism? It's either democracy or socialism, America or Russia. If it's your right to like Russia, why isn't it ours to like America?!'
> 'It's what the people want that matters,' Ṣafwat replied seriously.
> 'What"people"?'
> 'The people, the lower classes, the ones you don't know.'
> Disgust and bitterness, hatred and anger overwhelmed Ḥasan. At that moment he hated everything, even that garden filled with the perfume of orange blossom, that

lovely cool night, along with Ṣafwat Murjān and his wife Nihād al-Raḥmanī too, 'But be patient,' he told himself, 'for any moment some unimaginable disaster might well strike ...' (p. 127)

Feelings of insecurity and distress stemming essentially from Egypt's so-called 'no war, no peace' policy of the period is shown to have resulted in a broad sense of discontent. Disbelief in the government-controlled media is expressed and there are occasional references to the high cost of living and to the extreme difficulties faced by young people planning marriage. One gets also a vivid sense of the terrible overcrowding in Cairo today. Various conflicts are seen to develop from contrasting views of the position and roles of women in society and in marriage. Perhaps the most sensitive if transitory issue raised in occasional dialogue is the dissatisfaction of the armed forces at civilian unwillingness to view them with sufficient respect, and the military situation with due seriousness.

Some passages of cryptic conversation are bitingly critical and sarcastic about Egypt's current position and the policies that led there. The following passage where ʿAshmāwī, the old coffee-house shoe-shine, complains to Ḥusnī Ḥijāzi is typical of these:

'By rights, disasters should be distributed with proper equality.'
'You're right' replied Ḥusnī.
ʿAbdhu Badrān objected:
'I don't get it!'
Ḥusnī looked at him quizzically, and so went on:
'Well, these times of disaster follow one another like rain falling.'
'We're at the very centre of the world, so what do you expect?'
'First the (British) occupation, then independence, then 1956, the Yemen, 1967, the occupation ...!' complained ʿAbduh.
Ḥusnī objected, trying to fend off the depression creeping over himself;
'The future will create a new nation.'
'I don't feel good about it.'
'That's because you're just back from visiting the hospital whereas you'd been preparing for a celebration.'
'Oh for my country!'
ʿAshmāwī interrupted:
'Some country of saints and holy men!'
And then ʿAshmāwī commented fiercely, with some of the vehemence of earlier days:
'You Arabs!' (p. 90-91)

Here and there in the novel, characters express open disgust for the Revolution. Responding to a comment on his past life, Ḥasan Ḥammūda the trial lawyer and from the old land-owning class replies:

> 'Well, I was never really free of pain and worries until disasters positively overwhelmed me when the glorious Revolution came along and cleansed me of pain with what was even more violent, more frightful ...'

This extreme dissatisfaction shared by so many elements with the political, social, and military experience of Egypt is shown to have resulted in fundamental changes in the moral and religious outlook of the characters. Quite early in the novel Maḥfūẓ has ʻAshmāwī put forward the simplistic but widely held view that times of national disaster coincide with and result from the breakdown of traditional religious and moral values in a society. But Ḥusnī Ḥijāzī comments to himself in reply:

> 'But what are morals? Your real crisis is that you're all in need of new morals!' (p. 34)

The point is illustrated in various ways. Munā specifically states her total rejection of her country's traditions. (p. 46) Even the abortion issue is seen to present no complex moral problem for ʻAliyyāt and Ḥusnī. Ḥāmid, her future husband, will marry her, moreover, despite his knowledge of her earlier pregnancy. Samrā' Wagdī's reported sarcastic comment that:

> '... the end of the age of innocence has coincided with the end of the reactionaries, feudalists, and imperialists.' (p. 126)

is seen to be an accurate reflection of the attitudes of most characters in this novel. Ḥusnī Ḥijāzī in particular makes frequent satirical and cynical comments covering a wide range of subjects. He counters, for example ʻAliyyāt's critical remark about Sālim ʻAlī's marriage to a prostitute with the observation:

> 'But that word no longer has any meaning'. (p. 87)

In one extraordinary scene somewhat reminiscent of a Greek chorus, consisting of snatches of enigmatic dialogue between unnamed young men, a whole range of sensitive areas are discussed, even including the expression of doubts on the very existence of God. Marzūq Anwar and a crowd of young friends engage in conversation over drinks in a bar. Following discussion of current sexual mores, someone comments:

> 'But that's all unimportant; what matters is does God Exist?'

'Why do you want to know?'
'Our hottest issues used to be "Arab Unity" and "African Unity".'
'What's that to do with the existence of God?'
'Now the hot issue is when and how to erase the effects of the aggression.'
'Please, just one moment for me: does He exist?'
'Oh, what days of glory there were!'
'They were a dream.'
'No, just mere imagination.'
'And people object to our relaxing a little in the street!'
'The dogs!'
'Well, if it's decreed for the Jews to leave, who is to remove them but us?'
'Who gets killed each day but us?'
'Who got killed in '56? And who in the Yemen? And who got killed in '67?'
'Old men think that to have a half-naked girl is everything.'
'It's up to us to start from scratch.'
'To clear away the nightmares.'
'But no one wants to answer me; does He exist?'
'Very well, friend, if we judge by the chaos rampant everywhere, He simply can't exist!'
'Isn't it possible He does have power but doesn't use it?'
'And yet Egyptians are still worshipping Him?!!!' (p. 36-7)

The scene ends shortly thereafter with a discussion of war. One character, unidentified like the rest, states:

'War is not the most frightful thing threatening the world.'
'There's something worse?'
'Individuals aren't completely secure even within their own families and families fear their neighbours; one's nation is threatened by a variety of other nations, while the world itself is encircled by another hidden world of destructive beings. The earth itself could be destroyed by faults in the solar system and the solar system could explode and disappear in an instant.'
'You're an idiot!'
'But anyway, we have to laugh and not allow anything to spoil our precious lives ...'
'Amen.'
'Amen.'
'Amen.' (p. 38)

In an atmosphere so charged with bitterness and insecurity it is not surprising to find many of the characters in this novel contemplating ways of escape from Egypt, a subject Maḥfūẓ also touched on in earlier works. Emigration is the subject of several conversations between the novel's upper class characters. Munā and ʻAlī Zahrān and Ḥasan the lawyer all showed they have considered the step seriously on ideological grounds. Munā at one point defends the idea of emigration as a matter of nothing less than *sunna*, a hallowed tradition. Ibrāhīm asks in response:

> 'Even if it were to the United States?'
> 'Even if to hell itself!' replied Munā defiantly. (p. 60)

Curiously, however, it is only Ḥusnī Ḥijāzī, essentially patriotic despite all his sexual amorality, who does emigrate. He is to leave for Lebanon at the novel's end purely because he fears police discovery and public disclosure of details of the private life in his so-called 'enchanted flat'.

Exploration of the feelings of guilt and frustration of his countrymen is another of Maḥfūẓ' major themes in this novel. Those characters who contemplate emigration are clearly ridden with guilt at the idea of abandoning their country while it is still under occupation and at war. Ḥusnī Ḥijāzī is seen frequently evincing feelings of guilt at his own hedonism and love of life, and frustration at his inability to serve Egypt. Marzūq similarly feels guilt at his deferment from military service and seeks to serve through his acting. ʻAbduh Badrān, in his sixties, regrets his lack of opportunity for public service at any time throughout his life; he had been too young for participation in the anti-British activities at the end of the First World War and was too old now. ʻAshmāwī's frustration is on a different scale. He clearly sees the conflict with Israel as a mere extension of those old neighbourhood troubles between Cairo's different religious and ethnic communities that he and his friends were so easily able to suppress, if not without violence. Now in his eighties, he can only express his impotent rage in passages of boastful bravado directly reminiscent of Kirsha in *Zuqāq al-Midaqq*. His sense of hurt is extreme when his neighbours remembering his legendary exploits of earlier days, naively appeal to him to gain revenge for the lives of local boys lost on the war front. He simply cannot comprehend the environment into which he has survived. At one point he bursts out:

> 'Whatever has become of the world? Women walking naked in the streets, jailbirds getting jobs in government service and the Jews as conquerors!' (p. 166)

It is clear, then, that Maḥfūẓ is highly successful in exposing in this work a large variety of the concerns engaging the attention of Egyptians over the last several years. To have accomplished all this within one short novel in a manner both aesthetically pleasing and intellectually convincing would have been a feat indeed; Maḥfūẓ does seem to display here a greater unevenness in style and arrangement, and to develop his characters and situations less impressively than in much of his earlier work. Individual scenes are skillfully developed but there does seem a lack of satisfactory cohesiveness to the whole.

In the early sixties, of course, Maḥfūẓ began using the 'stream of consciousness' technique as a method of revealing the thoughts and motivations of his central figures. In *al-Liṣṣ wa 'l-Kilāb* for example, the technique was used consistently and effectively to express the wanderings of the mind of his confused, and emotion-ridden, central figure. Here, however, we find the technique used only occasionally and somewhat inconsistently. In the greater part of the novel the unspoken thoughts and motivations of characters are generally revealed following introductory phrases such as: 'He told himself.' (p. 21) 'He recalled how ...' (p. 15) 'He went on to tell himself ...' (p. 11). The sometimes extensive stream of consciousness passages that occur mainly in the novel's second half seem unexpected and jarring, especially when they display the emotions of rather minor characters. In scene 26, for example, the transition is abrupt from a defensive comment made by Ḥasan Ḥammūda to expression of his anger and resentment. The passage reads:

> 'Oh no, my dear,' he replied, 'she could still have become a wife, or merely a madame in a house of prostitution, or a nun ...'
>
> 'Why were they bringing up this old emotional account for the sake of a past now dead and disregarding the hurt to my feelings, to my pride. ...Isn't Samrā' Wagdī a thousand times happier than I? Didn't our family lose a nephew in the deep penetration raids? Didn't my father die and our reputation and honour become tarnished?..' (p. 126)

In this novel too, perhaps because of its extreme compactness despite its many complexities of plot and character relationships, the reader feels uneasy at what seem melodramatic, even grotesque, plot developments. One character kills another with a single blow and the strangulation of Samrā' in full view in the café by a man she has never met before who is in his sixties and with no apparent record of violence, seems somewhat unlikely. Although often witty and entertaining, the dialogue does sometimes appear annoyingly obscure, if not inappropriate to the scene; the directness and finally the brutality of Rashwān's language and actions in his efforts to seduce Munā, for example, seem contrived and unconvincing. Perhaps Maḥfūẓ would insist that he is using such devices to underline the blackness of the mood and the scarcely suppressed violence of the Cairo he is describing.

Some aspects of Maḥfūẓ' novels that have appeared since the early sixties have given the impression that he is consciously developing scenarios for the film and television industries, as much as writing works to be read as literature. Filming of his novels and some of his short stories has become almost automatic. He was also, of course, professionally engaged in his earlier career in adapting for the screen a number of works of other Egyptian writers and for some years he held a high executive position in the television administration in Cairo. All this perhaps accounts for the paucity of physical descriptions of characters and places in his later works, in marked contrast to the full and meticulous descriptions of the early novels.

It is clear that in *al-Ḥubb taḥt al-Maṭar* Najīb Maḥfūẓ has attempted to continue to fulfill his self-imposed but widely accepted role as the vocal conscience of Egypt. By giving frank expression in his fiction to a whole range of psychological and social concerns, he is performing some of the functions of the free press and communications media in other societies, while at the same time critically portraying a mirror-image of the contemporary life in his country.

Since publication of this novel Maḥfūẓ has brought out two further works. A volume of eight short stories and a play appeared early this year under the title *al-Jarīma (The Crime)* and these were followed by *al-Karnak (Karnak)*, a series of scenes, character sketches and conversations of astonishing frankness set in a coffee-house of that name. Although both of these works are more modest in scope and objectives than the novel examined here, their vitality and the incisiveness of their criticisms and observations, suggest that Maḥfūẓ, now in his sixties, is still capable of building even higher his reputation as the unchallenged master of contemporary Arabic fiction.

Trevor Le Gassick

Classical Arabic on Stage

The world is a stage. Everything is acted out on it. Everything plays its own role. But such an observation began to be made only when the observer emerged from among the actors, when he said: 'I am acting the role of the observer, of the audience, before whom the spectacle of the world is being performed.' In brief, the world became a stage after there was a stage to accommodate it, after the planks of self-consciousness were laid underneath it. One could ask: How large has the stage of the world to be? Anywhere between the universe and the nutshell, perhaps? What matters is the point of view, the perspective, the row and the seat. Stages of all sizes and shapes were emerging when man began looking at his own performance, but it was only when he set up a pavement or put a row of planks together and raised them and then put himself there and acted out what he had seen happening, that the word stage, the name and the certainty of the experience was achieved. From up there he could then look around and say: The world is a stage.

Arabic cultural and social self-consciousness suspected all this, of course, from the beginning - certainly before the year 1848. al-Jāḥiẓ's world of marketplaces, alleys and tenements teeming with picturesque misers was then and there a stage for much wisdom and folly, for much that was life. al-Maʿarrī's afterworld was a fully consciously enjoyed spectacle, and the author's ironic tone leaves no doubt as to who is sitting in the orchestra. But this is one way of seeing the world as a stage. The other one remained unnoticed by the Arabs as literature, as spectacle and even as that work of carpentry which goes into putting the planks together. The magic platform on which human folly and human wisdom, hope and regret could again and again be enacted through movement and speech, through pauses and silences, through a precast image of things, the analogue of the ship of fools, the nutshell in the palm of the hand, that physical, dynamic thing called theatre - it did remain unknown to Arabic culture until 1848.

It is not the purpose of this paper to discuss the plots and the characters which with Mārūn Naqqāsh, and with those who followed in his footsteps, began to populate the newly assembled planks of the Arabic stage. Instead, I shall devote some attention to perhaps the most dramatic, the most torn and perplexed, the most taken-for-granted and misunderstood of all the characters to have acted out their drama on the Arabic stage, the Arabic language itself.

When plays were first written by the enormously well-intentioned Syro-Lebanese amateurs of the new art, the type of language they turned to was, as it were by a cultural reflex, the *al-Fuṣḥā*. It would be a compounded mistake to call that language 'classical Arabic' without further qualification. Indeed even the normally used term of *al-fuṣḥā* which is essentially qualitative, already presupposes a level of purity and correctness which those early dramatists were never able to give their language. In more appropriate terms, therefore, the language which first appeared on the Arabic stage may be called the mid-nineteenth century form of written Arabic - the end product of a waning literary culture.

Almost all the critics of the Arabic stage since Muḥammad Taymūr's precocious insights agree that the beginnings of the Arabic theatrical venture were severely marred by the inability of the early playwrights to give to drama its own, independent entity outside of the chaotic assemblage of musical spectacle.

Perhaps one ought to be lenient at this point, however. It may be even unfair and uncritical to expect satisfactory results in a creation *ex nihilo*. For Arabic drama to have been born in any more perfect semblance than the one given to it by Mārūn Naqqāsh would have come close to being a literary miracle. An exceptional creative genius would have been needed even to have theoretically envisaged the totality of the requirements for the kind of theatre with which successive generations could live in inner comfort. As it was, Arabic theatre was born and went through its infancy enveloped in the externally undoubtedly obtrusive and vulgar, but internally protective, mantle of song, music and dramatically inconsequential flourish. Thanks to this non-dramatic bait and paraphernalia, however, Arabic theatre, at least as regards the social aspect of the availability of an audience, was not born still. The mere chronologically quantitative fact within modern Arabic culture that theatre - not just obscure literary attempts but the live, complex fact of the theatre - was the first one among the European artistic forms and genres to be adopted and cultivated uninterruptedly, should not be underestimated.

As far as our interest in the language of the Arabic theatre at that early stage is concerned, we must realise that the heavy emphasis on the sung word made certain that the painful fact remained hidden that Arabic as a literary vehicle did not yet possess its language of the stage. Indeed, one sighs with relief, thinking of the Arabic theatrical audiences of the nineteenth century - and of the decade or two of the present century - enjoying their money's worth of the musical numbers, being able to skip over, imagine or take for granted much of what might otherwise require complex dialogue or tightly motivated action. From song to song or dance to dance, the audience could be guided through plots which were labyrinths of disbelief, over lack of full understanding of speech, around an as yet undeveloped sense of plasticity of the stage. Music made all this novelty understandable, familiar, and certainly not least of all worth the expense. Arabic theatre could thus imperceptibly evolve from a cultural oddity to which the sophisticates of the foreign and diplomatic community would be invited for an escapade, into a cultural habit and a social reality.

It was only later, when playwrights, actors and audiences had ripened, that higher demands upon the Arabic theatre could be rightfully made. Indeed, it is not a coincidence that, as if marking that point of emerging consciousness of the real theatre, a critic like the young Muḥhammad Taymūr is raising his voice (1918). His most important demand is for Arabic theatre to rid itself of its overlong illegitimate affair with music.

Certain other significant things had happened then in the Arabic theatre almost simultaneously or only a few years apart. Serious dramatic companies like Jūrj Abyaḍ's and Yūsuf Wahbī's were established in Cairo. An autochtonous Arabic historical drama began to show signs of maturity. Faraḥ Anṭūn wrote his *al-Sulṭān Ṣalāḥ al-Dīn wa Mamlakat Urūshalīm* (1914) and Ibrāhīm Ramzī his *Abṭāl al-Manṣūra* (1915). The appearance of social drama imposed new critical postulations especially with regard to language. Thus both Faraḥ Anṭūn *(Miṣr al-Jadīda wa Miṣr al-Qadīma,* (1913) and Mīkhā'īl Nu'ayma *(al-Ābā' wa 'l-Banūn,* 1917) face squarely, even though producing arbitrary solutions, the problem of social authenticity in the dramatic use of the two available languages - the literary and the colloquial. Last but not least, the rapid rise of melodrama proved that the Arabic theatrical audiences were now ready to listen to dramatic dialogue and to let themselves be fully involved in the action which was unfolding on stage. The success of Yūsuf Wahbī's production of *al-Dhabā'iḥ* (1925) by Anṭūn Yazbak was more than an incidental moment in the process of shaping a new theatre-going public.

It is from this critical timespan on that one may confidently say that the spoken word both in its literary dimension and in its dramatic enunciation becomes a full-fledged maker of theatre in Arabic and at the same time one of its *dramatis personae*. The clarity and purposefulness with which the word itself now dominates the stage makes it difficult to disregard or to avoid the problems which it poses.

First of all there are two languages in Arabic, or two levels of speech, which claim their dramatic rights. Here I should like to dwell more on the second definition of a divided Arabic language as 'two levels of speech', rather than go into a tangential, linguistic discussion which the term 'two languages' would beg. What is dramatically important is that to the playwright, as well as to the audience, the difference between the literary, which is to say the written word, and the spoken or conversationally used word is less immediately one of grammatical properties, of correctness or incorrectness, as it is one of level of meaning and of style in the broadest sense of mode, manner, and level of being. In other words, a person who uses one language or another, means and becomes what that language imposes on him. The existence of these two levels of speech in Arabic thus still chains Arabic literature to some extent - and in a more particular way Arabic dramatic literature - to that antiquated mentality of a division of styles into higher and lower, with which Dante was trying to come to terms in his *De Vulgari Eloquentia*. In the adaptations of European dramatic literature in Egypt we find quite clearly indicative traits of this consciousness of levels of styles. Thus Muḥammad Mandūr in his *al-Masraḥ al-Nathrī* (p.36) draws not only a distinction between a free translation or adaptation which 'merits' the term *al-taʻrīb* and the other 'more dubious' handling of the problem, called *al-tamṣīr*. If *taʻrīb* were to denote only a more disciplined form of translation-adaptation as opposed to a totally rampant *tamṣīr*, matters would be fairly simple. Indeed, excessive distortion of the translated dramatic work may be condemned on principle as artistically undesirable. The difference between the two approached goes further, however. *Taʻrīb* is not only a rendition closer to the original - it is also a rendition into the literary language, and, what is particularly significant, it concerns itself almost as a rule with so-called serious drama. *Tamṣīr* on the other hand, as the term itself suggests, is an Egyptianization, a version of the taken-over word into a local language and a local milieu. One could go further and suggest that the end-product of *tamṣīr* would be something like a 'provincial' adaptation of something which in its original might have had a general validity. The term *tamṣīr*, therefore, might easily suggest, as it does to Muḥammad Mandūr, a value judgement. There is some justification for this value judgement, too, however, because the plays which were rendered into the colloquial idiom and which were most thoroughly turned local or 'provincial' were, once again almost as a rule, comedies, that means works which in the Aristotelian hierarchy of dramatic *genres* would fall 'below' the theatre of serious or lofty purport.

This survival of the existence of the two styles - the high and the low - implying the use of a different language in each instance, was an equal imposition of limitations on both languages, the literary and the colloquial. Borders were created which were difficult to cross from either side. On the one hand, outside of full *tamṣīr* or assimilation of characters and action into the local milieu, there existed, and to some extent goes on existing, a peculiar lack of faith in the colloquial language, reflected in the thought that, if a play is translated, its environment is foreign and therefore the *fuṣḥā*, the formal literary language, is more appropriately the vehicle of rendition. The colloquial language would immediately presuppose an environment which would be too closely defined. Indeed it took a long time for Arabic theatre-makers - the audience was never really asked for an opinion - even to begin imagining the possibility that a generally valid and perhaps unconnotative in the folkloric sense dramatic subject could be expressed in the language of common speech. That language was not to be generalized, and it was not transferable. It possessed a 'meaning' and a cultural and social connotation by just being the *ʿāmmiyya*.

On the other hand a similar lack of faith existed - and still goes on existing - with respect to the literary idiom, the *fuṣḥā*. This language was felt to lack qualities denotative of environment. It was almost its excessively non-denotative, neutral nature, therefore, which was rendering it appropriate for translations of plays with alien environments which at best can be expected to be rendered in an external, detached manner. The notion of 'universality by definition' which this feeling for the literary language was depositing in translator, playwright, actor, and audience, was thus imposing equally burdensome strictures on that language which in theory at least, and following the postulations of the Arabic literary canons, would have had to play the role of the all-inclusive dramatic vehicle on the Arabic stage.

When we pass from translations to original dramatic production, we encounter the same problems, only perhaps put into an even sharper focus. Play-writing in the colloquial language had at first, and for a very long time afterwards, only one domain open - that of comedy. Serious drama and tragedy were the domain of the formal literary language. Only at the high point of the melodramatic vogue *(al-Dhabāʾiḥ)* does the colloquial language cross the boundary into the other domain. On the Egyptian stage this was of course translated into a confrontation between Jūrj Abyaḍ and

Yūsuf Wahbī. Ukāshah's productions of plays which hesitated between comedy and melodrama, like the tragicomedy *al-Hāwiyah* by Muḥammad Taymūr (1921), were conquering for the colloquial language the kind of dramatic middle ground which was to remain perhaps most characteristic of the subsequent development of colloquial-dialogue theatre. The heavily theoretical bias against the colloquial language as the language of the Arabic stage - and in particular, one feels, as the language of a more serious or artistically ambitious theatre - may, however, be perceived in the rather wantonly expressed sentiment of pity by Muḥammad Mandūr over the fact that Muḥammad Taymūr should have written his plays in the colloquial language. Thus, beyond a purely theoretical position of principle, one must wonder why Muḥammad Mandūr voiced this fruitless, postmortem hope that, had Muḥammad Taymūr lived, he would have turned to the *fuṣḥā* as his brother Maḥmūd had done (*al-Masraḥ al-Nathrī*, p.117)? Did Muḥammad Mandūr have really the future of Arabic theatre in mind at this point, one wonders? Did he actually regard Maḥmūd Taymūr's theatre so highly? Of course, he knew that Maḥmūd Taymūr himself, at the decisive stage when he was still a creative playwright, was not at all certain which language had the real right to the Arabic stage, that therefore he was offering bilingual (colloquial and literary) versions of his plays. Simply enough, Maḥmūd Taymūr did not trust either language fully, and his defence and limitation of both had serious flaws in argumentation as to what constitutes the reading value of a work of the theatre and what the dramatic value - as if such a differentiation were at all legitimate, especially when coming from a playwright (*al-Makhba' Raqm 13*, Introduction).

Be that as it may in the realm of pseudo-dramatic critical discussions of the merits of one form of language over another, discussions which in reality belong to other stages of great import in modern Arabic cultural life, those of philology and ideology, in the realm of the ongoing drama of the theatre itself and on the planks of the only stage which decides dramatic value, the dramatic efficacy of at least one of the two languages, the colloquial, has managed to establish itself securely. In its case things simply took their natural course. A gradually growing silence of Arabic dramatic criticism about the fact that, as time went on, ever more and ever richer and better theatre was being written, produced, and enjoyed, in the colloquial language, only helped the process of the maturing of that language as a full-fledged idiom of the stage. In this case at least, we obtain an example of how beneficial the critical neglect of a seemingly imperative question can be, if I may be permitted the paradox.

What remains more in need of a critical consideration is the *fuṣḥā* as dramatic idiom, this self-assured protagonist of an ideal Arabic stage, whose dramatic qualifications were all too often taken for granted by critics with more sense of cultural pietism and loyalty, than concern for that protagonist's true performance on the real planks, before an audience anxious to undergo the experience of the theatre. Unfortunately, all too often the possibility of the failure of that protagonist was dismissed by maintaining that the whole thing, the dramatic experiment in the literary language, is in reality only a pretext, a play within a play, that nothing was meant to be performed, that we were facing literature, that very noble and unassailable creature which would suffocate in the sweaty, dusty, encroaching, physical air of a filled hall. Tawfīq al-Ḥakīm escapes in such a way from the real world of the theatre into the world of make-believe of a higher literary purpose. Maḥmūd Taymūr, in writing his double versions of plays, in effect abdicates responsibility. In his *fuṣḥā* versions he displays an uneasy psychological antiquarianism, as if he were creating something which he does not dare to put to the test dramatically, something which therefore may not have a real life as dramatic literature either, a type of theatre and of literature which from the start is condemned to being a museum piece.

If today, reading - and occasionally viewing - even some of the best achieved examples of Arabic drama written in the literary language we nonetheless continue reliving, even if it be in our hypersensitive critical awareness, those trials, tribulations, half-confessed fears and pains of birth which the creators of the Arabic literary drama had experienced, it is perhaps because we feel that the process of maturing of the *fuṣḥā* as the language of the stage is not over and that certain critical seams remain visible. But it is precisely because we acknowledge the accomplishment that we are alerted to the process.

In this process the development of a dramatic dialogue was the beginning and the final test of achievement. It is not that there was no dialogued story construction in literary Arabic before Tawfīq al-Ḥakīm, for example. There had been the translated theatre, some original historical drama and melodrama. But, analyzed more closely, that early theatre was precisely that: dialogued story. The declamatory, rhetorically constructed speeches of individual dramatic characters were monotonously arranged in a flat, stretched-out surface of addresses. The only variety in this flatness of speech was of a lyrical nature, as when lovers would go off into tender flights of mutual confessions of once again interchangeably flat words concerning feelings. The nature of speech in those plays seemed to have been determined prior to its use in specific dramatic situations. In simple terms, such language was borrowed, extrapolated out of other *genres*, and was never dramatized.

When in his searching years Tawfīq al-Ḥakīm appears to us so obsessed with the idea of forging for himself a dramatic style and with opening up for Arabic literature a new medium, we have the feeling that he is aware, albeit in theoretically quite broad terms, of this very problem. His first intimations of accomplishment, conveyed so well in his *Zahrat al-ʻUmr*, come with the writing of *Ahl al-Kahf* where a new, more individually determined, more internally motivated idiom makes its appearance. This idiom is not borrowed in *genre* terms, brought in from some other context, recognizable by other stylistic traits. It seems, tentatively, perhaps but quite indicatively, to be originating in the action of the play itself. This may have been the realization which gave Tawfīq al-Ḥakīm the feeling of having found 'his style.' Today we see perhaps a little more clearly, realizing that *Ahl al-Kahf* specifically is as yet quite a 'styleless' work as far as the language itself is concerned. At the same time it is unmistakably a work where for the first time in the history of Arabic dramatic literature conceived and executed in the *fuṣḥā*, an effective fusion of dramatic action and language takes place. It is therefore rather than the achievement of a personal style, the achievement of a play.

If, as we had noticed with respect to the colloquial language, a new, dramatic use of that formerly 'lower style' had progressed, reached diversification and depth in a process which went against the grain of all formal critical postulation, finally benefitting from critical neglect, in the theatre of the literary language matters were not quite as easily 'taking their own course'. Here, aside from the lack of dramatic directness and stage impact which the formal *fuṣḥā* deep underneath felt with respect to the spoken *ʻāmmiyya*, the severest tensions were of an internal nature. The burden of its own past was still pressing heavily on the *fuṣḥā*. Established *genre*-traditions and stylistic recourses once so easily applicable, were now perceived as jarring. Whichever way the new Arabic playwright turned in pursuit of the right dramatic tone and timbre, the imposing wealth of the old non-dramatic body of literature and its determining hold on the uses of the *fuṣḥā* would not yield what he so desperately needed. Neither the poetic nor the sententious-epigrammatic nor the argumentative nor the expository styles were of much use on stage, and yet they were forcing themselves upon the language-consciousness of the new playwright. Most heavy was the burden of the oldest and the most literary of Arabic styles, the poetic one.

With that burden on his shoulders, the Arabic playwright writing in the *fuṣḥā* had - and still has - two things to keep in mind while constructing his dramatic dialogue: one was the difficulty of producing low key, naturally sounding or everyday idiom - something which would remain discreetly in the background of the audience's attention, that something which would convey the flow of dramatic action without burgeoning in volumes of words.

The other was the complexity of approaching the elevated style in a dramatic way. Through the use of the *fuṣḥā* as the 'elevated' language by name and definition, all elevated diction has become top-heavy in Arabic. On stage such a language is typecast and is rendered dramatically ineffective. It inevitably tempts the mind in the easy chair and the actor on stage to speak it with an inflated chest. Its idioms and rhetorical devices are too easily recognizable poetic borrowings. Arabic poetry being prevalently lyrical, such borrowings are automatically charged with other *genre* connotations, with contexts which are not dramatic - and certainly not traditionally suggestive as part of the dialogue.

Thus the dramatist who wants to raise the literary-aesthetic level of his dialogue and who wants to bring it into the foreground of the audience's awareness as speech has to fight an internal stylistic battle which will be an attempt to come to terms in a new way with an inherent self-contradiction. He will have to raise the rhetorical and meaningful level of his speech while at the same time denying himself access to all the traditional notions of such a raised level of speech. The Arabic playwright's discomfort with the formal language becomes particularly acute when he has to raise the emotional level of speech. To which model will he turn? To the old moulds of rhetorical pathos? It is of interest to notice that Alfred Faraj, for example, while maintaining the dialogue in his play *'Alī Janāḥ al-Tabrīzī* (Cairo 1968) in the literary language rather consistently, will nevertheless introduce here and there an expression or a whole line of dialogue in colloquial, solely motivated by the need to indicate that a given dramatic character has found himself in a heightened emotional state. Thus we come across the author's tone indications like *munfa'ilan* (with agitation) (p.104), after which a transition to an utterance in the colloquial language takes place. This may appear like a rare moment of psychological honesty on the part of the Arabic author, one must admit; but how to fit it into the psychology of the *ghayr munfa'il* dialogue? What seems to be happening in such cases is that the Arabic playwright prefers to skirt the issue of whether it is possible, or how effective it would be, if he attempted to introduce an 'agitated' speech in the formal language which, undeniably, is so rich in agitated utterances of the old poets and orators.

Having attempted to enunciate some of the live, dramatic problems which face the Arabic literary language as it becomes a language of the new venture of the Arabic theatre, I realize that I have so far failed to do what had been at the back of my mind as the germinating thought of it all: to place the Arabic literary language on the planks of the stage, to let it sound and play itself and become, in the words of Ezra Pound, the theatre's true medium, not the black and white of ink on paper but the total thing of 'people moving about on a stage and using words.' (*The ABC of Reading*, London 1951, p.46).

Indeed, how does theatre in the *fuṣḥā* actually sound? How does the *fuṣḥā* act out its own role on stage as a physical entity of sonorous volume?

The sound of the word on stage is expressive to the extent to which it is interpretative - very much in the fashion of music. Theatrical audiences receive a rendition of a dramatic work not unlike concert-going audiences receive renditions of works of music. Here as there, the productive intermediary, the performing artist, is an essential part of the artistic achievement.

The Arabic theatre audience, in the case of theatre in the literary language, contrary to habit, receives not what it reads, but what it hears read to it. It must also be prepared to hear speech delivered according to some current, established form of enunciation. It must share with the actors on stage a certain notion of Arabic stage language. The sound of the *fuṣḥā*, while being unfamiliar in life outside the theatre, must become familiar to the audience as it reaches it from the limelights. There rests therefore on the shoulders of the Arabic theatre-maker - the actor and the director - the responsibility of giving the audience a kind of language which is at the same time to an intelligible degree familiar in sound, in agreement with the formal notion of what the literary language must be phonetically in order to remain literary, and theatrically, dramatically, effective and fulfilling as medium of interpretation and expression.

As far as intelligibility and familiarity of sound are concerned, they are achieved perhaps only up to that certain level which might be called intuitive and empathetic. Theatre audiences being as they are - diverse, that is - are not always able to grasp the precise meaning of every word in the *fuṣḥā* which rushes at them from the stage. They are even less prepared to distinguish the virtues of specific classicist syntactical constructions. Mostly, therefore the stage *fuṣḥā* is understood with reference to those expanded and flexible mental habits which form like a halo or a periphery of the other language, the *ʿāmmiyya*. Indeed, only from a minority which itself cultivates the habit of the *fuṣḥā*, is it realistic to expect a full understanding of a dialogue in that language. The familiarity of sound of the stage *fuṣḥā* is perhaps related precisely to that fluid level of its comprehension. It is an important part of that vast cultural residuum of the truly 'classical' Arabic language, which is the repository of pre-Islamic poetic sounds, rhythms, and symbols, the tongue of the daily prayers and the receding memory and proportionately growing fondness of that never quite defined beauty of Qur'anic words, which at an early age everyone had been taught to revere, as it were, outside of every value system. In brief, the evocative power of the literary language which reaches the audience especially in a sonorous dramatic enunciation, is the power of multiple cultural echoes. By cultural conditioning, the audience is expected to respond to the sound of that language in a wholly undramatic way, however. Its response will in the first place be one of warmth, love and respect for the language in itself, apart from the dramatic context. It will be lyrical. Indeed the Arabic theatre audience's attitude to theatre in the *fuṣḥā* is initially - and then finally as memory - lyrical. Somewhere in between, the drama has to impose itself. All this has inevitably its impact on that audience's overall response to the witnessed dramatic work, and in a particular way it is bound to influence any critical evaluation of the dramatic experience itself. It thus imposes upon the theatre an extra-dramatic set of values.

As regards the maintenance of the integral character of the Arabic literary language as it becomes the language of the stage, there do not arise any true difficulties. Broadening our context, we observe that stage languages are rather as a rule conservative entities. At least until the present hyper-realistic, studiedly vulgarizing vogue, the type of diction used on stage in any country with an established theatrical tradition was a slightly backward-looking one. With respect to articulation, some European countries had even produced distinct stage modalities which were meant to impose themselves upon disturbing regional divergences of speech. Such is the German attempt at a *Bühnensprache*. An Arabic *Bühnensprache* does not yet exist in any succinctly definable way. Indeed, isolated Arabic attempts, like Tawfīq al-Ḥakīm's *al-Ṣafqa*, point in the opposite direction. Such a language intends to be so flexible that it would permit the broadest possible approach to articulation. This would then place language outside any tradionally binding norm, giving it the semblance of relativity. Presumably an audience could dictate its own level of language. The prevalent tendency in the Arabic theatre which opts to remain literary is to disregard such oddities and to assume the somewhat formal, classicist air. The plays which are being written in the *fuṣḥā* seem to encourage the Arabic actor to prove his classicist leaning. They are still mostly historical, philosophical, or religious in theme, or expressedly poetical in style. Social prose drama and comedy in the *fuṣḥā* are, if not entirely an oddity, certainly not tone setting. Furthermore, their production on stage is even rarer than their appearance in print. Thus, if at present there is any notion of *Bühnensprache* or stage articulation in the *fuṣḥā*, it is a conservative and classicist one.

This brings us finally to the theatrically productive, interpretative aspect of the *fuṣḥā* as medium of a live, dramatic action. Here, as we sit back in our orchestra seat, all the previously mentioned 'lyrical' cultural considerations ought to be disregarded - at least as a clinical exercise in abstraction, so that we may obtain an isolation of the problem.

The first startling observation which we make as an audience is that the Arabic actor as he delivers his lines in the *fuṣḥā* does not seem to be making much of a distinction between what is supposed to be prose and what presumably is verse. His understanding of a fully enunciated *fuṣḥā* seems to obliterate this difference. Perhaps actual verse drama suffers less from this delivery of the *fuṣḥā*. Perhaps only the confines of its diction become somewhat blurred until the audience realizes what it is hearing. The effect which this confusion or this uniformity of the theatrical *fuṣḥā* has on theatre in prose is much more serious. To say the least, rather than to raise it to poetic levels, it drowns it in oppressive monotony.

In his critique of the theatre of Aḥmad Shawqī and ʻAzīz Abāza, Lūyis ʻAwaḍ accuses both poets - to the extent to which this affects them as playwrights - of suffering from the *muʻallaqa* complex, *ʻuqdat al-muʻallaqāt*, (*Dirāsāt ʻArabiyya wa Gharbiyya*. Cairo, 1965, pp. 99-106). How much more emphatically one should then accuse the Arabic actor and director of this ancient illness! The inadequacies of playwrights are of a nature which one had to accept almost as immutable facts. One has to learn how to live with the playwright - or how to live without him altogether. He is at the beginning of it all: he gives and he takes away. Some larger measure of critical tolerance toward the playwright as creative artist is conceivable, and the most constructive critical attitude towards shortcomings in plays is improvement through superior interpretation. And here comes our complaint - indeed more complaint than criticism - against the Arabic actor as interpreter of dialogue written in the *fuṣḥā*. Almost invariably his reading of the lines will be of an evenly sustained, secure and balanced volume, with tone inflections which never disturb the sovereign flow of sonority, that superb sonority which fills the stage and the entirety of the theatre and which never subsides throughout the duration of the play. The audience is wrapped up in it as it were in a comforter or a security blanket. As long as the sonority lasts, nothing else matters. No real understanding seems necessary, no dramatic response. The effect of catharsis is not just at the moment of crisis and resolution. Catharsis is a continuous process of being bathed in the sound of the language. From it alone the audience ought to emerge unburdened and cleansed. Is such then the feeling left behind by a dramatic experience? Is this musical, symphonic entrancement what theatre is meant to produce? Or rather, is this not a confusion of the media?

The explanations of such excesses in acoustic indulgence which one hears most often about Cairo, for instance, is that no doubt the melodramatic phantom of Jūrj Abyaḍ still lives on. At first one accepts Jurj Abyaḍ as a convenient scapegoat, but then one wonders. Is the melodramatic acting style really the root of all evil? And here mere complaint ends, making room for one critical suggestion: the Arabic interpreter of prose theatre in the *fuṣḥā* ought to re-examine his entire approach to the dynamics of the *fuṣḥā* as language of the stage.

We do realize the fact that theatre in the colloquial language is capable of absorbing even the melodramatic acting style. Indeed, that style had once quite handsomely availed itself of the *ʿāmmīyya*. On the other hand we notice that verse drama especially can operate effectively through the medium of a rigorous *fuṣḥā* - at least there is no doubt that a few scenes from Aḥmad Shawqī's plays may still be salvaged and put forward as instances of theatrical achievement. Furthermore, we now seem to be experiencing an upsurge of dramatic writing in freer verse forms which yet observe modified traditional metres.

As suggested by the colloquial example, a language with dramatic capabilities ought to be able to outgrow melodrama as it learns from it. Melodrama, therefore, is the wrong kind of scapegoat. We also know that verse drama demands the *fuṣḥā* for more reasons than just its elevated diction. It needs it for the very essential - in verse, at least - reason of its measurability, its agreement with the Arabic system of poetic metres.

Where then does the prose play in the *fuṣḥā* stand with respect to the two extremes above: the colloquial in prose and the *fuṣḥā* measured? The answer is a very simple one, rather too simple to be anything less than a paradox: the *fuṣḥā* prose play stands, or ought to stand, precisely in the middle. But for it to stand in the middle it must deny an important aspect of its language medium in order to receive an equal measure of that which makes the colloquial language so dramatically effective. It must change in tone the moment it steps on stage without changing even by one letter in the printed text. The element which has to be exchanged, or balanced, is that of the accepted by Arabic philological tradition idea that the *fuṣḥā*, in order to be *fuṣḥā*, has to insist on a quantitative syllabic measure. Anywhere but on stage, this insistence remains of little relevance. On stage, however, it balloons into almost grotesque proportions.

The Arabic actor, trained in the *fuṣḥā* largely on poetic examples, transfers to the stage the full weight of that *mu'allaqa* complex of which Lūyis 'Awaḍ spoke, only that here, in the spoken word, its perniciousness becomes even more apparent. It generates not only monotony through the imposition of a stream-like, horizontal sense of rhythm which lulls and draws in, rather than animates and dramatizes by expelling to the surface of awareness - but what is more - it alienates the stage *fuṣḥā* from the qualitative rhythm of spontaneous accentuation which has become the only valid rhythm of the spoken language. A shying away from full accentuation in stage *fuṣḥā* by following the poetic rhythmic patterns of quantitative measure is what stops stage *fuṣḥā* from being a medium of drama. When read - and interpreted - as poetry is read, the *fuṣḥā* will remain a poetic medium, and the only way it will be possible to fit it into dramatic dialogue will be by imposing upon it a lengthy series of extra-dramatic conventions and presuppositions, all of which will only try to reason away the problem. But the moment an actor steps on the stage, all explanations remain behind. The problem is still how to draw dramatic speech away from that archaic stream of sound, of language as something following its own course, governed by its own unyielding rhythm of flow, beating with its own unchanging pulse, and make it the property of the speaker, of the individual at the very moment of his need to say what only he, at that moment and in his own unique way, desires to say.

Owen Barfield sees language which obeys quantitative rhythmic values as archaic and as poetic in the archaic sense. It is objective. In it quantitative rhythm is 'to some extent inherent in the language itself'. Accent in the language, on the other hand, 'is much more *a determination of the material part of language by the speaker's own peculiar meaning*' (*Poetic Diction, A Study in Meaning*, Third ed., Wesleyan University Press, Middleton, Connecticut, 1973, p.150). If 'the decay of quantitative values leaves us with prose', as Owen Barfield concludes (*Ibid.*, p.150), we do realize that above all it leads us to the dramatic dimension of speech, to the dynamically accentuated, profiled language of the stage.

The Arabic actor performing in the *fuṣḥā* will thus have to be retrained thoroughly before he is ready to interpret so much untried, or mistried Arabic dramatic literature which is all there, waiting. He will have to bring to the stage the literary language in a new sound - not in the sound of ancient poetry, of lyrical moods and rhetorical pathos, but in the sound of fully accentuated flexibility and plasticity. His loud outbursts of joy or pain will then not have to be lengthened in order to be stressed, and his language of delicate feelings might then go on forever in length of syllables in suggestive diminuendos, where before there would only have been possible a forced crescendo. Above all, accentuation will bring the *fuṣḥā* closer to the live linguistic sense of the audiences.

J. Stetkevych

Some Aspects of Modern Arabic Drama

For the past twenty years or so, Arabic has been engaged in an active search for an identity. The call for a special identity for Arabic drama was first articulated by the novelist and dramatist Yūsef Idrīs in the early 'sixties. In three articles published by the Cairo monthly *al-Kātib*, Idrīs pointed out the necessity for our drama to possess a soul and a formula of its own. At present we are lost amid dramatic theories imported from the West. These have helped us to produce some sort of theatrical activities for the past one and a half centuries or so, but will never enable us to create our own national drama. For this to be established, the writer went on to say, we have to abandon the Italian theatre form, and search for drama inherent in our culture. This alone can be truly expressive of our innermost feelings and inspirations.

The formula which Idrīs recommended for a truly national drama was one known as the *Sāmir*, a peasant theatre-in-the-round which for centuries had entertained simple folk of the countryside. It comprised many performing arts including word, song, story and dance. It allowed for a free interflow between performers and audience, thus creating what Idrīs calls *al-Tamasruḥ*, or complete involvement in the dramatic act, a state of spiritual elation in which both actor and spectator become one and the same. This state of complete identification is the only safeguard for us if we want to create a drama truly our own.

To support his case Idrīs came out with his very interesting play called *al-Farāfīr*, which was presented by the Cairo National Theatre in the season 1963-64. In the preface to the printed play Idrīs told his readers that by writing *al-Farāfīr* he aimed at raising Arabic popular drama to the artistic and aesthetic levels achieved by world drama. In this he was decidedly successful. In parts the play reminds one of the comic discussions of Aristophanes' plays. In others it is an approximation of some of the techniques of the Roman and Italian popular comedy. Like these it makes use of the comic duet of stupid master and intelligent slave, or servant, to shed ironic light on very many things indeed. These range from the plight of humanity at large, the inadequacies of various political régimes, to more personal matters concerning the marriage, birth and death of some characters taken from everyday life in Cairo.

al-Farāfīr makes considerable use of characters and situations taken from Egyptian popular comedy, such as the hen-pecked husband and his sharp-tongued wife; the match of abuse in which characters in Arabic popular comedy readily indulge, and which never fails to produce delicious laughter, as well as some slap-stick comedy and various comedy numbers. In all this, Idrīs has notably achieved his aim of raising Egyptian popular comedy to higher levels. All the same he does not prove his main contention that the *Sāmir* form is able to induce that rare state of mind in its audiences in which actor and spectator become one. This amalgam never actually took place in any of the performances. Writer and director alike had to content themselves with a compromise: actors pretended to be spectators and were put in the stalls and boxes to give the illusion of intercourse between audience and performers.

Prior to *al-Farāfīr* however, the *Sāmir* had proved its entertainment value and its ability to draw people to theatre halls when Tawfīq al-Ḥakīm's play, 'The Deal', was given in the year 1956. Based on an event taken from actual life, the play uses drama, song and dance to depict the simple life, customs and beliefs of peasants in a small Egyptian village. A rich landowner happening to pass by, the villagers think he has come to outbid them in the purchase of some land and to ward off this calamity, they bribe him off the deal with money they can ill afford to give away.

A more subtle use of the *Sāmir* was made in the mid-'sixties by the young playwright Maḥmūd Deyāb in his fascinating play called 'Harvest Nights'. Deyāb uses the *Sāmir* form to tell of the beautiful young woman Sanyūra, who has turned the heads of all men in her village, young and old, and started rivalries among them, and caused a bloody fight to take place between them and the inhabitants of a nearby village. In the course of events, one of her admirers loses his mind and kills an innocent woman in the belief that she is Sanyūra. Song, dance and outdoor games are used to entertain, and a measure of pretended improvisation is added, together with certain tricks from the narrator-impersonator form, (which form will be discussed presently), to give the play a deliciously illusive nature. The actors go in and out of their parts, from illusion into reality and back in true Pirandello manner, and at times the spectators do not quite know whether the actors are acting their parts or being the real human beings they pretend they are.

In his call for a truly national drama, Idrīs was soon followed by no less important a dramatist than al-Ḥakīm. In the mid-'sixties al-Ḥakīm came out with a little book he called *Our Dramatic Form*, in which he recommended yet another and, he claimed, a much older kind of drama: the narrator and impersonator form. The first introduced the play, linked up its events and commented upon them - a sort of one-man chorus. The second impersonated the part - more often the many parts - that fell to his lot, clearly pointing out to his audience that he was not acting but imitating the person or persons concerned. He was at one and the same time himself and the character he was impersonating. This form al-Ḥakīm found appropriate to our needs. For one thing it is easy to adopt. It is really a poor man's theatre, easy access for all sorts of people, and particularly convenient to strolling players and the like, who would be able to take it to the smallest village without much trouble or expense.

On the dramatic and aesthetic levels, the commentator-impersonator drama afforded double pleasure to its audiences. It simultaneously showed them actors impersonating given characters and being their real selves. This could not fail to flatter the spectators into paying more attention to the play, since it demonstrated to them that they had been taken into the confidence of the players who revealed before them the 'secrets' of their art. It also had the very modern advantage of doing away with illusion. No pretence was made in that kind of theatre that what went on was anything but a play. The audiences were kept wide awake, and were encouraged to take part in the show, either as judges and 'critics', or simply as lively spectators. This, in turn, made that particular dramatic form especially suited to critical comedy, a form of drama the Arabs seem to be particularly fond of. al-Ḥakīm did not himself write plays to prove this theory. He merely chose some episodes from Greek and modern drama and claimed that if those were presented in the narrator-impersonator style, they would clearly point out those advantages of the form alluded to above. It was left to young writers such as the Egyptian Naguīb Sorūr and the Moroccan al-Ṭayyeb al-Ṣiddīqī to prove al-Ḥakīm's case for him.

In 1963 Naguīb Sorūr presented his poignant play called 'Yāssīn and Bahiyya' to the Cairo pocket theatre, which produced it in its 1964-5 season. It is about the star-crossed love of the valiant young man Yāssīn and the beautiful Bahiyya. Both are peasants who live under the yoke of the repressive feudal Egypt of King Farouk. The feudal lord usurps the land of the peasants and moves on to try to rape Bahiyya. When on top of that tax-collectors come to confiscate the harvest against taxes the peasants have failed to pay, the whole village flares up into armed revolt in which Yāssīn, their leader, gets killed.

This simple story is given in the semi-dramatic form which story-tellers of old used to entertain their audiences at coffee-houses throughout the Middle Ages and right up to the early years of this century. The story-teller, or the *shā'ir*, told of the epic exploits of his heroes to the accompaniment of his *rabāb* - a primitive violin, mixing narration with dramatic elocution. This form is adopted in essence by Sorūr to tell the story of Yāssīn and Bahiyya. His *shā'ir* becomes both narrator and commentator, and the bits of story which the old *shā'ir* tried to dramatise by elocution are acted on the stage. A point of subtlety is achieved when, towards the end of the play, Sorūr pushes aside his *shā'ir* and starts to talk about his own plight, a self-exiled poet or *shā'ir*, unbefriended and starving in a far away land. And yet, the snowbound country he lives in is unable to distract his attention from events that take place under a very different climate. Sorūr establishes a link between the oppression which the Egyptian village suffers from and the political wrongs which drove him into self-exile. He thus becomes one of his own *dramatis personae*. Although this play seemed to many too static to be worthy of the title of a play, it actually succeeded in proving the validity of al-Ḥakīm's contention that the narrator-impersonator form could be an effective dramatic vehicle for themes truly national and consequently nearer our hearts. Sorūr proved the case by merging together the two traditional forms of story-teller and commentator-impersonator.

In Morocco, al-Ṭayyeb al-Ṣiddīqī wrote one of his very successful plays in this same form: 'The poems of Sidi 'Abdul Raḥmān al-Magdūb'. It is part-narration, part-dramatisation of the life of this popular 16th century poet who lived a very broad life, all spent in travels during which he recited his poems and displayed his wisdom to peoples of many lands. I saw the play given in a far away desert place called Wurzazat, in Morocco, whose inhabitants had seen very little theatre, if any at all. For more than two hours, this simple audience sat wrapt in wonder, their attention divided between listening to the sweet poems of al-Magdūb recited by the narrator, and following the acted portions of the life of this fascinating wanderer performed by actors. The form, it was unmistakably clear to me, accorded well with this particular audience.

In Syria, the young playwright Sa'ad Allāh Wanus cast his play: 'The Adventures of the Head of Mameluk Jābir', in the same form, though he introduced some alterations, and added some pretended improvisation. In the play the story-teller recites bits of the story and a troupe of actors, not impersonators, act the other sections. This is supposed to be taking place in a café, for the story-teller is the old traditional *shā'ir*, being asked repeatedly to recite a certain story they like, while he insists that that particular story is not suited to the times. Rather he would tell them of the fall of Bagdad, a more appropriate theme! This play also was appreciated by theatre-goers.

How are we to explain this active interest in traditional forms of drama on the part of Arab playwrights? I think one good reason for this is a deep sense of resentment felt by modern Arabs on account of what was thought to be the semi-total absence of drama from Arabic culture and literature. The Arabs were told, by others and by themselves, time and time again, that for a medley of reasons theatre was never born in their midst. Arab scholars of old could neither understand nor appreciate Aristotle's *Poetics*, and their rendering of the terms 'tragic' and 'comic' bore witness to this.

Modern Arabs of the mid-nineteenth century who came to be interested in the dramatic arts such as al-Naqqāsh, (1817-1855), al-Qabbānī, (1865-1903), and Ṣannū‘ (1839-1912) seem to have accepted this with resignation, and, instead of shedding unnecessary tears, made admirable efforts to make up for the loss. Hence their incredible enthusiasm for the theatre. al-Naqqāsh, a rich Lebanese tradesman, sets up a theatre in his own house, writes plays for it, invites over friends and supporters to witness the birth of the new art, and neglects his trade in the process, only to die later, tormented by a strong sense of frustration. For all his efforts, al-Naqqāsh felt that continued theatrical activities in Lebanon were most unlikely. al-Qabbānī, another enlightened tradesman, Syrian this time, is lured by the theatre to make dramatic writing and presentation his main occupation. Like al-Naqqāsh, he wrote his own plays, and depended for themes on popular tales and plays from world drama adapted to suit Arab audiences. They contained verse, song and dance. While Qabbānī dares to cast boys in the parts of women, he is decried as a dabbler in licentious activities, and is forced to leave the country for a more lenient climate in Egypt. Ṣannū‘, an Egyptian Jew, starts a dramatic company from scratch, in the year 1870, occupies himself with writing, producing, directing and stage-managing its plays. When he ventures to criticise polygamy, he incurs the royal displeasure of his patron, Khedive Ismā‘īl. He is summarily ordered to close down his theatre and put an end to his dramatic career.

Those courageous men were working under the rather painful feeling that an important manifestation of social, literary and artistic activity was denied to their people, and they sought to compensate for this loss by frantic efforts, thus submerging their resentment in useful work. There followed others who wanted to fill the great gap. ‘Uthmān Galāl, for example, who Egyptianised Molière's comedies and some of Racine's tragedies, feeling that he was thereby doing good service to the nascent Arabic drama, by making available to both theatre artists and audiences good models of dramatic works.

When Tawfīq al-Ḥakīm appeared on the scene in the early twenties of this century, he had to fight the double-battle of winning respect for the still despised art of drama and of writing sufficiently good plays to win serious attention for drama as a worthy literary and artistic *genre*. The under-tone of his dramatic and other works is one of restlessness and ill-hidden resentment. The great void that he was born into, a literature which knew neither novel nor drama - especially drama, his passion - caused him grave disquiet. This is how he expresses his feelings on the subject:

> Perhaps we were a generation of martyrs ... people who sacrificed themselves and wasted away their lives on an impossible quest, egged on by terror at the great dark chasm before them. Thus it was that we were forced to write and write, rendering black white sheets with useless scribblings.

By the early sixties, al-Ḥakīm had written well over fifty plays, among them many of his best. Well could Yūsef Idrīs afford to call a halt to dramatic writing in the land with a view to stocktaking. Enough had been done to plant the idea of theatre in the Arab, more especially Egyptian soil. For some years there had been an institute for dramatic arts, turning out theatre artists in various capacities: actors, directors, scene designers and the like. Many had been sent to Europe to be trained in the various dramatic arts. Theatrical activities had been supervised and financed by the state, and more especially by the newly-created ministry of culture. More important, al-Ḥakīm had moved from the position of the only devoted playwright to that of the head of a group of young dramatists, all enthusiastic and keen on serving; all full of good ideas and teeming with themes for plays which they eventually wrote. The moment was ripe in the early sixties for the kind of call which Idrīs sounded: the need for a truly national drama. With Idrīs it is no longer mere resentment because the date of birth of Arabic drama is not earlier than the mid-nineteenth century. There is a growing realisation that Arabic drama must have existed much earlier. Idrīs was inspired when he decided to turn to popular drama for a possible earlier date of birth.

Since the three articles published by *al-Kātib*, and even before, studies have appeared which strove to set a date for the birth of Arabic drama. In 1963, Dr. Ibrahim Ḥamāda, of the Cairo Higher Institute for Drama, edited and published the texts of the three shadow plays which are the only extant works of Muḥammad Jamāl al-Dīn Ibn Dāniyāl (1248-1311), who had come from Iraq to live in Cairo, bringing with him a remarkable talent for shadow plays. To find stories for his plays, or *bābāt*, as they are called, Ibn Dāniyāl went back to the rich stores of the *maqāmāt*. He also used his keen sense of observation of everyday life, especially life at the *sūq*, or market, to create some impressive characters that have been the stock-in-trade of Arab popular comedy ever since, such as the old procuress-matchmaker who is more concerned to make money than to arrange matches.

Ibn Dāniyāl seems to have been a man of the world, but he was also a conscientious artist. In the introductory words he addresses to one of his friends at the beginning of his *bāba* called: 'Ṭayf al-Khayāl', he describes his art in the following discerning words:

> I have written these *bābāt* of fun and licence. If you draw the characters therein and have them cut out and classified, then proceed to wax your screen and get your audience in the proper mood for intimacy, then you will meet a supreme art which by the very fact of substantiation, will supersede that which is mere imagination, (i.e. a merely imagined but as yet unrealised story).

The author of this paper was encouraged by these revealing words to look into the three *bābāt* and try to ascertain to what extent they can be considered dramatic. To do this with advantage, he also examined the *maqāmāt* of al-Hamadhānī and al-Ḥarīrī, which he had always considered as drama in embryo. The results of this investigation were published in a book called: *The Arts of Comedy from Shadow Plays to al-Rīḥānī*. In the first chapter of this book entitled: 'The Maqāma on Stage', an attempt was made to analyse the *maqāmāt* of both al-Hamadhānī and al-Ḥarīrī. Special attention was paid to Hamadhānī's *maqāma* called: 'al-Maḍrīriyya', which seemed to come closest to a one-act play. A careful analysis of this *maqāma*, it was pointed out, would indicate that, in point of fact it was a play which only religious restrictions deprived of the title of a play. Perceiving clearly the close relation between Ibn Dāniyāl's *bābāt* and the *maqāmāt*, the author concluded that Ibn Dāniyāl had brought with him what to all intents and purposes was an Arab theatre, the only theatre the Arabs were permitted to have. The significance of Ibn Dāniyāl's shadow plays is that they established this link between Arabic literature, (through *al-Maqāmāt*), and Arab shadow plays. These latter spread far and wide; to Turkey, North Africa, and more especially to Syria. In that country, towards the end of the last century, a popular actor and playwright by the name of George Dakhūl seems to have hit on the idea that it would be great fun if the shadow plays should be acted by men instead of by shadows.

Dakhūl must have had some training in popular comedy, possibly also Italian popular comedy. When he took his *fuṣūl* to Cairo, some time in the last decade of the nineteenth century, he enjoyed considerable success by presenting them in regular and makeshift theatres. Depending both on the technique of the shadow plays as well as on the art of improvisation, these had a profound influence on Egyptian popular comedy, and are clearly discernible in the writings of our established writers such as: Naguīb al-Rīḥānī, Ibrāhīm Ramzī, Badī' Khayrī, Muḥammad Taymūr, al-Ḥakīm and Idrīs. (Some of these *fuṣūl* were published in my book: *Improvised Comedy on the Egyptian Stage*, Dār al-Hilāl, 1968). What had been written in the 10th and 11th centuries as a theatre in the mind, to be imagined or only read out dramatically, had at last been permitted to be acted by men and women, thanks to the mediation of the shadow plays. A long and uninterrupted line of drama can thus be seen to extend over several centuries, and to say that the Arabs have known the theatre since the middle ages no longer need seem strange or provocative. The date 1848, when al-Naqqāsh wrote his first play in Beirut, already seems unduly modest. (See the insert on Arabic theatre in the Encyclopedia for the Young called *al-Ma'rifa*, issue 162, May 1974, where the shadow plays are considered the beginning of Arabic Theatre).

Immediately after the publication of 'The Arts of Comedy', the Moroccan actor-director and playwright al-Ṭayyeb al-Ṣiddīqī, who had read the chapter on *al-Maqāma*, took up the idea of tapping the *maqāmāt* of al-Hamadhānī for drama, and came out with a very interesting dramatic presentation based on *al-Maqāmā al-Maḍīriyya*, which I suggested should make good comedy on stage. al-Ṣiddīqī used other *maqāmāt* by al-Hamadhānī and when his work was presented at Damascus in the spring of 1973 the result was electrifying. Here, for everyone to see and witness was good, poignant, and very biting critical comedy in the tradition of *al-Shuṭṭār*, or picaresque literature. al-Ṣiddīqī merges time past into time present and uses the *maqāmāt* as a means of criticising the 20th and 11th centuries. For this he uses the style of the puppet theatre. His human beings are made to look and act as if they were puppets. The lighting, the dresses, and the masks he uses add to the effect. At times, one is strongly reminded of a Jonsonian play. That evening in Damascus left one with the reassuring feeling that the various efforts to discover an origin and an identity for Arabic drama were at last bearing fruit.

I have discoursed at some length on this subject for more reasons than one. First, because it seems to me that this quest for identity is the most important thing that is happening in the field of Arabic drama today. The quest does not stop at the search for traditional forms. It also embraces themes from the folk-lore. In 1963, without a manifesto or much theorising, Alfred Farag, who was then a beginner with only one play to his name, captured the imagination of critics and theatre goers alike by his deft use of two tales from the *Arabian Nights*, which he turned into two one-act plays on the same theme, under the title of: *The Barber of Bagdad*. The joint theme of the two comedies is the need for justice on earth, and the comedy emanates from the adventures of the busybody barber, who, though cowardly and defenceless, cannot help protesting against injustice, whether done to himself or to others. This lands him into one scrape after another, but the barber is both indefatigable and incurable. In the end all is well with him and with those he champions.

About five years later, Alfred Farag was to make more mature use of the *Nights* in his significant play: '‘Alī Janāḥ al-Tabrīzī and his Follower Quffa'. Here again the two tales from the *Nights* are merged together this time into one play, to that of the character of a dreamer who comes to a town and pretends he is the richest man alive. He claims that he has a caravan extending over all the way from Bagdad, heavily laden with rich merchandise and precious jewels. As ‘Alī Janāḥ is a remarkably persuasive man, all are soon taken in. Traders lend him money without reserve, and the king agrees to let him marry his only daughter, on the strength of his vaunted wealth. ‘Alī gives to the poor most of the money he borrows, thus effecting marked social and economic change. In the end, when it is discovered that no caravan exists, ‘Alī has barely time to flee, taking away with him the royal princess who has discovered hidden merits in him more precious than the wealth he does not possess.

The play raises many questions: to what extent can dreams be considered either lies or truths? Is a revolutionary who bases his beliefs on a myth and succeeds in creating good social change to be considered a prophet or an impostor? What is illusion and what is reality? The two attempts by Farag have done more to point out the importance of tapping traditional sources for drama than some of the theorisation that was afoot at the time. They also proved, through success with the critics and at the box-office, that going back to the sources can be good sound business, as well as added richness for Arabic drama. They, alongside other efforts by other dramatists, have shown that the search for identity, and the desire to move nearer the sources do not merely represent hankering after new literary and dramatic fashions. They have to do with that deep-rooted desire to remove resentment and make good the loss of centuries which many Arab playwrights felt as their duty.

In the course of the preface to his play: 'The Adventures of Mameluk Jābir's Head', the Syrian playwright Sa‘ad Allāh Wanus remarks on the gap that still exists between the Arab theatre and its clients. It is a gap, he says, which owes its existence to the fact that Arab audiences have not yet fully taken in the art of theatre. There is still something strange, something unfamiliar, which erects a certain barrier between theatre artists and theatregoers. Hence attendance at performances is not good enough. While this may be more the case in Syria where theatrical activities are neither continuous, varied, nor widespread, than in Egypt, for example, where the theatre is very much alive, the remark, nevertheless, is valid in general terms for all Arab countries. This is a problem with which an old hand like Tawfīq al-Ḥakīm had to contend: his extensive dramatic career is full of unremitting efforts to bridge this gap and reach for a wider audience. The plays themselves are cases in point. In one after another he tries to strike a balance between thought and entertainment, with varying degrees of success. When he tips the balance towards ideas, as indeed he does in plays like 'Scheherazade', 'The Cave Dwellers' and 'Oedipus', the result is 'fine' dramatic art acknowledged as such by critics, but very sparsely attended when given on the stage. al-Ḥakīm has always found this rather galling. Even today, when he is approaching the end of his career, he still feels as bitter about it as ever.

Wanus has suggested that one reason for the absence of strong support at the playhouses lies in the fact of novelty. Drama is not yet securely with us. It is not sure enough that its audiences will not fail it in favour of less exacting and easier to reach mass media entertainment. But this is only one reason for the gap. Another no less important factor is that the approach of a good many of our playwrights to drama is not the right one. They seem to think of a play more as a literary work than as a theatre piece, designed to please by visual action as well as by ideas. When a play that contains 'lofty' thought and deep observation fails to please, they blame this on the audience, not on their own defective dramaturgy. That the lack of strong support for Arab plays is in some cases attributable to insufficient command of the art of dramatic writing is, I think, palpable in the cases of those plays where dramatists have shown more care for the entertainment value of a play. al-Ḥakīm's 'The Deal, and 'The Sultan's Dilemma' each cast in the form of an operetta, (without music), and each containing stimulating ideas and good comedy, have drawn wide audiences to them, much bigger than those who usually attend al-Ḥakīm's more esoteric plays, such as 'The Tree Climber', a good play in itself.

Alfred Farag, who has always shown great care for the arts of dramatic writing and those of stagecraft, has been rewarded by good attendance whenever he has added some trick here and there, or introduced some comic elements or reverted to the storehouse of drama for a character or a situation. Thus his plays 'The Barber of Bagdad', and '‘Alī Janāḥ', have been both successful at the box-office without failing to stimulate the mind. The heart of the matter is that some of our playwrights need to recognise that dramatic writing is a trade to be learnt and practised before being put at the service of whatever social or ideological message they choose to deliver.

Arab men of the theatre have always recognised the fact that a dramatic piece should please in the first place. With Ibn Dāniyāl there was never any question of producing a show which did not entertain. He had either to entertain or perish. Even the 'importers' of drama - Naqqāsh, Qābbānī and Ṣannū' fully realised that their newly acquired art, unlike other forms, had to contend with live people, to cater for them and reap the reward of their satisfaction or feel the brunt of their displeasure. Hence they wrote and worked on the assumption that the audience was the real master and owner of the show. It is for this reason that Naqqāsh chose to cast his plays in what he believed to be the opera form, because he felt that his audiences preferred to see and hear verse, song, and dance within the scope of one work. al-Qabbānī did the same, while Ṣannū', who claimed to have written under the influence of Molière, Sheridan and Goldoni, did not hesitate to resort to the tricks of the Egyptian puppet theatre known as the 'aragoz', nor to use the sources of the *Arabian Nights* for entertainment.

Apart from the achievement, or lack of it, of the dramatists themselves, the reasons for the poor attendance at performances can be sought in the nature of dramatic practice in many Arab countries. In almost all these countries, theatre activities are dangerously concentrated in the capitals. The net result of this is that national talent runs the risk of being warped, or unduly curtailed. Moreover, the provinces which, whenever given the chance, have shown themselves not lacking in talent, are consequently reduced to the position of importers of theatrical fare from the capitals, while their own talent they lose to those same capitals, because limelight and fame exist only there. Efforts have been made to redress the balance, and under the auspices of the Ministry of Culture in Cairo, some provincial companies have sprung into existence, but not for long, and not strongly enough.

If this poses the question of whether to be metropolitan or national for the drama in each Arab country, there is another question allied to it, namely whether Arabic drama should be national or pan-Arab? The possibility for the creation of a truly Arab drama exists. The experiences and the themes treated by dramatists in each individual country are largely the same, and can be readily transported to other Arab countries, were it not for the fact that the majority of plays are written in one of the many dialects of Arabic that abound throughout Arab lands, and which are at times difficult to follow by those who are not born into them. This constitutes a real barrier for the national drama of a given Arab country, a fact which I myself tended to minimise until I came to attend Lebanese, Kuwaitī and Irākī plays. In each case I could only follow the very general lines of the play, while much of what the dialogue had to convey was lost to me. The problem is rendered more complicated by the fact that writing in classical Arabic, and more especially acting in it, seems to have become dying arts. In the season of 1959-60, the Cairo National Company revived Aḥmad Shawqī's verse play: 'The Death of Cleopatra'. Not only was the attendance scanty, but actors were finding it difficult to act. One of them, a truly talented actor, was particularly uncomfortable with Shawqī's sonorous lines!

Yet it is on using some sort of classical Arabic for writing plays that the ultimate hope for the creation of a pan-Arab theatre seems largely to depend. al-Ḥakīm had suggested, in the epilogue to 'The Deal', the use of a special form of Arabic, the 'second language' he called it. This should depend on a vocabulary usually thought by purists to be not classical, while in point of fact it is entirely legitimate Arabic. Because words in this vocabulary have the advantage of being widely used in everyday life, introducing them into a play would make it more understandable to the common theatre-goer. This special language has the added advantage of affording its user a choice between the dialect and the classical forms, since he is free to make use of the many licences normally allowed to poets, one of these being dispensing with declension al-Ḥakīm wrote 'The Deal' in this special language, but his theory was never put to the test, as the play was given in the Egyptian dialect only. However, despite present language barriers, drama in each individual Arab country is getting closer to other Arab drama, thanks to drama festivals in places such as Hammamet, Tunis (bi-annual), and the annual event in Damascus.

Besides looking forward to becoming pan-Arab, modern Arabic drama aspires to be internationally known. Some of al-Ḥakīm's plays have been translated into French and English, and have been presented in Europe and the United States. Through these translations, our veteran dramatist has acquired a certain international fame. But neither this, nor the fact that other writers have also had some of their plays rendered into world languages, would justify any belief that Arabic drama has achieved world recognition. The fault is in our plays, not in the world. Such Arab dramatists as Kāteb Yāssīn, of Algeria, and George Shehāda, of Lebanon, have gained world fame on account of the quality of their dramaturgy, not because they happen to be writing in French. This is a fact which ought to be remembered by those among us who believe that translating Arabic plays into foreign languages would, of itself, gain a world footing for Arabic drama. For this footing to be securely captured, we should have to work harder and write better than, at present, we are doing.

ʻAlī al-Rāʻī

Problems of the Egyptian Theatre

When a critic offers to discuss the problems connected with the culture of anything we tend to suspect that he will concentrate on certain grim, or, at best, negative aspects of culture in a given time or area, which usually evoke the pessimistic mood. But since we Egyptians are now wallowing, perhaps with good reason, in the optimistic mood, especially since the October War, let us try to describe our cultural problems as cheerfully as possible and maintain the present all too precious sense of euphoria. In order to do so, we shall have to assess as is the fashion to do, two theories:

a) that our present cultural problems are simply the hangover of our nightmarish recent past, and

b) that since the old order is fast breaking down giving way to new, we have reason to be confident about the future.

Let us be warned, however, that this may not be exactly the situation, for the old has not quite broken down, and there are not enough indications that the new will be a positive improvement on the old, unless by some mighty local effort and by some mighty international co-operation a different cultural ideal is enabled to replace the existing one.

Of all our cultural problems I shall select one set to discuss, namely, the problems of the Egyptian theatre. In a sense what holds true of the problems of the Egyptian theatre also holds true of the problems of Egyptian culture in general, not because the Egyptians are especially theatrical, as Yūsef Idrīs once claimed, but because the Egyptian theatre has in the last quarter of a century or so, for sociological reasons, become the most symbolic aspect of our Egyptian cultural life under the Nasser Revolution. Since the containment and eventual disfiguration of our intellectual leadership, once the pride of the country, and since the total control of mass media through the nationalisation of the press and the unification of political organization, those who did not wish to wear the mask of conformity had to wear the mask of the drama, which enabled them to bring to the surface with relative impunity the ambivalence of life under the Nasser, puritan, *petit-bourgeois* Revolution. It would be a prodigious task to try to discuss the main problems of the Egyptian theatre in the last century or so, i.e. since it became a perceptible force in Egyptian social and cultural life sometime in the seventies of the nineteenth century. I shall therefore concentrate on the two problems of the Egyptian theatre which I think are the most vital, namely the problem of language and the problem of social commitment.

After the inauguration of the Cairo Opera House in 1869 by Khedive Ismāʿīl with Verdi's *Rigoletto*, which marks the official, not to say the actual, birth of the Egyptian theatre, there was a distinctive polarization in the Egyptian theatre which coincided with the troubled reign of Ismāʿīl and the outbreak of the ʿUrābī Revolution (1882). The main protagonists of this polarisation were the revolutionary Yaʿqūb Ṣannūʿ and the courtly ʿUthmān Galāl. Ṣannūʿ, a kind of a less sophisticated Beaumarchais, identified himself with the insurgent Egyptian masses and squirearchy and wrote satirical sketches in the vernacular debunking the Khedival largesse, ostentation, and high-handedness which brought the country to bankruptcy. He was direct and almost artless in form, sociopolitical in content, and very close to the common man. Despite his delicious *naivete*, his may be regarded as the first experiments in social realism and of the creative *litterature engagee*. His use of the Egyptian vernacular and his concern with Egyptian themes not only place him at the heart of the 'Egypt for the Egyptians' movement, but also make him and ʿUthmān Galāl the true founders of Egyptian National Drama. His was the way of the *Commedia Dell'Arte*, of improvised theatre. After his exile ʿAbdulla Nadīm tried to continue his revolutionary tradition in both form and content, and his dialogues gave great impetus to the ʿUrābī revolutionary movement.

Ṣannūʿ's counterpart in the eighteen-seventies was Mohammed ʿUthmān Galāl who was probably the most cultured Egyptian of his period. His extant contributions are his adaptations of Aesop's *Fables* and of Bernardin de Saint-Pierre's *Paul et Virginie* and his translation into metrical Egyptian vernacular of four tragedies by Racine and four comedies by Molière, of which the best known until today is *Tartuffe* which he rendered under the title of *Sheikh Matlouf*. The anti-clericalism of *Tartuffe* must have appealed to the secular classes of Ismāʿīl's time, but what really added to its popularity is the fact that ʿUthmān Galāl, while being faithful to the original text managed brilliantly to cast the play in an Egyptian setting; characters, scenes and all.

ʿUthmān Galāl's political position is somewhat enigmatic, for we hear of him in 1868 issuing the first Egyptian literary review which was suppressed by Khedive Ismaʿīl after three issues, which suggests that at one period of his life ʿUthmān Galāl was a radical of some kind. In the following decade, when he published his translations of Racine and Molière, we find him writing panegyrics to Crown Prince Tawfīk who was to succeed Ismā'īl after his deposition in 1879. So also was the great Ṭaḥṭāwī. Even Afghānī and his circle were on excellent relations with Prince Tawfīk throughout most of the seventies. But the wily Prince Tawfīk had then posed as a good radical and democratic Moslem, so much unlike his despotic father Khedive Ismā'īl. He actually was Head of the Freemason Lodge in Egypt to which most of the revolutionaries of the period belonged. Tawfīk's first action as Khedive in 1879, however, was to banish Afghānī, clamp down on Afghānī's circle, and turn against all denominations of liberal and radical thought in Egypt, i.e. against the Egypt for the Egyptians Movement, against the Humanistic Parliamentarianism of Sharīf Pasha and against the Puritan pan-Islamic Reformation of Afghānī and his circle. In his life and death struggle with these three groups during the 'Urābī Revolution he brought in the British Occupation and revived Egypt's vassalage to the Ottoman Sultan-Caliph. Upon his death in 1894, he left Egypt virtually without a theatre. When the theatrical tradition came to be revived around 1900 onwards by Iskander Faraḥ, Naguīb Ḥaddād, Salāma Higāzī, George Abyaḍ and Aḥmed el-Shāmī it was no longer in the vernacular and it no longer had any social or political context. Most of these men were of Levantine origin, and the Levantine contribution to the Egyptian theatre is the use of classical Arabic as the medium of expression, the reliance mostly on adaptation, as opposed to translation, of European classics in what was then called 'Iqtibās' and 'Ta'rīb', and finally the choice of benign themes which have no social or political implications, like the themes of Saladin, Romeo and Juliet and Oedipus Rex.

The important thing about 'Uthmān Galāl is that, although he belonged to the new Egyptian aristocracy and although his sophisticated genius was naturally attracted to foreign climes and foreign themes like those of the *Iphigénie* of the *Femmes Savantes* and the *École des Femmes*, he unnaturally opted for the use of the Egyptian vernacular which did not lend itself easily, especially at that stage of the development of the language, to convey the dignity of French grand tragedy or grand comedy. This can only mean one thing: that 'Uthmān Galāl was working according to a theory of literary expression which assumes that the Egyptian vernacular is at least as good a medium as classical Arabic, and that there can be no true national literature in Egypt unless Egyptian vernacular becomes the accredited literary medium for all themes and genres and modes and not only for local, popular and realistic subjects as practised by Yacoub Ṣannū' and 'Abdulla Nadīm. Some wrong-headed scholars have persistently tried to establish a theory that the tradition of the use of the vernacular in Egyptian literature was only started when civil engineer Wilcox of the Aswan Dam translated around 1900 some of the

Scriptures into colloquial Egyptian Arabic to make them better understood by the semi-literate *fellāḥeen* of Egypt. Their contention is that that was part of an imperialist Christian design to undermine the sacred language of the Qur'ān. The experiments of Ṣannū', 'Abdulla Nadīm and 'Uthmān Galāl in the seventies of the nineteenth century prove that the movement of the Egyptian vernacular had been started a quarter of a century before the Englishman Wilcox, by a thoroughbred 'baladī' Egyptian Jew, a thoroughbred 'baladī' Egyptian Moslem and a gallicized, intellectual Egyptian Moslem all of whom were connected with the upsurge of Egyptian nationalism and Egyptian democracy in the decade preceding the 'Urābī Revolution of 1882. We must regard *Sheikh Matlouf*, the Egyptian *Tartuffe*, as an expression of Egyptian secular anti-clericalism as felt by the Egyptian intelligentsia during the reign of Ismā'īl.

The case for the use of the vernacular remained for a long time one of the main problems of the Egyptian theatre. The 1919 Revolution, being a popular revolution, revived interest in the vernacular and in *l'art engagé*. Two Egyptian dramatic schools gathered around the persons of Yūsef Wahbī and his *Teatro Ramses* (for the tragic Muse), and of Naguīb al-Rīḥānī and his collaborator Badī' Khayrī, (for the comic Muse). There was also 'Alī al-Kassār and his Rūḍ al-Farag *café-théâtre* or open-air *chansonniers* duplicated endlessly in the theatre row along the outer Shubrā bank of the Nile. There was also the traditional Azbakiyya Theatre directed by Zakī 'Okāsha at the heart of Cairo and the various operatic troupes and the *cabaret-theatres* operating in Sharia 'Imād al-Dīn and Sharia Alfī, of which the most famous was that of the singer Mūnīra al-Mahdiyya. Those (the 'twenties) were the times when Sayyid Darwīsh proved his formidable genius both in the *théâtre lyrique* and in folklore songs. Cairo was teeming with theatrical activity in the 1920s, and most theatrical activity was conducted in the vernacular. Serious romantic drama, still rife and potent, was still conducted in classical Arabic, but mainly translations or adaptations: there was the usual dose of Shakespeare, Cazimir de la Vigne's *Louis Onze*, Edmond Rostand's *L'Aiglon* and *Cyrano de Bergerac*, the younger Dumas' *La Dame aux Camélias*, adaptations of an Italian play entitled *The Confessional* and of another called *Rasputin*. Most of these melodramas and romantic dramas formed the basic repertoire of Yūsef Wahbī, George Abyaḍ, and Rūz al-Yūsef, throughout the 'twenties and eventually of Fāṭima Rushdī and 'Azīz 'Id in the late 'twenties and early 'thirties. The late 'twenties and early 'thirties crowned the Egyptian theatre with Shawqī's famous poetic dramas *The Fall of Cleopatra*, *Magnūn Laylā* and *Cambyses*. But while Shawqī's metrical compositions in classical Arabic were an astounding triumph of classical diction they, paradoxically enough, practically sealed the death of drama conveyed in classical Arabic for almost two generations. They helped to emphasize the ever-widening gulf between form and content in Egyptian life. With the ebbing away of the liberal revolutionary spirit the classical tongue, consciously or unconsciously, became increasingly an instrument of the Egyptian Establishment, a thing to conserve to underline the distinction between the masses and the élite, a distinction once consumed by the sacred flames of Egypt's liberal revolution of 1919. It was not an accident that the Royal Academy of the Arabic Language was founded in the early 'thirties by the Ṣidqī dictatorship to preserve the purity of the classical Arabic language and that about the same time State intervention was also deemed necessary to found the National Troupe in order to give a longer lease of life to an already expiring tradition, Egyptian or Egyptianized drama conveyed in the classical medium. When in 1933 Tawfīk al-Ḥakīm then making his splendid début in Egyptian letters, dared use the vernacular as a medium of dialogue in his novel *The Return of the Soul* and afterwards in some of his plays like *A Bullet in the Heart*, he was assailed right and left by the parties, led even by Ṭāhā Ḥussein, and condemned as a corrupter of the sacred tongue. He was so scared that he declared his apostasy, abstained from using the vernacular and eventually concocted his theory of the 'middle language', a kind of all-size Arabic especially designed for the drama and for dialogue in general that could be at once read as classical and spoken as vernacular. His compromise over the problem of language, and not his dramatic genius, earned him his seat in the Academy of the Arabic Language. The models of conservation were of course the Académie Française and the Théâtre National, better known as the Comédie Française.

The revival of interest in the use of the vernacular for dramatic purposes which was brought in by the 1919 Revolution was connected with the revival of the social function of literature and the arts. No doubt in those days they did not use the same aesthetic vocabulary which we use today, such as *engagement* or Social Realism. They simply used terms like: the theatre in the service 'of the country', 'of the people', 'of liberty', of the 'national struggle', maybe 'of society'. But it boiled down to what we call today 'commitment'. Harnessed to that was a degree of social realism. Riḥānī first established himself in the early 'twenties by creating the character of Kishkish Bey, the gullible Egyptian ʻUmda who comes to Cairo immediately after the cotton harvest to squander his money, i.e. the sweat and blood of the Egyptian *fellāḥ*, on the taverns of al-Alfī Street and on the *entraineuses* of ʻImād al-Dīn and Azbakīyya cabarets. He uses the jolly side of Naguīb Maḥfūẓ's absurdly serious al-Sayyid Aḥmad ʻAbdel Gawāb. In his context and epoch, Kishkish Bey was a corrective piece of social and political criticism. As for ʻAli al-Kassār, he typified the naīve but honest Nubian, nicknamed 'the Unique Berberi of Egypt', who harped on a famous theme, that of the unity of Egypt and the Sudan. Riḥānī and Badīʻ Khayrī adapted extensively and very freely, in Egyptian vernacular, the work of Marcel Pagnol and Georges Feydeau, much of which was not purely commercial theatre. It was also studies in bourgeois realism. Perhaps Rīḥānī's adaptation and rendering of the character of Topaze will always remain his greatest contribution to Egyptian bourgeois Social Realism.

None the less, all this happened within the sphere of comedy which lends itself easily to the vernacular. When Yūsef Wahbī decided to add to his foreign repertoire a thoroughly Egyptian repertoire he wrote a series of melodramas of which the best known were *Awlād al-Zawāt* ('Sons of the Nobility') and *Awlād al-Fuqarā'* ('Sons of the Poor'), two forceful pieces of direct social criticism. This Egyptian phase reached its peak in the 1930s. When Yūsef Wahbī did not produce social tragedies, he produced domestic tragedies, usually with some 'moral' point.

In the 'forties there was hardly any room for tragedy either in the vernacular or in the grand style, i.e. classical Arabic, probably on account of the war, and the Rīḥānī Theatre reached its apotheosis. It was accepted by all classes, including the ruling classes which it set out to criticize. The post-war period was teeming with turmoil and repression, and when Rīḥānī was decorated by King Farouk in his last days, we must construe this to mean that he had become part of the Establishment which must have seen in him a kind of lightning-conductor, and in social satire a useful deflector of public wrath. To laugh away one's anger has always been a valid mechanism to avert an explosion. However, with all his benign, sentimental satire, Rīḥānī was a good school in social realism for the radicals and the Egyptian left in general. When the Nasser Revolution of 1952 came, he was the most potent influence on the Egyptian theatre. We feel his fingerprints in the work of most of the radical playwrights of the Nasser Revolution, from the first-born Nuʿmān ʿAshūr to the latest-born ʿAlī Sālem, passing by Luṭfī al-Khūlī, Saʿdaddīn Wahba, Maḥmūd al-Saʿdānī. Because Rīḥānī had no 'literary' pretensions, he made the use of the vernacular in comedy and in tragi-comedy a living reality at least in Egypt, if not in the Arab World. After twenty years of the Nasser Revolution, it is no longer relevant to question the medium of comedy, farce and vaudeville, whether it should be in classical Arabic or in the vernacular. It has been a complete rout for the classicists.

Where did Tawfīk al-Ḥakīm stand in all this? Since his great embroilment in the 'thirties over the use of the vernacular in his plays, novels and sketches, al-Ḥakīm found an excellent exit in 'literary drama' for which he was pre-eminently gifted. He picked up the thread from where he left off in *The Dwellers of the Cave*

('Ahl al-Kahf'), and continued to write in that tradition from *Scheherezade* in the 'thirties down to *Praxa* in the 'forties, *Isis* in the 'fifties, *The Bewildered Sultan* in the 'sixties and *Dialogues with a Planet* in the 'seventies. He lost something which he never truly had, namely, spontaneity and the warmth of life. Even since *Ahl al-Kahf*, it was obvious that al-Ḥakīm's special gift was for discussion plays or the *drame-à-thèse* which could be equally conveyed in the vernacular and in simple straight-forward classical Arabic or in any language whatsoever. Though greatly revered as a dramatic genius, Tawfīk al-Ḥakīm never attracted a wide audience in the theatre. He is better read than performed, and one always feels that the annual quote of al-Ḥakīm on the Egyptian stage is only there for the sake of form. He has the making of a Pirandello, but he is confined by the limitations of the Arabic language. Unlike Rīḥānī, Tawfīk al-Ḥakīm has no progeny in the succeeding generation of playwrights except, perhaps Alfred Farag who is the only dramatist of importance of the Nasser period who has not turned his back on classical Arabic. In my view, he is the most 'artful' of them all and the most acquainted with the construction and the techniques of serious drama, but his restraint, his chaste language, his studied sophistication and his excessive attention to form, all curb his talent and make him equal to his peers who surpass him in other elements.

Four dramatists of the Nasser period have totally escaped the influence both of Rīḥānī and of Tawfīk al-Ḥakim. Those are Yusef Idrīs, Maḥmūd Diyāb, Rashād Rushdī and Shawqī ʻAbdel Ḥakīm. Being mostly tragic writers, it is understandable why they did not follow the mainstream of the Rīḥānī school. But being committed writers, each in his own way, they could not avoid expressing themselves in the vernacular. Even Rashād Rushdī with all his defence of *l'Art pour l'Art* and with all his onslaughts on *l'art engagé*, has been throughout the Nasser period the most militant and committed rightist dramatist in Egypt. He has conducted his anti-leftism with a finesse and dexterity unknown to hard-liners like ʻAlī Aḥmed Bākathīr. As a former Ibsenian, in his *Butterfly* ('al-Farāsha'), he needed no local models, though in the 'sixties when most of the leftist playwrights went Brechtian, he too went Brechtian, exploiting the Bard-Narrator or the Chronicler-Narrator technique and the folkloric setting. Of these four, there can be no doubt that Yūsef Idrīs is the most vital force and, if it were not that his power of dramatic construction fails him half-way through his plays, he might have become the greatest Egyptian dramatist of the Nasser era. The fact that Egyptian tragedy itself has shunned the nobility and grandiloquence of classical Arabic and chosen to clothe itself with the language of the people shows that the barrier between art and life has finally broken down. The early romantic and melodramatic experiments of the 'thirties, in vernacular tragedy such as Anton Yazbak's *The Sacrificial Offerings* (al-Dhabāʼiḥ) or the works of Yūsuf Wahbī had proved that a dramatist could bombast and bluster on the stage as high and as loud in spoken Egyptian as he could in classical Arabic. The contribution of Egyptian dramatists during the Nasser era has proved that as far as language is concerned, good or at least passable tragedy could be written in the vernacular without having to put the vernacular to such unnatural uses. Similarly, our comedy does not have any longer to rely on slapstick or on Būlāqism (Cockneyism) in order to be comic. The defects of contemporary Egyptian drama, for defects there are, are not defects of language or theme, but rather defects of construction and technique due to the absence of a long-standing tradition, such as that which European dramatists have at their command from early childhood, as well as defects of dramatic sensibility stemming from the relative absence of a sense of ambivalence in our vision of life. Drama is not Dialogue. It is not even a Duel between protagonist and antagonist. For that the epic *genre* has ample room. Drama is a synthesis arising from the interpenetration of opposites and the reconciliation of thesis and antithesis at a heavy price. It is an existential feeling, and not a cerebral understanding, of the dialectics of nature and life.

It must be noted, however, that the battle for vernacular drama was fought out on the ground of the National Theatre, the leading Stage Theatre which emerged under the Revolution from what had been formerly the National Troupe under the *ancien régime*. The last signs of resistance offered by the classicists was around 1960 when they brought tremendous pressure on Sarwat Okasha, then Minister of Culture, to place the National Theatre under the tutelage of the poet-dramatist ʻAzīz Abāẓa, a kind of dimunitive Shawqī with heavier wings and leader of the purists in the Academy for Arabic Language and in the Higher Council for Arts and Letters. This would have simply meant putting a ban on all plays written in the vernacular and the blackballing of such proven new talents as Nuʻman ʻAshūr, Yūsef Idrīs, Saʻdeddīn Wahba, Luṭfī al-Khūlī, Naguib Surūr, ʻAli Sālem, Maḥmūd Diyāb etc. and clearing the ground for their less inspired compeers of the traditional school: Fatḥī Raḍwān, ʻAlī Bākathīr, ʻAbdū Badawī, ʻAzīz Abāẓa himself etc. Even Alfred Farag would have been disqualified on account of his alleged political leanings, regardless of his subtle rhythme and his mellifluous Arabic. When the Minister of Culture resisted the pressure and decided to place Aḥmed Ḥamrūsh and later Amāl al-Marṣafī, two left-wing administrators of the officer breed, at the head of the National Theatre and to entrust the State Theatre Organisation to the leadership of Dr. ʻAlī al-Rāʻī, an enlightened and committed University lecturer, he in fact decided the fate of the Egyptian theatre for a generation to come. The leadership of these three men extended State patronage to young talents already unfolding in the private theatre, then known as the Free Theatre and enabled them to mature with the years. It also prospected for and discovered new talents and gave them the necessary impetus until they became fully established. Another private monument of the vernacular theatre is the political cabaret of Taḥiya Karyūkkā and Fāyez Ḥalāwa which, while being more relaxed in the observance of the canons of serious drama, has managed by its tenacious adherance to social and political *engagement* to rise above the status of the commercial theatre. It goes without saying that all commercial theatre in Egypt is vernacular theatre. There has always been a tradition in Egypt that translated plays are presented in classical Arabic, and therefore with very few exceptions have always yielded a very poor box-office (often as low as £E. 2 or £E. 5 per night for a Tennessee Williams or an Arthur Miller). But even here, the classicists were not safe in their own stronghold. In the last five years or so relatively successful experiments in the vernacular were made with *Fleur de Cactus*, *Croque-Monsieur*, a Jugoslav social comedy called *His Excellency the Minister's Wife*, Anatoly Sovronov's *A Smile Worth a Million Roubles*, Edward Albee's *All in the Garden*, etc., but the vernacular translations of Peter Weiss's *Lusitanian Bogey* ('Angola') and his *Marat-Sade* were an astounding success in the State-owned Pocket Theatre. As previously stated, the triumph of the vernacular in the Egyptian theatre during the Nasser period had two implications: first that the gap between art and life and between the creative artist and the masses was becoming narrower and narrower, and secondly that the principle of *engagement* could thus have a more democratic basis. It may be said, with a note of caution, however, that in the last two years the massive reorganization of our cultural life on conservative lines and the general unleashings of rightist tendencies in Egypt, have already shown symptoms of a relapse into the linguistic and cultural alienation of the past. Since the old models can never be revived, the dislocation of the new can only result in one thing: a vacuum. However, as nature abhors a vacuum, let us be confident that the present sterility will not last longer than nature allows.

With the massive nationalizations and with the declaration of the National Charter in 1962, the gulf between the Egyptian Left and the Nasser Revolution began to be bridged but never to the point of coalescence. As the Nasser Revolution, under the pressure of economic dialectics swung a little to the left, the Egyptian socialists found no difficulty in swinging a little to the right. After four years of internment, hard labour and Sadist treatment, they were released as fellow-travellers to put their 'literature' to the service of the New Society or the New Order. Actually, the Nasser Revolution, being essentially a bourgeois revolution, had set out to industrialize Egypt. The conception of the High Dam as a gigantic source of power, was the grandiose prelude to this industrialization policy, its agricultural benefits being a by-product and not a primary end. The Nasser Revolution would have broken down it if had failed in its industrialization objectives. Since the accumulation of capital in an under-developed country under the system of private ownership, with all the Protectionism in the world, was a slow and uncertain process, especially with the general feeling of insecurity engendered by confiscations and sequestrations, arbitrary or otherwise, private capital investment was found to be inadequate to cope with the massive industrialization programme of the Revolution. Industrialization had to be a State undertaking. This could only be done by the massive nationalization of the means of production. What is called Egypt's socialist experiment is, as far as appears to the naked eye, an experiment in State Capitalism to render possible the industrialization of the country. There is nothing new in it. It was tried before, successfully, by Muḥammad ʻAlī, with one difference, that Muḥammad ʻAlī had no local urban investment capital to nationalize, so he nationalized the land of Egypt and monopolized trade. There was another difference, however. It is the difference between 1813 and 1961. In 1813 nationalization could be effected in the name of the Wālī, the only known embodiment of the State. In 1961 nationalization had to be made in the name of the People, hence a certain measure of socialist jargon had to be introduced and even implemented to humanize the process. This was the area where the Nasser Revolution and the Egyptian Left could meet.

The tragedy of the Nasser Revolution, like the tragedy of Muḥammad ʻAlī is that Egypt has never been like Japan, in an out-of-the-way corner of the world where men could be left in peace to build and reconstruct in relative security. Egypt is the centre of whirlwinds from the East, from the West, from the North and from the South. Constantly engaged in combats, Nasser, like Muḥammad ʻAlī, depleted his own prodigious resources, some of which he acquired through his nuisance value, in sterile wars, 'liberation movements', offensives and counter-offensives, etc., to the detriment of his primary objective, an Industrial Egypt. Judged by results, his revolution was worse than a fiasco - it was a disaster. But was Ismāʻīl possible without a Muḥammad ʻAlī? And was a Zaghlūl possible without an ʻUrābī? The question that will always tantalize historians is: had Nasser, or Muḥammad ʻAlī or Ismāʻīl for that matter, left people alone, would they have left him alone?

What has all this to do with literature, dramatic or undramatic? It is very simple. We are now dealing, not with the area of agreement between the Egyptian Left and the Nasser Revolution, but with the area of disagreement for which they continued to go back occasionally, not *en masse* but individually, to their former loggias in limbo, at least for briefer periods, or suffer suspension from public activities in the Press and other media of information.

Even after their dubious reconciliation with the Nasser Régime, Egyptian leftist writers were fighting desperately to deepen public consciousness of the necessity for enhancing the socialist content of public ownership, as opposed to the State content, chiefly though advocating greater measures of popular control over the public sector, especially over the technocracy, the managerial class and the entrepreneur class. Foremost among them were the dramatists who used the masks of the theatre to point out that the inherent contradictions in the Nasser Revolution were denuding it of its revolutionary content. The ageing Ṭawwāf of Nu'mān 'Ashūr, symbol of the landless barefooted *fellāḥ* who raises with loving loyalty, like a mediaeval vassal, all the sons of his country squire, has only one dream in life and that is to have his two feet shod before he goes to the grave. Of course he is promised a pair of boots for Bayram by his loving young masters, but one Bayram passes after another and no boots are forthcoming. Finally, he is faced with the bitter truth: he is a silly old man. If he had spent the first seventy years of his life barefooted, what use has he for a pair of boots at the end of his life? Agrarian Reform, instituted by the Nasser Revolution for the benefit of the Ṭawwāfs has given them nothing, not even the little that had been promised to the *fellaḥeen*.

In Sa'adeddīn Wahba's *al-Sibinsa* (The Rear Van), meaning the proletariat or, if you like, the 'cattlevan' always stuffed with *fellāḥeen*, in sharp contrast with the first-class coach. The *fellāḥeen* are promised a first-class coach by the station-master. But all he does is to shunt the locomotive to the rear of the train. The *fellāḥeen* are still in the cattle-van which becomes the head of the train. Attempts are made to persuade the protesting *fellāḥeen* that it is all relative, all an optical illusion, that they are really in the first class, since what determines the first class and the third class is the position of the coach, whether it is at the head or at the tail of the train. So long as the poor are immediately behind the driver, that should be enough to make them feel privileged. Again, in Yūsef Idrīs' *Farāfīr* (The Figaros), the turbulent, famished slave has a heated argument with his corpulent, well-fed master. The Farfūr is sick and tired of doing all the work and of being all the time ordered about. The Master tries to persuade him that that is the natural order of things, but the Farfūr threatens to quit. To pacify him the Master accepts to experiment with new systems of relationship between them. They first try to be both Masters. The system collapses because no work is done. Then they try a situation in which there are no Masters and no Slaves, but this also breaks down because it leads to anarchy. They then try a situation in which the Farfūr becomes Master and the Master becomes Slave. This equally fails because the Master bungles the work of the Slave and the Slave spoils the orders of the Master. In short, they try all possible systems of government and they fail, and finally meet with a catastrophe in which they both find themselves dead, having both worked as grave-digging slaves for their bread and butter. When both wake up in the next world, supposedly a place of absolute inertness and absolute equality, they find themselves transformed into rotating bodies, like all the bodies of the firmament around them. To their surprise, they realize that the Farfūr is rotating around the Master like the Earth around the Sun or like the Moon around the Earth. When the unhappy Farfūr yells protesting against his destiny and helplessly threatens to stop rotating because he fails to see the logic of the situation, why it is always he who is rotating around the Master, the Master calmly bids him to resign himself to his destiny, since it is in the Order of Nature that by the inexorable Laws of Gravitation and Inertia smaller bodies have to rotate around larger bodies. What a pessimistic comment on the egalitarian dreams of any working-class revolution! Yet in Yūsef Idrīs' total rejection of all systems of government he approaches the nihilistic position.

In Alfred Farag's *'Alī Ganāḥ al-Tabrīzī and his Attendant Qoffa* we are dealing with an enigmatic Mediaeval merchant who comes upon a large city and is able to impress its council of merchants that his huge caravan of a thousand camels all laden with the finest goods is to follow him in a matter of days, having been unsuccessfully intercepted on the desert road by gangs of highway robbers. He is given a royal reception in the city and the most expensive gifts are showered upon him in anticipation of his caravan which is expected to replenish and enrich the merchants of the city. He is such a charmer when he describes his forthcoming merchandise that merchants vie to be his favoured friends. What adds to his credibility is that he finds strangers who confirm to the people of the city that they had seen such a wondrous caravan heading for their city. When days pass and no caravan arrives and men begin to feel restless, 'Alī Ganāḥ al-Tabrīzī simply vanishes from the city, leaving behind him a great question mark: Was he a gifted swindler? Was he a munificent but unlucky merchant whose splendid caravan was pillaged by desert thieves? At any rate, we more often get the impression that Tabrīzī is simply a dream-vendor. The parallel with the Nasser Revolution is too striking to need comment.

Examples can be multiplied endlessly. It is a great tribute to the Egyptian dramatists of the Nasser era that they courageously employed, very often taking tremendous personal risks, the masks of comedy and tragedy for an intensive auto-critique of the so-called Socialist Egyptian Revolution. From Maḥmūd al-Sa'adānī's play *The Ordnance* to Luṭfī al-Khūlī's film *The Bird* is a good ten years. They both tell a similar story, that of the plunder of public property in the name of patriotism or socialism. Our playwrights, mostly leftists or radicals, because of rigorous censorship and repressive security measures, instead of using the techniques of Social Realism, have opted for the alternative techniques of Socialist Symbolism which normally flourish under reigns of terror. They have used parables and allegories, symbols and vast metaphors, to be able to smuggle their intentions through, something in the order of what Brecht was doing in the grim days of the German nightmare. It is certain that their masks and veils, like Brecht's, have been too transparent, and therefore more effective with an audience not too used to ambiguity and oblique expression.

The job of the committed dramatic writer became extremely difficult after the *débacle* of 1967 for various reasons. In the first year or two of the shock there were no difficulties to speak of, since the national resilience and the refusal to admit defeat, which expressed itself politically in the people clinging to the symbolic name and person of Nasser, expressed itself artistically in a series of dramas saying more or less the same thing in different terms: that Nasser brought ruin on the country because he was an idealist who entrusted the destinies of the Egyptians to a pack of rogues. It was a time when the patriotism of the Egyptians and not their gullibility made them instinctively delay the settlement of internal accounts in order to be able to face up to the greater danger. It began with Sa'adeddīn Wahba's *al-Masāmīr* ('The Nails') in which the setting is pushed back to the period of the national struggle during the 1919 Revolution. There we have the people of a certain village in revolt led by a heroic youth ('Abdulla), and to everybody's dismay, they find out that it was the ruling class of the village and the governing administrators who were betraying the people to the British and thus trying to abort the Revolution. The play ends with the classic Khaḍrā' or 'Azīza or whatever her name might have been, the great maiden of the village and of every village, and symbol of Egypt herself, invoking 'Abdulla to hit hard and to cleanse the house of all the traitors, shaking off the proverbial sentimental compassion of the Egyptians. It was in fact an invocation to Nasser to purge his foul entourage. Then there was Rashād Rushdī's *Baladī, yā Baladī* ('My Country, O My Country'), where the scene is in Mediaeval Egypt at the time of al-Sayyid al-Badawī, the great Moslem saint who was so absorbed in worship and pious teachings that he left the affairs of his followers in the hands of his hypocritical, corrupt and cynical assistants. The result was national chaos and general disintegration. Again it was a matter of exculpating Nasser from any direct responsibility for the national disaster, but in Rashād Rushdī the gloom is universal and there is no ray of hope, no forthcoming Horus or ʿAbdulla to save the situation. There was also ʿAlī Sālem's *It Is You Who Killed the Beast* treating the same theme against a different background, using the myth of Oedipus. We are in the Egyptian Thebes where Oedipus, having slain the Sphinx, is universally acclaimed ruler of the land. But this Oedipus is a towering contemplative genius, the embodiment of goodness itself, who shuts himself up in his palace living in utter solitude, trying to invent great things both material and intellectual for the benefit of his Theban people. In the process, he delegates all his powers to the corrupt and sadistic Minister of Public Security, called Kawāleh, who fleeces the people and throws them into dungeons by the thousand, supposedly because they speak evil of Oedipus. When the people revolt against these unspeakable abuses, Oedipus finally awakens to his own alienation, chases away Kawāleh and his henchmen. The penitent leader is at last reconciled to his people and they live happily ever after! A fourth play which belongs to the same period is *Yāssīn Waladī* ('Yasseen my Son') by Fāyez Ḥalāwa. It is probably the finest of that series. It was written and staged immediately after Nasser's death and is a kind of anguished but sober epitaph on the leader of the 1952 Revolution. There Yāssīn has all the dimensions of a tragic hero. The tragic flaw in his nature was that he talked like a Messiah, preaching impossible virtues and attempting impossible things like the equality of men and like national unity while counter-revolution was lurking in every corner to overthrow him. It succeeds in doing so through the great betrayal of Sinai. He is smitten with grief. Yet the play ends with a vision of resurrection, not of Nasser, but of Egypt.

As soon as the country recovered its balance, our dramatists re-assumed their role of auto-critique. In the painful process of the *examen de conscience*, they came to the conclusion that there was something rotten in the State of Egypt, and that it was nothing less than the Nasser Régime itself which relied on the counter-revolutionary to effect the revolution, on the Kulaks to effect agrarian reform, on the capitalists to effect socialism; it relied on the reign of terror to extinguish free thought, to quell the sacred ire of the masses and to shield public thieves and treasonable characters. ʿAbdulla did not seem to cleanse the house. In 1970 as many as five plays were banned by the Socialist Union, even before they were tried on the stage, one by Nuʿmān ʿAshūr, *Sirr al-Kawn* ('The Secret of the Universe'), one by Yūsef Idrīs, *al-Mukhaṭṭaṭīn* ('The Striped Ones'), two by Saʿadeddīn Wahba, *al-Ustādh* ('The Master') and *Sabʿa Sawāqī* ('The Seven Water Wheels'), and, oddly enough, Shakespeare's *Antony and Cleopatra* supposedly because it depicted a dark period of our national history under a foreign invader and a foreign queen! There was a sixth play which was rejected by The State Theatre Organisation, no less than Aeschylus' *Persae* on the grounds that it was the Persians who were routed and not the Greeks! All this happened in 1970, and since then nothing of real importance happened on the Egyptian stage except an almost pirate performance in January 1973 of *Marat-Sade* which was soon to be called off by the Ministry of Culture.

It is difficult to say what effect the general optimism brought about by the October War will have on the Egyptian Theatre. There can be little doubt that the formal abolition of censorship by President Sadat may help to create a better climate for dramatic freedom, but it is also difficult to see how our committed leftist or radical dramatists, whose main function in the last twenty years was to undertake critique and auto-critique, can survive in an atmosphere where optimism has become a national duty and private enterprise has become the order of the day. It is certain that commercial theatre will avail itself abundantly of the new optimism and of the promised *laissez-faire*. Great is the challenge to serious dramatists of the Nasser era. Should their stamina prove insufficient to cope with the new situation, a younger race of serious dramatists will, by the recuperative power of nature, rightfully claim their place for itself. Let us therefore end on this cheerful note of optimism.

Louis 'Awaḍ

The Contributors

R. C. OSTLE - *Editor*

Lecturer in Arabic and Islamic Studies in the Department of the Near and Middle East, School of Oriental and African Studies, University of London.

ROGER ALLEN

Lectures in the Middle East Centre of the University of Pennsylvania, and a specialist in Modern Arabic Literature. One of the editors of *Edebiyat*, a journal devoted to Middle Eastern literatures.

M. M. BADAWĪ

Lectures in Modern Arabic Literature in the University of Oxford, and has written extensively on both English and Arabic literature. Is an editor of the *Journal of Arabic Literature.*

SALMA KHAḌRĀ' JAYYŪSĪ

Well known as a poetess throughout the Arab World, and recently has held teaching posts in Arabic Literature at the University of Khartoum and the University of Algiers.

M. A. S. ʿABD AL-ḤALĪM

Lectures in Arabic and Islamic Studies in the Department of the Near and Middle East, School of Oriental and African Studies, University of London.

P. J. CACHIA

Lectures in Arabic in the University of Edinburgh, and is well known as a specialist in literary studies. One of the editors of the *Journal of Arabic Literature.*

ṢABRY ḤĀFEẒ

A leading figure amongst the younger generation of writers and critics in Egypt, with a particular interest in the short story. Broadcasts frequently, and contributes extensively to Middle Eastern periodicals on literary topics.

ḤAMDĪ SAKKOUT

Currently lecturing in Arabic Literature at the American University in Cairo, and is engaged in a bio-bibliographical research project on Twentieth Century Egyptian Writing.

ḤALĪM BARAKĀT

At present holds a post in the Lebanese University and Centre for Educational Research and Development in Beirut. He lectures in sociology, and is the author of novels and short stories in Arabic.

TREVOR LE GASSICK

Lectures in Arabic at the University of Michigan, and is known in particular for his translations into English of Arabic novels.

J. STETKEVYCH

Lectures in Arabic in the University of Chicago, and is one of the foremost authorities on the Modern Arabic Language and Literature.

ʿALĪ AL-RĀʿI

Currently lectures in the University of Kuwait, and is recognized as one of the leading scholars and critics of the theatre in the Arab World.

LOUIS ʿAWAḌ

One of the leading men of letters in Egypt, with a widespread reputation as a scholar and a journalist. Has been literary editor of *al-Ahrām* since 1962, and has written numerous books in English and Arabic on a large variety of literary topics.

Index